PITTSBURGH THEOLOGICAL
MONOGRAPH SERIES

Dikran Y. Hadidian
General Editor

32

REFORMATIO PERENNIS

Essays on Calvin and the Reformation
in Honor of Ford Lewis Battles

REFORMATIO PERENNIS

*Essays on Calvin and the Reformation
in honor of
Ford Lewis Battles*

Edited by

B. A. Gerrish

In Collaboration With

Robert Benedetto

THE PICKWICK PRESS

Pittsburgh, Pennsylvania

1981

Library of Congress Cataloging in Publication Data
Main entry under title:

Reformatio perennis.

   (Pittsburgh theological monograph series : 32)
   Includes bibliographical references.
   Contents: Ford Lewis Battles / Donald G. Miller
-- Christ, the law, and the Christian / I. John
Hesselink --The ecumenical intention of Calvin's
early Eucharistic teaching --[etc.]
   1. Calvin, Jean, 1509-1564--Addresses, essays,
lectures. 2. Reformation--Addresses, essays,
lectures. 3. Church and state--Addresses, essays,
lectures. 4. Battles, Ford Lewis--Addresses,
essays, lectures. I. Battles, Ford Lewis.
II. Gerrish, B. A. (Brian Albert), 1931-   .

III. Benedetto, Robert.   IV. Series.
BX9418.R36   270.6   81-1007
ISBN 0-915138-41-7   AACR2

CONTENTS

FOREWORD

After a long and courageous struggle with declining
health, Ford Lewis Battles died on Thanksgiving Day, 1979.
He would have been sixty-five on 30 January 1980. He knew
that a number of friends and colleagues were preparing a
collection of essays in his honor, and the title is essentially one that he himself proposed. A fitting appreciation
appears as the first chapter. But I think it will be forgiven
me if I preface the book with a personal word of thanks for
the double bond between the editor and the man we honor, a
bond that goes back to our first meeting--neither in his New
England nor in my old England, but in Göttingen, West Germany.
One side of it was recorded in the preface to my little book
of creeds and confessions, and it grew over the years, as we
continued to share our sometimes very different perceptions
of Calvin and Calvinism. The other side is attested in my
daughter's *Taufschein* from Göttingen's Reformed "temple" (as
the local inhabitants call it), dated 24 March 1963 and neatly
signed by the godparents, Ford and Marion Battles.

It was because of this double bond, sacramentally sealed
on that occasion, that I was asked by Dikran Y. Hadidian and
Robert Benedetto to act as general editor for this volume.
And of course I was delighted to do so. Everyone who knew
one or more of the many gifts of Professor Battles will be
grateful for the tribute paid to him by a long-time friend,
Donald G. Miller (chap. 1). Scholars and students will also
welcome the detailed bibliography compiled by Peter De Klerk
(pp. 195-209), all the more so because many of Professor Battles' writings have not been widely circulated. In the remaining chapters of the book, scholars pay tribute to the scholar
by offering samples of their own research in his prinicpal
field. Although "Calvin and the Reformation" by no means exhausts the professional interests of Ford Lewis Battles (he
also, for instance, worked extensively in patristics), it is
certainly as a Calvin scholar and a Reformation historian that
we mostly think of him.

Of the four essays on Calvin, the first, by I. John
Hesselink (chap. 2), argues that the norm of Christian living
is not, for Calvin, the Decalogue literalistically interpreted, but Christ, who is the end of the law. Calvin's
evangelical treatment of moral norms is then brought into
relation with present-day discussions of situational ethics
and ethics of moral principles. A parallel christological
direction appears in the essay by Joseph N. Tylenda (chap. 3),
who shows that the central meaning of the Lord's Supper in
Calvin's early eucharistic teaching lies not so much in what
he says about the mode of Christ's presence as in his view
of the sacrament's "finality": Christ as the nourishment of
the soul. But Calvin did not succeed in commending this view
as a bridge between the Lutherans and the Zwinglians.

The other two Calvin essays are both concerned with his
thought in relation to modern theological developments.
Partly through a comparison of Calvin and William Temple,
John H. Leith (chap. 4) proposes that we may think of the
doctrine of the will in the *Institutes* as a profound analysis
of Christian experience—but in the language of Calvin's own
day. Theologies from different situations may be very much
the same in substance but still not translatable without remainder into the language of another day. According to B. A.
Gerrish (chap. 5), an appreciation of Calvin's concern for
"piety" should rectify some misapprehensions of his doctrine
of God, and the similar (not identical) concern of Schleiermacher points to a closer relationship between Reformation
and liberal Protestantism than is commonly recognized.

The next three essays turn to the course of the Reformation in lands beyond Geneva: in England, Scotland, and
Poland. Robert S. Paul (chap. 6) does not seek to analyze
the rival ecclesiologies of the English Reformation, but to
explore the situation that fostered them. Unwittingly,
English experimentation with the doctrine of the church provided a matrix for the religious pluralism of America. James
K. Cameron (chap. 7) shows how, north of the border, the sixteenth-century Scottish reformers could not persuade Parliament to practice the intolerance which they believed, in
principle, was right. Strangely, Scotland did not have its
own Servetus case until the end of the seventeenth century,
when a Restoration act against blasphemy was confirmed and
implemented in the trial and execution of Thomas Aikenhead.
George Huntston Williams (chap. 8) then turns our attention
to eastern Europe, where Calvin himself was more directly
involved, and argues that it was Calvin's misplaced confidence in John Łaski that robbed the Reformed church of its

chance to become a major and abiding entity in the Polish-
Lithuanian world. Theological talent was what the situation
required, and Łaski's strengths lay elsewhere.

It is with a theological problem that the final two
essays of Part 2 are concerned: the problem of church and
state. Neither essay is concentrated upon Calvin. Robert M.
Kingdon (chap. 9) concludes that Peter Martyr Vermigli's *Loci
Communes*, second in importance only to Calvin's *Institutes* as
a source of Reformed theology, do not always give decisive
weight to scriptural arguments on political matters, but
appeal also to arguments drawn from Roman civil law, the
constitutional law of his own day, and even Roman Catholic
canon law. A case in point is Vermigli's view of resistance
led by inferior magistrates: he justifies it from German
constitutional theory. But it is the appeal to Scripture
that is the theme of the next chapter. Markus Barth (chap.
10) does not address himself directly to Reformation sources,
but to a central biblical text in Reformation debates about
secular government. He holds that, if interpreted in their own
context, Paul's words in Romans 13 justify neither political
submissiveness nor social indifference. For the "powers that
be" do not represent an autonomous natural order but from the
beginning have been subject to Christ.

As always happens with symposia, not all of those who
were invited to participate found themselves able to do so,
though they wished they could and wished Professor Battles
well. As also happens, not everyone who began with the best
of intentions was able to bring his essay to completion. And
there are many others whose names might equally fittingly be
among the contributors. These will all join us, I am sure, in
gratitude to Ford Lewis Battles for *his* contributions to our
common enterprise.

Finally, I would like to convey the contributors' as well
as the editor's thanks to Dikran Y. Hadidian, of the Pickwich
Press, who watched over everything to do with the production
of this volume, and to Robert Benedetto, of The University of
Hawaii, who took charge of the copy-editing of the manuscripts.

B. A. Gerrish
The University of Chicago

ix

FORD LEWIS BATTLES--AN APPRECIATION

Donald G. Miller

I first met Ford Battles on a social evening in a colleague's home. My first impression was of his naturalness and lack of self-consciousness. There was no pose, no attempt to impress, no artificial self-assurance, nor any ploys to attract attention to himself or his achievements. Here was a man who met his fellow human beings just as a human being, not as one who sat on a pedestal of scholarship, or had just descended from the Olympian heights of *Academia*.

In spite of this, the second impression was of the depth and breadth of his learning. No subject came up which did not draw from his well-stocked mind some quotation, or allusion, or parallel thought, or humorous circumstance relating to the matter in hand. One had the impression of a skilled horticulturist effortlessly plucking the ripest intellectual fruits from his well-cultivated orchard of erudition. Or, to change the figure, he wore his learning easily. The garments of knowledge fit the man so naturally that one was unaware of them.

A third impression was of a humble, chaste, disciplined man, whose quiet but firm convictions and dedication to the things that matter to the Kingdom of God came through unobtrusively, yet unmistakably. Here was a man whose gifts seemed to be put to the service of his Lord without religious ostentation or exhibitionism, and with no concern for self-glorification or personal reward. Here was a wholly authentic man, a transparent man, "an Israelite who deserves the name, incapable of deceit."

The impressions of that evening needed no readjustment as I came to know him more intimately through the years as a colleague and friend.

I. Scholar

Ford Lewis Battles was born to be a scholar, a scholar's scholar. Scholarship was flowing in his veins through ancestors who had pursued the disciplines of medicine, literature, and theology. His intellectual ability surfaced early, when he completed four years of High School work in two years, his courses heavily loaded with the Classics and Mathematics. His university and graduate study furthered his intellectual development and determined the direction of his future scholarly work. He majored in Classics at West Virginia University, after which he held a teaching fellowship in English at Tufts University. There he did a graduate thesis on Neo-Platonism in the theology of John Colet, indicating the bent of his mind toward theological studies even while laboring in other fields. After two years of graduate study and teaching at Tufts, he was appointed a Rhodes Scholar to Oxford University, where he enrolled at Exeter College. While at Oxford, he was drawn to C. S. Lewis, with whom he worked on the allegory of temptation. An invitation by Lewis to come "to his rooms" to discuss his paper was generally followed by a period of satisfaction. A few hours later, however, he realized that his tutor had gracefully taken his work apart before his very eyes. The indirect character of Lewis' pedagogy, while naturally congenial to Ford's temper, found its way, sometimes a puzzling way, into his own teaching method. · More importantly, however, Lewis first introduced him to the Church Fathers, which turned his interest toward the history of the Church and shaped his subsequent career perhaps more than any other single factor.

An enlistment in the Second World War interrupted his studies for a period of four years and took him first to Panama where he became an authority on the Third Locks Program of the Panama Canal and then to Washington where he was in charge of airfield intelligence under the Joint Chiefs of Staff preparing monographs for the invasion of Japan. In Washington he met and married Marion Davis, a legal analyst for the Office of Strategic Services. When the war ended, he returned to teaching English at West Virginia University. After one year, however, he took leave of absence to pursue graduate courses in Bible at Hartford Seminary Foundation. The lure of his research there led him to resign his teaching post at the University to carry through a Ph.D. program. He began by preparing himself in the biblical languages, intending to major in Old Testament studies, but his interest in the Church Fathers finally turned him in the direction of Church History. His doctoral thesis was a translation and critical study of the Homilies on Ezekiel of Gregory the Great. He was then asked to join the faculty at Hartford as Associate Professor of Church History, and later was installed in the Phillip Schaff Chair of Church History.

His interest was soon turned toward the works of John Calvin. In 1951, the editors of the *Library of Christian Classics* invited him to undertake a definitive translation of the 1559 edition of Calvin's *Institutes of the Christian Religion*. The seven years of labor on this, including a sabbatical leave spent in Lausanne, Switzerland, were the beginning of a process which has made him one of the world's authorities on Calvin. Thereafter, a Guggenheim Fellowship enabled him to spend a year in Göttingen, Germany, where he produced a translation of Calvin's *Commentary on Seneca's De Clementia*. This was followed by a *Computerized Concordance to the Institutes*, a herculean task involving 50,000 or more computer cards, laboriously prepared under the difficulty of incessant changes made in computers through the years. The first English translation of Calvin's 1536 edition of the *Institution* was published in 1975, followed by *The Piety of Calvin*, the first English translation of *The Enchiridion* of Johannes Eck, and a monograph on Calvin's method entitled *Calculus Fidei*, prepared for the Calvin Congress in Amsterdam in 1978. Here Calvin is set off clearly from the Scholastics in method, and is shown to have anticipated what later came to be known as the theory of limits in Newtonian mathematics. In addition to these publications, countless periodical articles on various aspects of Calvin's thought and work have come from his pen, along with translations of several of the works of the Church Fathers and many study outlines prepared for Seminary students and for pastors in continuing education courses. Most recently he was at work analyzing and translating the 1500 extant prayers of Calvin. Aware for many years of the crucial place of Peter Lombard's *Four Books of Sentences* in the formation of scholastic theology and the subsequent reaction to it, he undertook the translation of Book III of this work, for the first time in English. Recently he was working on the translation of Calvin's 1539 edition of the *Institution of the Christian Religion*. It will be seen from this partial list of Ford Battles' publications why he was a scholar's scholar. Thoroughly familiar with the Classical languages, he worked with original sources on difficult tasks for which few men have either the linguistic or historical preparation, and which taxed both energy and time in a fashion that only the most thorough and disciplined scholar could endure.

When I was seeking information concerning Ford with a view to extending him a call to Pittsburgh Seminary, I inquired about him from those who were expert in the field. One of his mentors, the late Matthew Spinka, told me that "many of us in his field consider him to be a bit of a genius." The late John T. McNeill, considered to be the Dean of Church historians in his day, when I asked how Ford compared with another scholar in the field, replied: "Well, it depends on what you want. The other man is a good popularizer and will have more public appeal; but if you want a scholar, the two are not in the same league."

In a conversation with a visiting lecturer and a colleague following an address on Shakespeare, Christopher Marlowe's name was mentioned. Ford immediately spoke of a good article on Marlowe in a leading journal. His colleague told me that he went to look up the article. He searched back through all the numbers into the '40's, and did not find it. He thought to himself, "Well, Ford's memory has slipped him for once." He spoke of it to Ford, who said, "Oh, it was in the early '30's!" His colleague went back to the library, and there it was! In telling me of this, he just shook his head, as much as to say: "How can the rest of us compete with a mind like that?"

Here was a Church historian who was a superb linguist, who knew mathematics, was familiar with computers, had a broad grasp of English literature, was at home with the early Greek philosophers, was well trained in the theory of music, had a wide acquaintance with hymnology, and could speak with some authority on mechanics and physics. His curious mind was always filled with new ideas, and was forever plotting paths of research for which he could not find time, and branching out into fields beyond that of his own specialty.

A call was extended in 1977 by Calvin Theological Seminary to join the faculty as visiting professor of Church History. One of Ford's main tasks was to bring into being a Center for Calvin Studies. Despite failing health in 1979, he worked feverishly to finish the translation of Book III of Lombard's *Sentences* into English. His love of teaching enabled him to teach his seminar on the *Institutes* until three weeks before his death, holding classes in his home when too weak to make the trip to the campus. His brief tenure at Calvin Seminary was marked by a sense of finding a theological home in a community which understood and appreciated what he sought to do for the Reformed tradition.

It has been a blessing to the Church that such a rich mind has been dedicated to helping us understand our past, so that knowing whence we have come, we may better understand where we are, and how we should face the future.

II. Teacher

Some scholars can learn, but cannot teach. I once knew of an erudite professor who lectured dully year after year, covering the same ground in the same way. Once, a student skilled in shorthand took down the lectures practically verbatim, then mimeographed them and distributed them to all the members of the following year's class. One of the students showed the professor the mimeographed copies of the lectures. When he learned that the students already had copies of his lectures, he said: "Well, then, what's the use of me lecturing?" The student replied: "That's just what the rest of us were wondering!"

This was not so with Ford Battles. He approached each course in a fresh way, continually changing his method of dealing with a subject, presenting the material in a fashion which both challenged the curiosity of the student and made him delve into the subject on his own. He never wrote out his lectures; there is no corpus of lecture notes in his literary output. Each term called forth fresh imagination to enable students to enter into past debates and struggles in the Church as though they were going on at that time, and were living realities of the moment. He showed how the issues faced in the past confront the Church today in different garb, but with all the potential for both good and evil which they embodied in past centuries. He strived to give students a grasp of the developing thought of the Church through the ages by which they could measure both the deviations and the authentic insights of the present. For those in the Reformed tradition, he rescued Calvin from the misunderstandings and caricatures which have grown up through the years on the part of people who have not taken the trouble to study Calvin himself, and enabled the student to keep company with the vast mind and warm heart of the great Reformer at firsthand. For adherents of other traditions, he made the other Reformers and the Church Fathers into human beings whom to know has not only antiquarian interest but current significance.

Ford was particularly adept as a mentor of graduate students. Early in his career at Hartford, he was appointed as a reader of all the graduate dissertations, and not long thereafter became head of the Ph.D. program. During his tenure at Pittsburgh, he spent several years as coordinator of the Ph.D. program which the Seminary established in conjunction with the University of Pittsburgh. He was not only gifted in enabling graduate students to learn how to do research, but had that rare quality of inspiring them with enthusiasm for their task. His rigorous demands for scholarship were matched with a personal interest both in the student and his subject which fostered diligence on the part of the candidate and brought encouragement when his spirit flagged.

The late John T. McNeill remarked that Ford's excellence as a guide to graduate students was to be seen in the number of those to whom he has been *Doktorvater* who are engaged in responsible teaching positions and who have already become authors in their own right.

III. *Churchman*

Ford Battles' life has been so identified with service to the Church that many are surprised to learn he was a layman. Without taking orders, he has been "under orders" from a Higher Source to devote his life unstintingly to the welfare of the Body of Christ. For him, scholarship within the Church was not an end in itself. It was a gift to be put wholly at the disposal of those who claimed fealty to his Lord.

For seven years he worked as a member of the Hymnal Committee of the United Church of Christ in preparation of a new Hymnbook. Here again, his imaginative quest for new approaches was put to service in finding new texts for new tunes. Wherever he went, he tried to stimulate people to try their hands at the writing of hymns, which resulted in the incorporation of a number of new hymns in the new hymnbook. At the opposite end of the spectrum, he culled from the writings of the Fathers, such as Gregory Nazianzus, prose passages which he cast in poetic form as "new" texts. These were often combined with commissions to church musicians to compose musical settings. He also served in an advisory capacity to hymnal committees of other denominations.

He participated in countless continuing education activities for ministers, often painstakingly working out for them

new courses of study produced in pamphlet form, with appended
bibliographies, rather than falling back on materials prepared
for other occasions. His love of printing enabled him to
spend long hours at the keyboard of his special typewriter,
whose variety of type fonts were to him as a palette to an
artist. Frequently he was called on to offer courses to laymen in local churches, through which he was able to awaken an
interest in historical and theological study on the part of
many who had never been introduced to any serious religious
study beyond the level of the Church School.

He served on many occasions in conducting worship services in local Churches, often writing the hymns for the service to coordinate the worship of the congregation with the
Scripture lessons and the theme of his sermon. When not leading worship, he was to be found in the pew as a worshipper on
Sundays, and frequently during the week he labored faithfully
as a member of various congregational committees. The Church
was the central concern of all his labors.

IV. Human Being

We might expect that one whose scholarship was so deep
and whose life so disciplined might be lacking in human
traits, but this was not so with Ford Battles. True, he had
small interest in sports, indulged little or no time in tele-
vision programs, and was hard at work when most men were seeking leisure. In this regard, he reminded one of John Wesley
who wrote in his *Journal* one day that he and leisure "had
forever parted company." This was rooted in the same conviction as Wesley's, that the tasks to which he was committed were
of such interest and importance that he simply did not have
time to be diverted by other things. His personality was not
grave, nor forbidding, nor morose, and underneath his disciplined exterior lay a jovial and lighthearted disposition.
He never gave an air of superiority, never shut himself off
from a brother who sought his help, was never pompous nor
arrogant. He had the capacity for love within his family,
and for warm friendships. He was a man with few enemies.
Anger or indignation were seldom stirred in him, and then
only in the face of what he conceived to be unfair or unjust
or out of character with the Lord he served. His delightful
sense of humor graced a social occasion, and his sense of
the ludicrous was sharp.

The quality of his humanity was developed out of broad

experience and diversified interests. He early learned to
work with his hands, and greatly enjoyed splitting wood for
his fireplace, or working on the plumbing of his small farm-
house in Vermont, or planting a vegetable garden. Two years
of experience as a dormitory proctor at Tufts University gave
him a good insight into the follies and quirks, as well as the
excellencies, of youth. Experience in the military intelligence service during the war furnished him with a world grasp
of politics, an intimate view of the Washington scene, and a
close observation of men in high office, many of whom he
briefed on matters pertaining to his field of responsibility.
Vigorous activity in student political clubs during his Rhodes
Scholarship days at Oxford as the Second World War was shaping
up gave him an intimate look at the inner working of the Com-
munist Party which was particularly active in student affairs
in England at that time. A summer spent in forest service
brought him into close touch with nature in the vast expanses
of our West. Fellowship with many foreign nationals in the
Missions School at Hartford, and periods of sabbatic leave
in Germany and Switzerland, brought him into close touch with
the life of the world Church and with many of the leading
Church scholars of our day. The responsibilities of a family
of two daughters kept him in touch with the practical realities
of life, and the recent addition of two grandchildren deepened
the joys of his family life.

Those who join in honoring Ford Lewis Battles in this
volume have been greatly enriched through their fellowship
and work with this scholar, teacher, churchman, and delightful
human being. We are representative of countless others who,
if their voices could be heard, would rise up to call him
blessed.

PART ONE: JOHN CALVIN

CHRIST, THE LAW, AND THE CHRISTIAN:

AN UNEXPLORED ASPECT
OF THE THIRD USE OF THE LAW IN CALVIN'S THEOLOGY

I. John Hesselink

I. *The Question of the Third Use of the Law*

It is well known that the law of God plays a prominent role in Calvin's theology. He, more than any other reformer, stressed in particular the continuing need of the law as a norm and guide in the Christian life. This, the so-called third use of the law *(usus tertius legis)*, was for Calvin the "principal use."[1] This third and positive use or function of the law is not unique to Calvin; it was also propounded by Melanchthon[2] and appears in the Lutheran Formula of Concord (1577).[3] Nevertheless, this positive function of the law as a norm and guide has come to be associated primarily with Calvin and is considered a special characteristic of Reformed ethics and piety. Many Lutherans, in fact, regard this as a fundamental difference between Luther and Calvin, although others, such as the Danish ethicist, N. H. Søe, conclude that there "was no essential difference between the two Reformers on this question."[4]

The notion of a continuing, positive function of the law for Christians continues to be rejected by certain types of Lutherans, liberals, and fundamentalists (especially dispensationalists), who are convinced that "the ethic of Jesus" or the principle of Christian freedom as propounded by the Apostle Paul does away with any such use of law. Others, who would not fit any of the above classifications, are equally adamant that "the New Testament knows nothing of a third use of the law."[5]

II. *The Recent Rejection of Laws and Principles by Ethical Situationalists*

This animus toward the third use of the law was trumpeted with particular boldness in the 1960s when situation ethics and a general reaction against tradition and authority dominated the theological scene. It may be only a coincidence that the three most outspoken situationalists were Anglicans: Professor Joseph Fletcher,[6] Bishop John A. T. Robinson,[7] and Canon Douglas A. Rhymes,[8] the former two also proclaiming a "new morality" and the last named being even more radical. Their fans and followers, however--and they were and are legion--on both sides of the Atlantic represented most denominational backgrounds.

Fletcher, Robinson, and Rhymes do not appear to know about Calvin; at least, they don't bother referring to him. But their attacks against laws, rules, and general principles, as well as traditional morality, if valid, would be devastating for Calvin's concept and use of the law. For in the ten commandments Calvin found principles which are valid forever. These commandments, he repeatedly affirms, are the rule of life *(regula vivendi)* which God has given to the universal church.[9] For Calvin there is nothing worse than trying to live the Christian life without definite, revealed norms or rules. This is why God's law, as revealed in the Scriptures, is indispensable and crucial for living the Christian life. "For unless he prescribes to us what his will is and regulates all the actions of our life according to a certain rule *(certam regulam)*, we would be perpetually going astray."[10]

Other ethicists, writing in the 1960s, were more aware and appreciative of Calvin's viewpoint, but sought to move beyond it. Paul Lehmann's *Ethics in a Christian Context*[11] appeared the same year as Robinson's *Honest to God* (1963). His contextual, *koinonia* ethic is more moderate and more carefully reasoned than Fletcher's situational approach. He quotes Calvin frequently and usually with favor, but it is significant that at one crucial point he criticizes the reformers for slipping "back to a preceptual reading of the law."[12] This is not incidental, for there are several aspects of his position, particularly his eschewing of moral principles in general, which are inimical to Calvin's understanding of the law. The same can be said of the Princeton ethicist, Paul Ramsey, a sharp critic of situationalist ethics. In his

Deeds and Rules in Christian Ethics (1965)[13] he in effect
defends the third use of the law, but not in Calvin's terms.

Of all the criticisms of situational and contextual
ethics,[14] one of the most balanced and perceptive was that
of Professor James M. Gustafson, then at Yale University and
now at the University of Chicago. In 1965, in the midst of
all the furor about the new approach to ethics, he wrote an
essay which has been reprinted elsewhere and cited frequently:
"Context versus Principles: A Misplaced Debate in Christian
Ethics."[15] The debate between situationalists and those who
stress objective moral principles is "no longer a fruitful
one," maintains Gustafson, both because it is difficult, if
not impossible, to know who belongs to which camp, and, more
importantly, because in responsible decision making no one is
simply a situationalist or traditional moralist.[16] Gustafson
concludes his essay with a question which brings us back to
the key issue being dealt with here in regard to what are the
ultimate norms for Calvin in living the Christian life, namely,
"Is there one normative starting point, or base point, for
work in Christian ethics around which other discussion ought
to cohere?"[17]

III. *The Issue at Stake*

This debate about context versus principles, and rules
versus a "love monism," confused certain basic issues in
Christian ethics, but sharpened others. Above all, the debate
forced ethicists to clarify how responsible and meaningful
moral or ethical decisions could be made in an exceedingly
complex age. Calvin, of course, could not have anticipated
some of the issues which defy neat and simple answers, such
as abortion and euthanasia. However, my thesis is that Calvin
is surprisingly evangelical and flexible in his treatment of
this fundamental issue of norms.

Many of the critics of Fletcher and Robinson have pointed
out the inadequacy of affirming that love is the only binding
obligation and that love must not be regarded as a principle.
When Fletcher insists that "the ruling norm of Christian decision is love: nothing else,"[18] the question inevitably
arises, "And how do we know what love is?" According to the
New Testament, "love is the fulfilling of the law" (Romans 13:
10), but Fletcher and Robinson--and many others--assume this
means that love abrogates the law. The appeal is often to the
teachings of Jesus or the example of Jesus himself. But in

the former case we are back to principles of some sort, and in the latter case one must ask, "Which Jesus?" In either case, the result is a modern version of an old-fashioned antinomianism not too different from that taught by Luther's critic, Agricola. Love and love alone, or love plus the situation (Fletcher's solution), do not provide us with a solution, for "'love,' like 'situation,' is a word that runs through Fletcher's book like a greased pig."[19]

Love without law is a vacuous thing. Moreover, as Elton Eenigenburg, among others, reminds us, "Love is not everything!" There is also justice and righteousness and the obedience of faith. Jesus himself said that he did not come to destroy the law and the prophets but to fulfill them (Matthew 5:17). "He did so with a love unsurpassable in its depth and embrace. Love as instrument is secondary and functional to that primary thing, God's revealed will."[20]

This is precisely where one must begin with Calvin in seeking to determine what is the ultimate norm for the Christian, or what we today would call responsible decision making. The answer, for Calvin, is surprisingly subtle, one which even Calvin scholars have overlooked.

IV. *The Law as an Expression of the Will of God*

Calvin in various connections either speaks of the law as an expression of the will of God or simply directs all of our activity to the will of God as the ultimate and most comprehensive norm of the Christian life. To illustrate this, we could point to such statements as, "He alone has truly denied himself who has so totally resigned himself to the Lord that he permits every part of his life to be governed by God's will."[22] In short, Christians "are taught to live not according to their own whim but according to God's will."[23]

This much is almost self-evident and would hardly be a point of controversy. For it is generally agreed that the Christian life is to be lived, insofar as possible, in accordance with God's will. The matter becomes more complicated and more problematic, however, when we try to determine how and where God's will is to be known--especially when facing difficult and often ambiguous ethical decisions. Yet for Calvin it would seem as if the answer were relatively easy; for he simply affirms that "the precepts of the law ... comprehend the will of God."[24] "God has revealed his will in the law."[25]

In the law he has delineated his own character;[26] here his
will, so to speak, is placed before our eyes.[27] Moreover, not
only does God reveal in the law what kind of God he is, but
there he also "lays down what he demands from us, and, in short,
everything necessary to be known."[28]

In some of the above references the word "law" may refer
to the Mosaic revelation or the Pentateuch. Nevertheless,
Calvin does not hesitate to speak in the same way about the
moral law as comprehended in the decalogue.[29] Since it contains "a perfect pattern of righteousness," it is the "one
everlasting and unchangeable rule to live by."[30]

It is at this point that Calvin and the other reformers
are often criticized; for in their catechisms in particular
they give the impression that the only norm for the Christian
life is the decalogue. The "reduction" of the will of God to
the decalogue without any consideration of the Sermon on the
Mount, the apostolic exhortations and injunctions, etc., is
held to be an unfortunate hangover from the earlier Catholic
tradition. Moreover, it is pointed out that this approach is
also unbiblical since the Old Testament law rather than Jesus
Christ is declared to be the sole source and norm of the Christian life. These criticisms can be found in a published doctoral dissertation by a Swiss scholar which is critical of the
whole tradition of giving a central place to an exposition of
the decalogue in catechical instruction.[31] In regard to Calvin,
however, this critic, Hugo Röthlisberger, finds a different
approach in the *Institutes* from that in his Catechisms. In
the former he finds *two* norms for the Christian life, viz.,
the law and Christ, whereas in the latter he maintains that
only the law is the norm.[32] That this is not an adequate understanding of Calvin's approach will be shown below. Emil
Brunner also chides the reformers for having overlooked the
fact that in the New Testament the decalogue scarcely appears
to be the norm for the Christian Church.[33]

The question then is whether Calvin limits the knowledge
of the will of God to the law and further, whether he unconsciously operates with two norms (the law and Christ). A related question is whether Calvin in practice overlooks Christ
and the new insights of the gospel in his treatment of the
third use of the law. In sum, what is the concrete content
of the will of God? There is no simple answer to these questions, but a perusal of Calvin's interpretation of the decalogue, together with an examination of what is normative in
his exposition of the Christian life in Book III of the *Institutes*, will shed light on these questions.

V. *Christ the Best Interpreter of the Law*

Calvin's high estimate of the decalogue and praise of the law in general can be grossly misunderstood if his three principles for interpreting the ten commandments are overlooked. The first and crucial principle is that in interpreting and applying the law we must follow "Christ, its best interpreter."[34] The implications and consequences of this affirmation are extremely significant. For what Calvin proceeds to do is to interpret the various commandments in the light of the New Testament. He eschews a literalistic interpretation of the commandments--"He who would confine his understanding of the law within the narrowness of the words deserves to be laughed at";[35] he seeks behind the negative commands their positive implications;[36] and he stresses the significance of the division of the law into two tables[37] and accordingly concentrates on the sum of the law or great commandment where we are commanded to love God and our neighbor. Not only does he conclude his exposition of the decalogue with a discussion of the principles of the law in the light of Christ's teaching,[38] but his whole treatment of the decalogue is suffused with the spirit of the New Testament.

Hence, although there is no separate treatment of the Sermon on the Mount (nor is there in most contemporary dogmatics), Chapter VIII of Book II (the exposition of the ten commandments) is in effect a treatment of many of the themes in the Sermon on the Mount.[39] Thus it is quite unjust to declare that "unlike Jesus, he (Calvin) conceived of the will of God in terms of biblical literalism and set up a legalistic moral code."[40] And it is equally far of the mark to assert that his "whole outlook on life is tinctured with the spirit of Moses rather than Christ ...."[41] It would be closer to the mark to make the opposite complaint, namely, that Calvin has so christianized the law[42] that the norm of the Christian life is not so much the ten commandments as the teaching of Jesus! Calvin, in any case, would acknowledge no such polarization as law over against Christ, the ten commandments over against the Sermon on the Mount. As Paul Lehmann observes, "Indeed, on the basis of an inner meaning of the law, the reformers were right in seeing an intrinsic parallelism between the Sermon on the Mount and the decalogue."[43]

VI. *A More Precise Principle*

The three uses of the law are discussed briefly in Book
II of the *Institutes*; but whereas the civil or political use
is taken up again in Chapter XX of Book IV ("Civil Government"),
at first glance it appears that the third and "principal use"
is dropped after the brief treatment in sections 12 and 13.
(There is also an allusion to this function of the law in III.
19.2). This, however, is not actually the case, for Calvin
takes up the third use of the law again in his discussion of
the Christian life in Book III, particularly Chapters VI and
VII. There is no explicit reference to the third use of the
law in either of these chapters, but rather incidental references to the law at the beginning of both chapters indicate
that Calvin is presupposing the discussion of the law in Book
II, Chapter VII. As Paul Jacobs has pointed out, "The treatment of the doctrine of sanctification, the so-called ethic
of Calvin's, is an unfolding of the doctrine of the *tertius
usus legis*."[44]

In Chapter VI, where Calvin collects various scriptural
data relevant to the Christian life, after noting the object
of regeneration he states: "The law of God contains in itself
that newness by which his image can be restored in us."[45]
But that is the last reference to the law in this chapter!
He continues: "But because our slowness needs many goads and
helps, it will be profitable to assemble from various passages
of Scripture a plan for the regulation of our life *(rationem
vitae formandae)* in order that those who heartily repent may
not err in their zeal."[46]

Calvin concedes the impossibility of doing justice to
this subject in one short chapter, so he tries to find some
"universal rule" *(regulam)* which aids the believer in living
a "rightly ordered life."[47] Since we have been adopted as
sons by God in order to live in harmony with him, the first
principle must be a love of righteousness or holiness on our
part. The goal of our calling is that we should be holy because our God is holy (Lev. 19:2; I Peter 1:15, 16).[48] "The
beginning of living rightly is spiritual, where the inner
feeling of the mind is unfeignedly dedicated to God for the
cultivation of holiness and righteousness."[49]

But Calvin proceeds to make another significant qualification in this chapter. He acknowledges that in many places
in Scripture we are exhorted to live righteously, but he finds

a stronger motive for holy living in the redemptive work of
Christ. Consequently, "to wake us more effectively, Scripture
shows that God the Father, as he has reconciled us to himself
in his Christ, has in him stamped for us the likeness *(imagi-
nem)* to which he would have us conform."[50] Later, in refuting
the charge that the doctrine of justification by faith stifles
the zeal for good works, Calvin lists more than ten scriptural
motives (or "spurs") for arousing us to fulfill our calling.
The first is one of gratitude to "reciprocate the love of him
'who first loved us'" (I John 4:19).[51] For no one will truly
pursue holiness unless he has first "imbibed" the doctrine
that we are justified by Christ's merit alone.[52]

The prime motive for the Christian life is thus the grace
and forgiveness we have received in Jesus Christ. He is also
the model of the Christian life. For Christ "has been set before us as an example *(exemplar)* whose image *(formam;* French,
l'image) we ought to express in our life."[53] Does Calvin then
operate with two norms, the law and Christ, as Röthlisberger
maintains? Hardly. Granted, in III.6.1 Calvin says that we
have been adopted as sons so that his image may be restored
in us through the *law;* and in III.6.3 he says that we have
been adopted as sons (note the identical language) on the condition "that our life express *(repraesentet) Christ,* the bond
of our adoption." But there is no contradiction here. Since
Christ is the "very soul" *(vere anima)*,[54] the life,[55] the goal
and end (fulfillment) of the law,[56] "the law in all its parts
has reference to him ... indeed, every doctrine of the law,
every command, every promise always points to Christ."[57]
Christ is thus not only the best interpreter of the law; he
is also its substance and fulfillment.[58] Hence, for Calvin
there is no inconsistency in referring sometimes to the law
and other times to Christ as the norm or rule of godly living
and as the expression of the will of God. Nevertheless, it is
not without significance that in his discussion of the Christian life, he prefers to refer to Christ, rather than the law,
as the model and image to which God would have us conform and
whose life we are to emulate.

We find much the same approach in Chapter VII of Book
III: "The Sum of the Christian Life: The Denial of Ourselves."
Again Calvin begins with a reference to the law (its third
use), and again he quickly passes on to "an even more exact
plan" *(accuratiore etiamnum ratione).* "Even though the law
of the Lord provides the finest and best-disposed method of
ordering a man's life *(constituendae vitae),* it seemed good
to the Heavenly Teacher to shape his people by an even more
exact plan (or precise principle) to that rule *(regulam)*

which he had set forth in his law."[59] Note that as in the
beginning of Chapter VI the law is spoken of in the highest
terms. Calvin has not forgotten the law; nor is he about to
reject it in favor of some alleged antithetical New Testament
insight or principle. He knows no either/or, i.e., either
the Old Testament or the New Testament, either the law or
Christ. At the same time, however, he tacitly acknowledges
that in the law we have not exhausted the meaning and purpose
of God's will for our lives.[60] Hence, in both chapters the
praise of the law is followed by a crucial qualification. In
Chapter VI he spoke of a means by which God awakens us "more
effectively,"[61] and in Chapter VII he speaks of a "more exact
plan."[62]

The "beginning of this plan" (*principium rationis*) in
Chapter VII is found in Romans 12:1, 2. For Calvin this is a
programmatic text of special significance: "I appeal to you
therefore brethren, by the mercies of God, to present your
bodies as a living sacrifice, holy and acceptable unto God,
which is your spiritual worship. Do not be conformed to this
world but be transformed by the renewal of your mind, that you
may prove what is the will of God ...."[63] After citing this
passage Calvin proceeds to elaborate the nature of the Christian life in terms of a repeated contrast: "We are not our
own ... we are the Lord's" (see Romans 14:8; I Corinthians
6:19). This is Calvin's "Christian philosophy" (*Christiana
philosophia*) which "bids reason give way to, submit and subject itself to the Holy Spirit so that man himself may no
longer live but hear Christ living and reigning within him"
(Galatians 2:20).[64]

In the above section Calvin also refers to Ephesians 4:
23, another key text in his understanding of the Christian
life. For in Ephesians 4:22-24 he finds the two basic principles of Christian living, namely, putting off the old nature
and putting on the new nature. (These are also the two elements of repentance, i.e., mortification and vivification.)[65]
In reference to this passage Calvin refers to two rules for a
godly and holy life. The first is "the denial of ourselves
and the regeneration of the Holy Spirit." The second--and
here again we have an echo of III.7.1--is "to live, not by
our own spirit, but by the Spirit of Christ."[66]

These are not the only texts which Calvin considers important for a "well-ordered life" (*vitae bene compositae*).
In the *Institutes* he also points to Titus 2:11-17[67] and "the
rule of love" as found in I Corinthians 13:4, 5.[68] But the
important thing to keep in mind is that this is what Calvin
means by the third use of the law![69] It does not mean that

we live according to the spirit of Moses and the Old Testament, but rather that with the law and the prophets as our foundation we live in Christ, for Christ, and by his Spirit. This is the will of God and the ultimate end of the rule of the law which is the rule of love.[70]

NOTES

1. *Institutes of the Christian Religion* (henceforth simply *Institutes*) II.7.12. In general I am using the translation of Ford Lewis Battles in the Library of Christian Classics series edited by John T. McNeill (Philadelphia: The Westminster Press, 1960). For Melanchthon and Luther the second use of the law, the *usus elenchticus* or *theologicus* is the "proper and principal use" (*"Secundum officium ac proprium legis divinae et praecipuum est ..."*) (Melanchthon, *Corpus Reformatorum* XXI, 405.) Luther uses the same terminology in his later (1535) Commentary on Galatians (WA, XL, 168, 481-483, 528) and further calls it "the true ... most important and the highest" use of the Law (WA, XL, 533); cf. the English translation by Jaroslav Pelikan in Luther's Works, Vol. 26 (St. Louis: Concordia Publishing House, 1963), pp. 91, 310-313, 345, 348. It is unlikely that by using similar terminology to describe the *third* use of the law Calvin was engaging in a polemic against Luther although Werner Elert, the late Lutheran theologian from Erlangen, was convinced that this was indeed Calvin's purpose. See his *Law and Gospel* (Philadelphia: Fortress Press, 1967), p. 44. This is a translation of an essay which originally appeared in a larger work of Elert's: *Zwischen Gnade und Ungnade: Abhandlungen des Themas Gesetz und Evangelium* (Munich, 1948).

For other parallels in Melanchthon and Zwingli see the long, valuable note on pages 334-335 in Ford Lewis Battles' English edition of the *Institution of the Christian Religion* (1536) (Atlanta: John Knox Press, 1975).

2. In his *Loci Communes,* both the second and third editions (C.R., XXI, 406). Cf. the English translation of the 1555 edition of the *Loci Communes* entitled *Melanchthon on Christian Doctrine,* edited by Clyde L. Manschreck, in A Library

of Protestant Thought (New York: Oxford University Press, 1965), pp. 122-128.

3. Section VI is entitled: "The Third Function of the Law." See *The Book of Concord*, edited by Theodore G. Tappert (Philadelphia: Fortress Press, 1959), pp. 479f.

4. See his essay, "The Three 'Uses' of the Law," in *Norm and Content in Christian Ethics*, edited by Gene H. Outka and Paul Ramsey (New York: Charles Scribner's Sons, 1968), p. 310.

5. Emil Brunner, *The Christian Doctrine of the Church, Faith, and Consummation*, Dogmatics: Vol. III (Philadelphia: The Westminster Press, 1962), p. 301. Brunner here reverses a position taken earlier in his ethics, *The Divine Imperative (Das Gebot und die Ordnungen)* (Philadelphia: Westminster Press, 1937), p. 149. See my discussion of this question in relation to the treatment of the law in Part III of the Heidelberg Catechism in *Guilt, Grace, and Gratitude*, edited by Donald J. Bruggink (New York: Half Moon Press, 1963), pp. 149ff.

6. See his *Situation Ethics: The New Morality* (Philadelphia: Westminster Press, 1966), the best known and most widely read and discussed representative of this movement.

7. One of the most controversial chapters in his best seller, *Honest to God* (London: SCM Press, 1963), "The New Morality," is indebted to an earlier, programmatic essay by Joseph Fletcher. Cf. Robinson's later work, *Christian Morals Today* (Philadelphia: Westminster Press, 1964).

8. See his *No New Morality* (London: Constable and Co., 1964).

9. *Institutes* IV.13.12.

10. Commentary on Jeremiah 32:33 (*Calvini Opera* = CO 39, 20); cf. Preface to Commentary on Isaiah (CO 36, 19); Commentary on Acts 2:23 (CO 48, 40).

11. New York: Harper and Row, 1963.

12. *Ibid.*, p. 78, n. 2.

13. The first edition of this work was published in Edinburgh in 1965; an enlarged version, which included a

response to Fletcher was published in 1967 by Charles Scribner's Sons. This work represents a considerable shift in thinking--and a marked improvement--vis à vis his earlier *Basic Christian Ethics* (New York: Charles Scribner's Sons, 1950).

14. Cf. three valuable symposia: *The Situation Ethics Debate,* edited by Harvey Cox (Philadelphia: Westminster Press, 1968); *Storm Over Ethics,* by John C. Bennett, James M. Gustafson, E. Clinton Gardner, *et al.* (Boston: United Church Press - Bethany Press, 1967); *Norm and Context in Christian Ethics,* edited by Gene H. Outka and Paul Ramsey (New York: Charles Scribner's Sons, 1968).

15. This essay first appeared in the April 1965 *Harvard Theological Review* and was reprinted in *New Theology No. 3,* edited by Martin E. Marty and Dean G. Peerman (New York: The Macmillan Co., 1966).

16. *Ibid.,* pp. 70ff.

17. *Ibid.,* p. 99. Gustafson deals with this in his outstanding book *Christ and the Moral Life* (New York: Harper & Row, 1968). Calvin is treated here in a perceptive and sympathetic manner, but Gustafson does not deal explicitly with the question I pose.

18. *Situation Ethics,* p. 69.

19. James F. Gustafson, from "How Does Love Reign?" originally a review in the *Christian Century,* May 12, 1966, and reprinted in *The Situation Ethics Debate,* p. 81. Cf. his essay "Love Monism" in *Storm Over Ethics.* Here he compares the "love monism" of Fletcher and Ramsey and concludes: "For both writers love is king; how he reigns, however, makes a lot of difference," p. 37.

20. "How New is the New Morality?" in *The Situation Ethics Debate,* pp. 220-221. This appeared originally in the *Reformed Review,* Vol. XX, No. 3 (March, 1967).

21. In contrast to ethicists (and historians) who simply label Calvin a legalist and find in him "a streak of ethical fundamentalism" (so N. H. G. Robinson, *The Groundwork of Christian Ethics* [Grand Rapids: Eerdmans, 1971], p. 20) it is refreshing to find one of America's foremost ethicists recognizing that in his understanding of the moral life "Calvin is more complex" than either Luther's or the Catholic approach (James M. Gustafson, *Theology and Christian Ethics* [Philadel-

phia: United Church Press, 1974], p. 173).

22. *Institutes* III.7.10.

23. III.8.4.

24. I.17.2.

25. II.8.59.

26. II.8.51.

27. Commentary on Jeremiah 9:15 (CO 38, 41).

28. Commentary on Isaiah 8:20 (CO 36, 184).

29. See *Institutes* II.8.5; IV.13.12; Genevan Catechism, Questions 130-132, *Opera Selecta* = OS 2, 96.

30. *Institutes* II.7.13.

31. *Kirche am Sinai*--"Die Zehn Gebote in der christlichen Unterweisung," by Hugo Röthlisberger (Zürich: Zwingli Verlag, 1965). See especially pp. 130f., 143f.

32. *Ibid.*, p. 101.

33. *The Christian Doctrine of Creation and Redemption.* Dogmatics: Vol. II (Philadelphia: Westminster Press, 1952), p. 219.

34. *Institutes* II.8.7.

35. II.8.8. Here Calvin is employing the principle of *synecdoche*, a figure of speech in which a part is used for the whole. For example, a commandment such as "Thou shalt not kill" is by *synecdoche* only a partial statement of what God fully intends by this commandment.

36. *Ibid.*

37. II.8.11.

38. He does this both in his Commentary on the Last Four Books of Moses (CO 24, 721-728) and in the *Institutes* II.8.51-59.

39. Actually, there are numerous references to Matthew 5 in this chapter of the *Institutes*. See especially II.8.7, 26, 57, 59.

40. Georgia Harkness, *John Calvin, The Man and His Ethics* (Nashville: Abingdon Press, paperback reprint, 1958), p. 63.

41. *Ibid.*, p. 113.

42. So Paul Wernle, *Der evangelische Glaube*, Band III, Calvin, p. 397. His actual words are "das verchristliche Gesetz."

43. *Ethics in a Christian Context* (New York: Harper & Row, 1963), p. 78.

44. *Prädestination und Verantwortlichkeit* (Darmstadt: Wissenschaftliche Buchgesellschaft, 1968--a reproduction of the first edition of 1937), p. 103.

45. *Institutes* III.6.1.

46. *Ibid.*

47. *Ibid.*

48. *Institutes* III.6.2.

49. III.6.5.

50. III.6.3. "The apostle teaches that God has destined all his children to the end that they be conformed to Christ (Romans 8:29)" (*Institutes* III.8.1). The context here is the key to the Christian life, viz., bearing the cross and sharing Christ's sufferings.

51. III.16.2.

52. III.16.3.

53. III.6.3. Beveridge translates *exemplar* as "model," cf. Commentary on Philippians 3:17 (CO 52, 54). I have concentrated on the commentaries, but Ronald Wallace notes that, "throughout his *Sermons* he frequently refers to Christ as the '*patron*' (i.e., "pattern") after which the children of God must be modeled (*configurez*) or to which they must be conformed (*conformez*)" (*Calvin's Doctrine of the Christian Life* [Edinburgh: Oliver and Boyd, 1957], p. 41). A good example is found in a sermon on Ephesians 4:23-24 (but not cited by Wallace): "Let us know that our Lord Jesus Christ is given us for an example (*example*) and pattern (*patron*), and moreover, that it is his office so to reform us by the Spirit of

God his Father, that we may walk in newness of life ...."
(CO 51, 623; cf. CO 51, 619).

54. Commentary on The Acts 7:30 (CO 48, 144); cf. Commentary on John 1:17 (CO 47, 18) and 5:38 (CO 47, 124).

55. Commentary on 2 Corinthians 3:16 (CO 50, 45).

56. Commentary on Romans 10:4 (CO 49, 196); *Institutes* II.7.2.

57. Commentary on Romans 10:4 (CO 49, 196).

58. James Gustafson, in his book *Christ and the Moral Life*, designates five ways in which Jesus Christ influences or determines the moral life: as the Lord who is creator and redeemer, as the sanctifier, the justifier, the pattern, and the teacher. He refers to Calvin in the discussion of all five categories, but finds him particularly illuminating in the last two. This corresponds to my own findings except that if space permitted, it could be shown that Calvin stressed growth and progress in the Christian life much more than Luther and therefore should receive more attention in the chapter, "Jesus Christ, the Sanctifier."

59. *Institutes* III.7.1.

60. Even though in another context he affirms, "Now it is certain that God's law has not taught us by halves *(a point enseignez à demi)* what we have to do, but God has shown us in it a right rule *(choite reigle)* to which nothing can be added, nor anything taken from it. For in these two points [love of God and neighbor] all our righteousness is contained ...." (Sermon on Ephesians 4:23-24 [CO 51, 622]).

61. *Institutes* III.6.1.

62. III.7.1.

63. *Ibid.*

64. *Ibid.*

65. See *Institutes* III.3.5-9.

66. Commentary on Ephesians 4:22-23 (CO 51, 208); cf. *Institutes* III.7.10.

67. *Institutes* III.7.3.

68. III.7.5-7.

69. This is by no means an exhaustive answer to the question of norms and decision making in regard to Calvin's treatment of the third use of the law. Two other facets of Calvin's approach which are significant are the role of the Christian community, the church, and the Holy Spirit. In the case of the former, Calvin comes close to Paul Lehmann's *koinonia* ethic. In fact, many years ago Paul Jacobs described Calvin's ethics as a *Gemeinschaftsethik (Prädestination und Verantwortlichkeit bei Calvin,* p. 91). The role of the Holy Spirit in decision making is immediately apparent in Calvin's frequent use (especially in the commentaries and sermons) of phrases like "the leading or guidance of the Spirit." See *Institutes* III.14.9 ("sancti Spiritus ductu"); IV.19.6 ("ductore et director"); Commentaries on Acts 17:11 (CO 48, 401); Romans 11:34 (CO 49, 231); I John 4:1 (CO 55, 347); Sermons on Ephesians 2:16-19 (CO 51, 418); 4:23 (CO 51, 617); 4:29-30 ("nous conduise et gouverne" [CO 51, 654]).

70. See *Institutes* II.8.49, 57; III.7.5.

3.

THE ECUMENICAL INTENTION OF CALVIN'S

EARLY EUCHARISTIC TEACHING

Joseph N. Tylenda

While in pursuit of a legal career, Calvin, still obedient to his father's injunction to put the clerical life aside, left Orléans in 1529 for Bourges.[1] The nineteen-year old student, together with many other young lawyers-to-be, was attracted to Bourges by the famous Italian jurist, Andreas Alciati, who had recently received an appointment there. While the young Calvin was on his way or only recently arrived, the city of Marburg was playing host to the German-speaking Reformers, Luther, Zwingli, and their associates. The differences between the Reformers had their most bitter expression in the area of eucharistic theology and the Landgrave, Philip of Hesse, proposed a religious colloquy to be held at Marburg to mend the crack in the common evangelical front. Philip envisioned that the reformed movement would issue forth united and reinvigorated, but his vision was never to be realized.

Unfortunately for the history of the reformation, neither Luther nor Zwingli attended Marburg with hearts ready for conciliation or compromise. They arrived as enemies and left as foes.[2] Both were firm on the meaning of the words "This is my body." Luther maintained that a bodily presence of Christ in the Eucharist was essential to the proper understanding of the Lord's Supper, while Zwingli considered such a presence nonessential. On this point no agreement was forthcoming. But rather than depart from the conference in so negative and inimical an atmosphere, Philip requested Luther to draft articles of faith which would express the beliefs held in common by the two opposing parties. Zwingli subscribed to Luther's articles,[3] and the difference of opinion on Christ's presence in the Supper is noted in the fifteenth article. On five of six points in that article there was genuine agreement, but

the sixth point was the critically important one. "And although at this time, we have not reached an agreement as to
whether the true body and blood of Christ are bodily present
in the bread and wine, nevertheless, each side should show
Christian love to the other side insofar as conscience will
permit, and both sides should diligently pray to Almighty God
that through his Spirit he might confirm us in the right understanding. Amen."[4]

Marburg was a failure, and the outcome of the colloquy
was regrettable. Though Luther and Zwingli shook hands as
they departed from Marburg, it was a handshake of friendship
but not of brotherhood.[5] The movement for reform was divided,
and divided it was to remain. When did Calvin first hear of
the colloquy and what were his reactions?[6] Unable to pinpoint
the event as we would like, it remains, nevertheless, certain
that the failure at Marburg served as an incentive to Calvin
to try his best to achieve what Luther and Zwingli could not
achieve.

The intent of this essay, therefore, is to examine Calvin's earliest attempts to achieve a unified doctrine on the
Supper, from the first edition of his *Institutes* in 1536 to
his *Short Treatise on the Lord's Supper* in 1541, and precisely
on the very point that divided the disputants at Marburg.
Calvin sincerely believed that his understanding of the Supper
was the solution to the Luther-Zwingli impasse, and he would
labor to effect a union between the Reformers.

I

Calvin first gave expression to his reflections on the
Lord's Supper in his *Institutes* of 1536.[7] In this edition the
young Calvin holds a position different from that of the sen-
ior Reformers, Luther and Zwingli. Calvin felt that they gave
undue emphasis to an aspect of the Supper that actually did
not merit it, and consequently they minimized its true force.
The true meaning of the sacrament, for Calvin, is known from
its very name. It is called the Lord's Supper precisely because in it the Lord feeds his faithful--partaking of the Supper means to be fed spiritually by Christ.[8] This spiritual
feeding is "the entire force of the Sacrament" and this we
learn from the words, "Take, eat, drink; this is my body which
is given for you; this is blood, which is shed for forgiveness
of sins."[9] By telling us to take and drink, Christ wants the
benefits gained by his crucified body to be ours, and by choos-

ing the elements of bread and wine he underlines the meaning
of the sacrament, or his purpose in instituting it. The bread
and wine show that his body and blood are meant to be life and
food for us. As bread nourishes and sustains the body, so
Christ's body supports and nurtures us spiritually; as wine
imparts warmth and gladness, his blood strengthens and exhila-
rates us. As food maintains life, gives growth, and makes us
healthy, so Christ, the food of the soul, protects us, invigo-
rates us, and grants whatever is necessary to live the Christian life.

Calvin would have preferred if Luther and Zwingli paid
more attention to this important facet of the Supper rather
than spending their efforts on how Christ's body and blood
were present. It is true that in this 1536 exposition Calvin
may not give the idea of spiritual nourishment an extended
treatment--this will have to wait for future editions of the
Institutes--but he does bring it to the forefront so as to
make it the cornerstone of his eucharistic theology.

Writing only a few years after the Marburg colloquy and
with the contemporary scene in mind, Calvin noted with sadness
the dissensions that existed among Christians with reference
to the Supper. In 1536 he wrote:

> If this force of the sacrament had been
> examined and weighed as it deserved, there
> would have been quite enough to satisfy us,
> and these frightful contentions would not
> have arisen which of old, and even within
> our memory have miserably troubled the
> church, when men in their curiosity endeavored
> to define how Christ's body is present in the
> bread.[10]

The young reformer is gentle in his criticism of his
elders and it is fitting that he should be so. Such frightful
contentions have arisen because men have set aside Christ's
meaning of the Supper and have fallen victim to their own
curiosity. The cause of the dissension lies not in Christ's
teaching but in the interpreters themselves. Calvin's underlying argument is quite simple--abandon your curiosity and
return to the Word, then there will be union. By referring
to others' curiosity, he couches his censure in palatable
terms, but he really means that to try and define how Christ's
body is present in the bread is to go beyond Scripture. Such
an explanation is the product of man's own devising and hence
idle speculation. Calvin continues his text:

> Some men, to prove themselves subtle, added to
> the simplicity of Scripture: that he is 'really'
> and 'substantially' present. Still others even
> went farther: they said he has the same dimen-
> sions in which he hung on the cross. Others de-
> vised a wondrous transubstantiation. Others
> said that the bread itself was the body. Others,
> that it was the bread. Others that only a sign
> and figure of the body were set forth.[11]

Any reader of the above, familiar with the eucharistic theologies of Calvin's day, and earlier, would have had no difficulty
in recognizing the positions of the Roman Catholics, Lutherans,
and Zwinglians. Calvin is setting himself against all these
positions, but since he is a budding theologian and recently
come upon the scene, he does this respectfully without giving
names. Nonetheless, he accuses his opponents of being unsatis-
fied with God's Word and this dissatisfaction has led them to
make additions to the sacred text. Calvin is an acute observer
of the reformed scene and dares to accuse Lutherans and Zwinglians of the very charge they bring against the Roman Catholics,
i.e., adding to Scripture. While others make additions, Calvin
prefers to keep to Scripture's simplicity. He hurriedly leaves
this catalog of opinions to return to what he considers of
greater importance.

> This is indeed an important matter, over which
> great disputes, of words and minds, have arisen.
> So indeed it is commonly established; but those
> who feel thus, do not pay attention in the first
> place, to the necessity of asking how Christ's
> body, as it was given for us, became ours; how
> his blood, as it was shed for us, became ours.
> But that means to possess the whole Christ cru-
> cified, and to become a participant in all his
> benefits. Now, overlooking those highly impor-
> tant matters, in fact neglecting and well-nigh
> burying them, our opponents fight over this one
> thorny question: How is the body devoured by
> us.[12]

The question of Christ's presence in the Supper is indeed
important and on this point Calvin approaches Luther's opinion
rather than that of Zwingli, who thought it nonessential. But
its importance is a relative importance, that is, relative to
the Supper understood as spiritual nourishment. To overempha-
size eucharistic presence to the detriment of eucharistic finality, i.e., spiritual nourishment, is to obscure, even do
away with the Supper's true meaning.

When Calvin speaks of Christ's presence he chooses not to call it a "real" or "substantial" presence. This is the language of his opponents. In his dedicatory letter to Francis I, introducing the 1536 *Institutes*, he marshalls patristic evidence to support his claims, e.g., "It was one of the fathers who said that the true body was not in the sacrament of the Supper, but only the mystery of the body .... Therefore they overstep the bounds when they make it real and substantial."[13] To refer to Christ's presence as "real" and "substantial" is to go beyond proper limits. Consequently, rejecting the Catholic and Lutheran expressions on Christ's presence, and setting aside Zwingli's mere sign or figure, Calvin endeavors to settle into a middle position advocating a presence which is not a bodily presence, but at the same time not such an absence of the body which would render the Supper a mere sign or figure.

Calvin solves this problematic by asserting that because the promises of Christ are united with the sacrament "we must certainly consider him truly shown [*exhiberi*] to us, just as if Christ himself present were set before our gaze and touched by our hands."[14] Since the Supper's focus is spiritual, "the Lord willed to feed not our bellies but our souls, and let us seek Christ in it, not for our body ... but in such a way that the soul recognizes it as it were present and shown forth [*exhibitum*]. In short, we have enough to obtain him spiritually."[15] A spiritual reception of Christ's body necessarily implies his presence and Calvin has no doubt in this matter, just as he has no doubt that if Christ were physically present this would then entail a physical eating. But Christ cannot be physically present because "he has taken his flesh from us, and in the body has ascended into heaven .... Thus uncircumscribed, Christ can exert his power wherever he pleases, in heaven and on earth; he can show [*exhibeat*] his presence in power and strength ...."[16] It is in this manner, then, that "the body and blood of Christ are shown [*exhibetur*] to us in the Sacrament."[17]

In the above citations Calvin uses various forms of the verb *exhibere*. It is a favorite word of his, and since he uses it so frequently it indicates its importance to him. It is not always easy to translate, and one has to struggle to be sure that Calvin's underlying meaning is properly expressed. Calvin certainly does not use it as a synonym for *adesse*, to be present, because this word indicates a real, physical presence. *Exhibere* does not bring about a presence but presupposes a presence and manifests it.[18] Therefore, the bread and wine of the Supper are *signa*, not *signa repraesentativa*, signs representing something absent, but *signa exhibitiva*,[19] signs

manifesting something present. Calvin will never abandon
this word, and will use it throughout his career when speaking
of the Supper.[20]

Though Calvin intended his 1536 *Institutes* as a summary
of the reformed faith for his countrymen in France, so that
they might know what to accept and what to reject in the matter of religion, he really did not envision himself at this
time as an arbiter between Lutherans and Zwinglians. But in
point of fact, the eucharistic teaching of 1536 is his solution to the Marburg impasse. Nor did Calvin deliberately ex-
cogitate this intermediate position just to bring about a
union of the Protestants, but he honestly saw his teaching as
the teaching of the sacred text. Referring to his interpretation of Christ's words of institution, he says: "But if we
so tenaciously stick to the words, the words also splendidly
support me."[21] All Calvin intended to do was to give the
simple truth of the Word.

II

For the two years that followed the publication of his
Institutes, Calvin was involved in establishing the reformation in Geneva. In 1538, because of a dispute with the Genevan magistrates about using the customs of Bern in adminis-
tering the Lord's Supper, Calvin was forced to leave the city.
Eventually, he came to reside in Strasbourg, where he would
remain for the next three years. These years proved to be
among Calvin's happiest; they afforded him the friendship of
Bucer, freedom from consistorial harassment, peace in which
he could minister to his French congregation, and leisure to
write his *Commentary on Romans* and revise his *Institutes.*

Every friendship involves mutual exchange and influence,
and Calvin's friendship with Bucer was no exception. But the
degree of this influence has not yet been fully delineated.[22]
While still in Geneva, Calvin became familiar with Bucer's
attempts at union with Bullinger and the theologians of Zurich,
and now that he was in Strasbourg at Bucer's side, he was to
become a part of this movement.[23]

On the occasion of Bucer's visit to Germany in October
1538, to speak with Luther and the Landgrave of Hesse, Calvin
gave Bucer a letter for Philip Melanchthon together with
twelve articles. Unfortunately, the letter and articles have

not survived. Referring to these, Calvin wrote to his intimate friend, Guillaume Farel: "If he grants these to me, I
would demand nothing more from him or from Luther."[24]

A conference of political leaders and theologians was
scheduled for February, 1539 at Frankfurt--the questions to
be discussed were the great issues of the day, religious
peace for Germany and war against the Turks. Three months
had passed and Calvin still had not received word from Melanchthon about his articles; but he did receive a letter from
Bucer, then in Germany. Upon reading Bucer's letter, Calvin
was taken with an overwhelming desire to go to Germany immediately and help him, but he was especially interested in
meeting Melanchthon and talking with him about religious matters and his articles.[25] In mid-February Calvin set out for
Frankfurt where he represented the Strasbourg church, and
finally met Melanchthon. Calvin wrote his impressions of the
Frankfurt conference to Farel.[26] With reference to the war
with the Turks, it still remained a possibility; with regard
to the question of religious peace in Germany, the matter was
suspended until a future date when approved men would assemble
and discuss the religious topics now under controversy.[27]
And of his meeting with Melanchthon? "I spoke with Philip
about many things. I had previously written him about the
question of agreement so that we could with certainty declare
their opinions to other good men. With this end in view, I
had sent a few articles in which I briefly summed up the entire matter. He himself agreed without contradicting any of
them, but admitted that there were some in the party who de-
manded something more gross [crassius], and with such stub-
bornness and even imperiousness, that for some time he seemed
to be in danger since they saw that he was of an opinion different from theirs .... But as for himself, there is no doubt
that he completely agrees with us."[28] The exact subject matter of the articles sent to Melanchthon is unknown, but it
would not be far-fetched to conclude that at least one dealt
with the Supper, perhaps the very one on which Melanchthon and
Calvin agreed, while others took a more gross view.[29]

In addition to this basic agreement, Calvin also spoke
to Melanchthon on the question of ceremonies, obviously connected with the administration of the Supper. "I did not dis-
guise the fact that the abundance of ceremonies displeased me,
and that it seemed to me that their present form was not far
from Judaism. As I pressed on, he did not want to discuss
this point but granted that many of their ceremonies were
either absurd or at least superfluous, and held that he was
forced to make this concession because of the obstinacy of
the canonists."[30]

In October, Bucer received a letter from Luther in which
he sent regards to Calvin and Sturm and asked that they be informed that he had "read their books with special delight."[31]
Calvin naturally appreciated Luther's praise, and in a letter
to Farel, dated November 20, 1539, he ebulliently tells his
friend of Luther's kind remark and adds, "Just think of what
I have said there about the Eucharist, and see Luther's in-
genuousness."[32] Calvin understood Luther's comment as not
having taken offense at his contrary position on the Supper.
In Luther's letter to Bucer, he did not actually identify what
he had read of Calvin, but he does speak of Sadoleto, and must
be referring to Calvin's answer to the cardinal. But in this
answer Calvin does not treat the Eucharist. Luther may also
be referring to the 1536 *Institutes,* and perhaps its revised
and augmented version that had appeared in August of 1539.
In any case, Calvin applies Luther's remark to his teaching
on the Supper. Continuing in his letter he tells Farel of a
letter he had received from Melanchthon in which Philip told
him how certain individuals, bent on irritating Luther, had
pointed out to him certain passages from Calvin's writings in
which Luther and his friends were criticized. Luther read the
passages and felt that they were indeed intended for him and
said: "I hope that Calvin will one day think better of us;
but in any event it is good that he should now have a proof
of our good will towards him."[33] Calvin was profoundly affected by Luther's moderation.

So, as the year 1539 was coming to a close, Calvin had
reason for hope. Melanchthon agreed with him on the Supper,
and Luther, fully knowing that Calvin's view of the Supper
was different from his own, nevertheless took no offense but
remained cordial and sincerely interested in him. With both
leaders of the German reformation so amicably disposed toward
him, Calvin may have thought that the time had come to write
an ecumenical treatise on the Eucharist.

Frankfurt was Calvin's first taste in international ecumenical dialogue, and his remaining months at Strasbourg were
taken up with union activities. Since the Frankfurt conference
had decreed a future religious colloquy, Charles V convoked
it for June 1540, at Speyer. But Speyer was suffering from
an epidemic and the site was changed to Hagenau. Calvin attended the colloquy,[34] but Melanchthon, on his way to the conference, unfortunately suffered a complete breakdown, and had
to return home.[35] The colloquy was a failure; its purpose was
to prepare a common agenda for a future general conference,
but the Catholics had their agenda and the Protestants theirs,
insisting that it be the Augsburg Confession and Melanchthon's
Apology. Neither side would yield in compromise. Seeing no

way out of the impasse, King Ferdinand resolved to interrupt the colloquy and have it continue at Worms in three months time.

That of Worms was another failure since it did not achieve its goal. It was convoked for October 29, 1540, but discussions between both parties never began until January of the following year. This time the basis for the discussion was the Augsburg Confession, and the plan was to study it article by article. Beginning with the Trinity, there was immediate agreement; original sin followed and here were the first conflicts. After four days of discussion, a committee of four was named to formulate a common statement, then, to everyone's astonishment, a letter of the Emperor was read adjourning the conference until the Diet of Regensburg (Ratisbon). It appeared that Charles V wanted to promote the work of reunion by his own presence.[36]

Now, the Augsburg Confession presented for discussion at Worms was not that of 1530; it was a new version produced by Melanchthon precisely for the Worms colloquy to facilitate negotiations and to make it easier for the Protestants to present a united front. Looking upon the Confession as his handiwork, Melanchthon made changes in it wherever he willed. When the Confession was originally approved Melanchthon vigorously defended Luther's teaching on the real presence, but his 1540 version was a definite deviation from the original. Article 10 of the 1530 reads: "Our churches teach that the body and blood of Christ are truly present and are distributed [quod corpus et sanguis Christi vere adsint et distribuantur] to those who eat in the Supper of the Lord. They disapprove of those who teach otherwise."[37] The 1540 reading is as follows: "On the Supper of the Lord they teach that the body and blood of Christ are truly exhibited with the bread and wine [cum pane et vino vere exhibeantur corpus et sanguis Christi] to those who eat in the Supper of the Lord."[38] Within a period of ten years Melanchthon set aside the real presence and is tolerant of other opinions regarding Christ's presence.

Inasmuch as the *adsint* and *distribuantur* of 1530 became *exhibeantur* in 1540, the word used by Calvin in his 1536 *Institutes*, it is but natural to inquire whether Calvin had any influence on Melanchthon in this change, not only in word but also in the understanding of Christ's presence in the Supper.[39] In later years Calvin will speak of how this change came about saying that Melanchthon dropped *adsint* for *exhibeantur* at the insistence of some of the delegates, of whom he was one.[40]

Calvin approved Melanchthon's new version, called *variata*

to distinguish it from the original *invariata;* in 1557 he
wrote: "I do not reject the Augsburg Confession which I long
ago willingly and with pleasure subscribed to, as the author
himself explained it."[41] Whenever Calvin speaks approvingly
of the Confession, he means the *variata,* and insists that his
understanding of it is identical with that of its author.
For Calvin, Melanchthon was its only legitimate interpreter,
and now that he and Melanchthon were in agreement, Calvin had
reason to have joy in his heart. The breakthrough with the
Lutherans had been made.

From Worms the colloquists went to Regensburg. The session began on April 5, 1541, and the basis for the discussion
was the Regensburg Book, twenty-three articles of tentative
agreement, the product of Gropper, Bucer and others, written
under the direction of the Emperor. Though the evangelical
party would have preferred to use the Augsburg Confession
(i.e., *variata*), nevertheless, in deference to the Emperor
the Regensburg Book was accepted as the starting point, but
this did not keep the evangelicals from formally presenting
their Confession at the beginning of the Diet. The discussion
began where they left off at Worms, on original sin.[42] Next,
they had a spirited debate on justification arriving at a
common formula; then on to the church, where differences were
such that the discussion was discontinued. When it came to
the Supper, transubstantiation proved such an insurmountable
obstacle that it effectively brought an end to all further
progress.

Narrating the events of Regensburg to Farel, Calvin tells
how the Protestants rejected transubstantiation,[43] and how the
Catholics would not yield on this point. Though Bucer worked
enthusiastically for agreement he now became indignant, while
Melanchthon would do nothing to endanger the hope for religious
peace. The evangelicals were then summoned together each to
make known his opinion. Calvin notes that he was unable to
understand what the others had said since he did not know German, but nonetheless, he was asked to share his opinion and
this he did in Latin and fearlessly, not caring whether he
would be going counter to any of the previous speakers. The
evangelicals unanimously rejected transubstantiation. "We
teach that with the bread after it has been consecrated, the
body of Jesus is given [*donné, exhiberi*] to those who receive
it; we do not say that this comes about by transubstantiation."[44]
Melanchthon drew up a statement, but it was rejected. Then
Bucer and Melanchthon joined in producing an "ambiguous formula" concerning transubstantiation to see whether they could
satisfy the Catholics but at the same time yield nothing.
Calvin truthfully admits to Farel that this mode of action

was not altogether pleasing to him, but he assures Farel that
both Melanchthon and Bucer had good reasons for so acting; in
fact, both of them were filled with the best of intentions
and their only view was to promote the kingdom of Christ.[45]
Convinced that nothing else was going to come out of Regensburg, Calvin returned to Geneva.

III

The Genevans had been trying for months to lure Calvin
back to their city; they finally achieved their goal and Calvin returned September, 1541. Shortly after his arrival, his
Short Treatise on the Lord's Supper was published in the city.
Though printed in Geneva, it was written in Strasbourg probably
in 1540,[46] and since Calvin gives no details about its composi-
tion, one wonders whether it was written prior or subsequent
to Calvin's approval of Melanchthon's new version of the Augsburg Confession. It was first written in French, and had a
Latin translation in 1545.[47]

Calvin introduces his *Short Treatise* recognizing a plurality of opinions then current on the Supper, and that this
plurality has given rise to contentious disputes. Because of
the disputes, individuals, whose consciences are weak and who
of themselves are unable to resolve which view they should
hold, have unfortunately suspended judgment waiting for the
day when the contentions would come to an end and the theologians come to some agreement. Since that day has not arrived,
and since such a state is dangerous, Calvin feels obliged to
set forth the fundamentals that need to be known on the Supper.
His intention, then, is not to deal with the disputed questions, nor to solve them; rather, to give the rudiments of
eucharistic theology, showing there is a common ground which
could well serve as the foundation for the theologians in dispute to come together.[48]

Calvin divides his treatise into five parts, and it is
only in the fifth part that he speaks of Luther and Zwingli,
and shows less interest in the content of the dispute than
in the manner in which the dispute was carried on. In the
first part, Calvin writes of Christ's purpose in instituting
the Supper: "But as the life into which he has regenerated
us is spiritual, so the food for preserving and confirming us
in it must be spiritual."[49] The second part deals with the
benefits of the Supper, indicating that "the peculiar consola-
tion we receive from the Supper [is] that it directs and

conducts us to the cross of Jesus Christ and to his resurrection ... being made partakers of the death and passion of Jesus Christ, we have everything that is useful and salutary for us."[50] The third section deals with the right use of the Supper, that it ought to be observed according to the institution of Christ and celebrated frequently.

Almost half of the entire treatise is devoted to the fourth part, which is Calvin's polemic against the Catholic teaching on the Supper. Calvin covers the usual topics of transubstantiation, sacrifice, communion under both kinds, ceremonies, etc. But what is of note is that while Calvin argues against the Catholic position on the presence of Christ's body and blood, he keeps silent about Luther's holding a similar teaching.[52] Calvin is totally silent on other Lutheran issues connected with the real presence, e.g., whether the words of institution are to be taken literally or figuratively, the teaching on ubiquity as well as that on *manducatio indignorum*. Calvin deliberately withholds discussion of these divisive topics so that he can show a common and united front against the Catholics.

It is in the fifth part that Calvin approaches the dispute between Luther and Zwingli and desires to be the bridge-builder. Calvin has to face the fact that there have been and are differences, but he must not lay the blame at anyone's feet; he has to admit that they were in error but, nevertheless, they were not totally wrong; he wants to correct them, but still he wants to keep from offending them.

In calling the readers' attention to the recent disputes, Calvin asks them not to be offended because differences have arisen among God's servants, rather they must realize that the Lord has chosen to leave these servants in some ignorance and it was ignorance that led them into contention, but this is only a temporary situation. On the other hand, the readers are asked to see the depth of the darkness in which these religious leaders had been brought up before they took up their ministry, so even with God's illumination, it is no wonder that they could not know everything from the beginning.[53]

As for Luther's opinion on Christ's presence, Calvin recalls that Luther rejected transubstantiation, but said that "the bread was the body of Christ, insofar as it was united to him." Calvin finds fault with the similes Luther used to explain his opinion, but makes allowances saying that Luther "did so by constraint, because he could not otherwise explain his meaning. For it is difficult to give an explanation of so high a matter, without using some impropriety of speech."[54]

On the other hand, Zwingli and Oecolampadius, intent on counteracting the teaching on transubstantiation, gave such great emphasis to the ascent of Christ's humanity into heaven that "they forgot to define what is the presence of Christ in the Supper in which one ought to believe, and what communication of his body and his blood one there received."[55] Because of this "forgetfulness" Luther concluded that they intended to leave nothing in the Supper but bare signs. Thus the dispute began.

Calvin then advances to the manner in which the unfortunate dispute took place, and here he is more truthful to the facts. He notes that the discussions should have been done in a peaceful frame of mind, but they were not; rather than coming together in good will and to listen to each other, their only intent was to refute. He accuses Luther of bitterness of speech, impatience, violence in attack, exaggeration in words; Zwingli is guilty of referring to Christ's presence in the bread as superstitious, fantastic, and perverse.

Admitting these human frailties in the disputants, Calvin concludes that we ought not forget the gifts that God has bestowed on them, and the blessings which he has distributed through them. Being grateful for what we owe them, we can pardon them these excesses without blaming them: "Since we see that they were and still are distinguished by holy life and excellent knowledge and by conspicuous zeal to edify the Church, we ought always to judge and speak with modesty and reverence."[56] Finally, he suggests, "it has pleased God at last ... to bring to an end this unhappy disputation, or at least to calm it, in anticipation of it being quite resolved. I say this because there is not yet any published formula in which agreement has been framed, as would be expedient. But all this will happen when God is pleased to bring into one place all those who are to draw it up."[57]

Calvin undoubtedly felt that his teaching on the Supper was the solution; if it did not actually bring an end to the dispute, it could at least bring it calm until an agreed statement could be formulated. Calvin sincerely looked forward to such a future statement. It is not altogether strange for Calvin to think that he had the solution; in the *Short Treatise* he expresses this obliquely and with modesty, but in his 1536 *Institutes* he expressed it with the brash arrogance of youth, saying that in this matter few persons had "hit the nail on the head" as he had.[58] By the end of 1541 there was no unified teaching on the Supper, nor was it foreseen when such an agreement would be had. Calvin's *Short Treatise* made it clear that unity could be reached on the fundamentals of eucharistic

teaching, but unfortunately the very issues in the dispute
were very much cherished by the Lutherans and Zwinglians.
Each party saw its teaching as being conformed to Scripture;
for them to set these questions aside, as Calvin would want
because he saw them as mere subtleties, would be to go against
the Word of God.

The *Short Treatise* was translated into Latin by des
Gallars in 1545, and Luther is said to have seen a copy of
it in a Wittenberg bookstore. The shopkeeper informed Luther
that he had just returned from the Frankfurt fair with the
book, and that in Frankfurt everyone spoke of Calvin as a
young man, learned and godly. Luther picked up the book,
read the first few pages and last few, those dealing with the
dispute. Then Luther said, "This is certainly a learned and
godly man, and I might well have entrusted this controversy
to him from the beginning. If my opponents had done the same
we should have been reconciled."[59] Luther is more probably
referring to Calvin's ecumenical spirit rather than his acceptance of Calvin's teaching on the Supper.

In the years following the *Short Treatise,* Calvin continued to labor towards eucharistic unity. He hoped that
Melanchthon's view of the Supper would one day prevail among
the Lutherans. But in 1544, Luther unfortunately published
his *Brief Confession Concerning the Holy Sacrament,* in which
he renewed his vehement attack on Zwingli and his followers.
But with Luther's death in 1546, there was the renewed hope
that Melanchthon, now guiding the German movement, would have
his opinion finally accepted.

In 1549, Calvin and Bullinger published their *Consensus
Tigurinus,* a mutual agreement on the sacraments. While the
Swiss churches were successful in achieving unity, the Lutherans were suffering from internal division. Those who followed
Luther's hard line set themselves against those who preferred
Melanchthon's liberalizing tendencies. A minister from the
former group, Joachim Westphal, initiated a pamphlet war with
Calvin on the Supper.[60] Where Calvin had been reticent in
his early *Institutes* and his *Short Treatise* about making known
his true opinion of the Lutheran teaching on the real presence
and ubiquity, the minister's treatises afforded Calvin's polemic pen the opportunity to bring his opinions out in the open.
Referring to the Lutherans in his 1559 *Institutes,* Calvin
writes: "And surely certain men would rather manifest their
ignorance to their great shame than yield even the least parti-
cle of their error. I am not speaking of the papists, whose
doctrine is more tolerable or at least more modest."[61] This
praise of the Catholic position may indicate that Calvin was

beginning to relinquish hopes of a united reformed movement.

In 1564, Calvin died, and not only was his dream of unity not realized, but the Protestant front was, perhaps, more seriously divided than ever. Foreseeing that their internal strife could mean the demise of their movement, the Lutherans courageously took the means to gather themselves together. In 1567 they condemned Melanchthon's *variata*, equivalently rejecting Calvin's understanding of the Supper, and returned to the 1530 Augsburg Confession, inserting it into the official *Book of Concord*.[62] Thus the Lutherans regained their original unity, but they were as distant from the reformed churches of Switzerland as Luther was from Zwingli when they departed Marburg.

NOTES

1. Cf. Émile Doumergue, *Jean Calvin: Les hommes et les choses de son temps*, Vol. 1 (Lausanne: Bridel, 1899), p. 141.

2. For a description of the events at Marburg, cf. Walther Köhler, *Zwingli und Luther*, Vol. 2 (Gütersloh: Bertelsmann, 1953), pp. 66-163, also Hermann Sasse, *This Is My Body: Luther's Contention for the Real Presence in the Sacrament of the Altar* (Minneapolis: Augsburg, 1959), pp. 187-294.

3. Luther did not expect Zwingli to sign the articles, but he signed them not because he was in full agreement with their doctrinal content, but because he believed in the need of achieving solidarity with the Wittenbergers. Cf. *Luther's Works*, Vol. 38 (Philadelphia: Fortress, 1971), pp. 12-13.

4. *Luther's Works*, Vol. 38, pp. 88-89.

5. Cf. James Atkinson, *Martin Luther and the Birth of Protestantism* (Baltimore: Penguin, 1968), p. 274.

6. Jean Pannier, in his edition of Calvin's 1541 *Institution de la religion chrétienne*, Vol. 4 (Paris: Société

d'édition "Les Belles Lettres"), p. 300, suggests that Calvin heard about the colloquy from Melchior Wolmar, an acquaintance of his from his days in Orléans, who moved to Bourges sometime in 1530. Also see Alexandre Ganoczy, *Le jeune Calvin: Genèse et évolution de sa vocation réformatrice* (Wiesbaden: Steiner, 1966), pp. 49-50.

7. Cf. *Joannis Calvini opera selecta*, ed. P. Barth and G. Niesel (Munich: Kaiser, 1926-1928), Vol. 1, pp. 132-162. The 1536 edition has been translated by Ford Lewis Battles under the title *Institution of the Christian Religion* (Atlanta: John Knox, 1975), and the matter touching on the Supper will be found in pp. 139-168. References to the former will be designated by *OS*, those to the latter by *Inst.*

8. Cf. *OS* 1:136. Of course, Calvin also admits it is called the Eucharist because by it we give thanks to Christ for his kindness towards us, but Calvin has greater emphasis on spiritual nourishment than on thanksgiving.

9. *OS* 1:137-138; *Inst.* 140. Calvin uses a variety of words connected with eating to describe this facet of nourishment, e.g., *pascimur, edite, bibite, manducare, vitam ac alimentum, alit, cibum, potum, vescamur, gustum* and *saporem*. All these words appear in the first paragraphs introducing his teaching on the Supper.

10. *OS* 1:139; *Inst.* 141.

11. *OS* 1:139; *Inst.* 141-142. Further identification of these opinions can be found in the notes of *OS* 1:139 and *Inst.* 369-370.

12. *OS* 1:139; *Inst.* 142.

13. *OS* 1:28; *Inst.* 10. On Calvin's preference for the word "true" rather than "real," cf. J. Tylenda, "Calvin and Christ's Presence in the Supper--True or Real," *Scottish Journal of Theology* 27 (1974) 65-75; for his understanding of "substance," see J. Tylenda, "Calvin on Christ's True Presence in the Lord's Supper," *American Ecclesiastical Review* 154 (1966) 321-333, esp. pp. 325-327.

14. *OS* 1:137; *Inst.*140.

15. *OS* 1:139-140; *Inst.* 142.

16. *OS* 1:142; *Inst.* 145.

17. *Ibid.*

18. Boniface Meyer, "Calvin's Eucharistic Doctrine: 1536-1539," *Journal of Ecumenical Studies* 4 (1967) 42, n. 11, says that *exhibitio* "combines the two basic elements of visibilization and actualization." Does Meyer mean that *exhibitio* actualizes, brings about, the presence and then manifests it?

19. C. L. A. R. Hope, in reviewing the Battles' translation of the 1559 *Institutes (Zeitschrift für Kirchengeschichte* 74 [1964] 404) notes the difficulty in translating the word *exhibere*, and recognizes that it is a key word in Calvin's eucharistic theology. In the review Hope calls attention to an article of his on a letter of Bucer to Jan Laski ("Martin Bucer's Letter to John à Lasco on the Eucharist," *Journal of Theological Studies* 48 [1947] 66) wherein the Strasbourg reformer uses the expression *signa exhibitiva*. Hope concludes in his review that Calvin's use of *exhibitio* and *exhibere* stems from Bucer. But the Bucer letter to Laski dates from 1545 and Calvin was using the word in 1536! Therefore, if anyone insists on making Bucer the source of Calvin's use of *exhibere*, the task is to show Bucer's influence on Calvin prior to 1536.

20. In Book IV of the 1559 *Institutes*, Calvin uses the word 17 times in chapter 17, twice in chapter 18, and once in chapter 19. Cf. Ford Lewis Battles, *A Computerized Concordance to Institutio Christianae Religionis 1559 of Joannes Calvinus* (1972).

21. *OS* 1:143; *Inst.* 146.

22. For Bucer's influence on Calvin in the area of liturgy, cf. Doumergue, *op. cit.*, Vol. 2, pp. 488-504, and the bibliography there given. See also W. Pauck, "Calvin and Butzer" in his *The Heritage of the Reformation* (Glencoe, Ill.: Free Press, 1961), pp. 85-99.

23. For an overview of Calvin's union activities, see John T. McNeill, "Union Activities of Calvin and Beza" in his *Unitive Protestantism: The Ecumenical Spirit and Its Persistent Expression* (Richmond: John Knox, 1964), pp. 178-220.

24. *Joannis Calvini opera quae supersunt omnia (OC)*, edited by Baum, Cunitz and Reuss, 59 Vols., (Brunswick, 1863-1900); the reference will be found *OC* 10b:279. See also Doumergue, *op. cit.*, Vol. 2, p. 537.

25. *OC* 10b:322-323.

26. Cf. the letters of March 16, 1539 (*OC* 10b:322-329) and the end of March (*OC* 10b:330-332).

27. Cf. *OC* 10b:327.

28. *OC* 10b:331.

29. Doumergue, *op. cit.*, Vol. 2, p. 539, is of this opinion as is J. Janssen, *L'Allemagne et la réforme* 3: *L'Allemagne de 1525 à 1555* (Paris: Plon, Nourrit, 1892), p. 419. For Janssen's discussion of the Frankfurt conference see pp. 419-426.

30. *OC* 10b:340.

31. *OC* 10b:402 and 432.

32. *OC* 10b:432.

33. *Ibid.*

34. For Calvin's report on this colloquy see his letter to du Tailly (*OC* 11:64-67); on the conference in general, cf. Doumergue, *op. cit.*, Vol. 2, pp. 604-605, and Janssen, *op. cit.*, pp. 473-474.

35. Cf. Sasse, *op. cit.*, p. 311.

36. For a description of the Worms conference, cf. Doumergue, *op. cit.*, Vol. 2, pp. 611-620, and Janssen, *op. cit.*, pp. 475-476.

37. *The Book of Concord: The Confessions of the Evangelical Lutheran Church*, translated and edited by Theodore G. Tappert (Philadelphia: Fortress, 1959), p. 34.

38. *Melanchthons Werke 6: Bekenntnisse und kleine Lehrschriften*, edited by Robert Stupperich (Gütersloh: Bertelsmann, 1955), p. 19. Cf. also W. Maurer, "Confessio Augustana Variata," *Archiv für Reformationsgeschichte* 53 (1962) 97-151.

39. Clyde L. Manschreck (*Melanchthon: The Quiet Reformer* [Nashville: Abingdon, 1958], p. 241) holds that Melanchthon had come to a belief in the spiritual presence even before Calvin had come upon the scene, but admits that Melanchthon's new wording allowed for an interpretation which Calvin would accept.

40. On November 13, 1554, Calvin wrote to the Ministers of Zurich (*OC* 15:305): "Worthy brethren, the reasons why I can hardly agree with you with regard to the Augsburg Confession are these: that it proceeded from Luther is improbable to me, nevertheless, because of the constant urging of certain individuals at Worms, Philip was influenced to drop a word from that chapter. When the new version appeared the Papists raised an outcry calling us Zwinglians and forgers. Among the men in our party, Brenz was one who was unfavorable, but had already become more tractable. I brought Cruciger entirely over to our side." Also see W. Nijenhuis, "Calvin and the Augsburg Confession," in his *Ecclesia Reformata: Studies on the Reformation* (Leiden: Brill, 1972), pp. 97-114.

41. *OC* 16:430. Nijenhuis, *op. cit.*, p. 108 notes other changes in the Confession that could hardly have been acceptable to Calvin, e.g., free will.

42. Calvin's views on the Diet of Ratisbon are found in his letters to Farel dated March 28, 1541 (*OC* 11:174-180), April 24 (*OC* 11:202-204), May 11 (*OC* 11:215-216), May 12 (*OC* 11:217-218), July (*OC* 11:250-252), and to Viret, August 3 (*OC* 11:261-263).

43. When Calvin returned from the Diet he published *Les Actes de la journée imperiale tenue en la cité de Regespourg, aultrement dicte Ratispone, l'an mil cinq cens quarante et un, sur les differens qui sont auiourdhuy en la religion 1541.* The section of the Regensburg Book dealing with transubstantiation reads: "After the consecration the true body and the true blood of the Lord are truly and substantially present, and they are distributed to the faithful under the appearance of bread and wine, that is to say, they are changed and transubstantiated into the body and blood of our Lord" (*OC* 5:541). Note that the above statement avoids speaking of a real presence.

44. *OC* 5:567, the Protestant articles on certain points in the Regensburg Book. Calvin's French translation of the acta uses *donné* for "give," but the Latin word is *exhiberi*. The Latin reads: *"Ita nos docemus, cum pane consecrato exhiberi corpus Christi sumentibus: nec docemus fieri transsubstantiatio ..."* (quoted from Hope, *op. cit.*, p. 404).

45. *OC* 11:217.

46. In a letter dated March 17, 1546 to Veit Dietrich of Nürnberg, Calvin wrote, "I am very glad that my little book on the Supper was not displeasing to you. It was written in French

ten years ago" (*OC* 12:316). If the ten years are to be taken literally it would then mean that it was written in 1537 when Calvin was still in Geneva. The French version of the treatise may be found in *OS* 1:503-530; an English translation may be found in *Calvin: Theological Treatises*, translated by J. K. S. Reid (Philadelphia: Westminster, 1964), pp. 142-166. References to this translation will be by *ST*.

47. The fact that it was first written in French is a puzzle, especially if one wants to view the treatise as a deliberately ecumenical statement. Since the Lutherans and Zwinglians were unable to read French, these theologians hardly seem to be the intended audience of the treatise. Since it was in French, then his countrymen must have been the audience for whom the treatise was written.

48. Cf. *OS* 1:503; *ST* 142.

49. *OS* 1:504; *ST* 143.

50. *OS* 1:506-507; *ST* 145.

51. *OS* 1:508; *ST* 147.

52. Cf. *OS* 1:520f.; *ST* 157f.

53. Cf. *OS* 1:526-527; *ST* 163-164.

54. *OS* 1:527; *ST* 164.

55. *OS* 1:528; *ST* 165.

56. *OS* 1:529; *ST* 166.

57. *Ibid.*

58. *OS* 1:140; *Inst.* 142.

59. T. H. L. Parker, *John Calvin: A Biography* (Philadelphia: Westminster, 1975), p. 137; cf. also Doumergue, *op. cit.*, Vol. 2, pp. 572-573.

60. Cf. J. Tylenda, "The Calvin-Westphal Exchange: The Genesis of Calvin's Treatises Against Westphal," *Calvin Theological Journal* 9 (1974) 182-209.

61. *OS* 5:388, and *Institutes of the Christian Religion* (Philadelphia: Westminster, 1960), translated by Ford Lewis Battles, Book IV, chapter xvii, section 30.

62. F. Bente, *Historical Introductions to the Book of Concord* (St. Louis: Concordia, 1965), p. 26, says that Melanchthon had composed the *variata* in the interest of his irenic and unionistic policy but by so doing he weakened and made ambiguous the clear sense of the original Confession.

4.

THE DOCTRINE OF THE WILL

IN THE *INSTITUTES OF THE CHRISTIAN RELIGION*

John H. Leith

Calvin's understanding of the human will stands very close to the center of his theology both in popular appraisals and in fact. Many of the controversies that have focused on his theology and that have excited widespread response have to do with the nature of the human will: predestination, the perseverance of the saints, and total depravity. Some have found Calvin's doctrine of the will a sign of the profundity of his thought, but others have found it to be a mark of absurdity.[1] The doctrine of the will deals with a concrete dimension of human experience which we not only observe in its various effects but also of which we are immediately conscious. Hence, the doctrine of the will is clearly subject to one of the primary tests of the validity of any theology or faith, namely the test of intelligibility. Is actual human experience intelligible in the light of this theology? Here the rubric "Faith seeks understanding (intelligibility)" surely applies.

This discussion will concentrate upon the doctrine of the will in the *Institutes of the Christian Religion*. Its thesis is that Calvin's doctrine of the will is a profound analysis of Christian experience and that this analysis illuminates Christian experience today. At the same time the intelligibility of Calvin's treatment of the will is dependent upon its particular cultural and religious context and cannot be translated without remainder into the idiom of contemporary human or religious experience.

I

John Calvin was not given to self-analysis. One of the
difficulties in biographical studies of Calvin is the paucity
of introspective, personal reflections. Calvin's theology
focused attention upon God, not upon the human soul. Calvin's
energies were concentrated upon his work. He was temperamentally different from those great psychologists of the Christian
tradition--Augustine and Kierkegaard. Yet, Calvin utilizes
and builds upon Augustine's understanding of the human self.[2]

Calvin was aware of the discussions of the philosophers
about the nature of the soul. For Calvin's purposes their discussions were too subtle. "For the upbuilding of godliness a
simple definition will be enough for us."[3] It was enough for
Calvin's purposes to hold that "the human soul consists of two
faculties, understanding and will."[4] The function of the understanding is to distinguish between objects as each seems worthy
of approval or disapproval. The function of the will is to
choose and follow what the understanding pronounces good and
to reject what it disapproves. The understanding is the leader
and governor of the soul, and the will is always mindful of the
bidding of the understanding and in its desires waits the judgment of the understanding. Calvin included sense under understanding. For Calvin the soul is the subject, the I, the self,
which is embodied and which expresses itself through the body.
The understanding and the will are the primary dimensions of
the self.

God created man good. Calvin is adamant on this point.
In this original "integrity, man by free will had the power,
if he so willed, to attain eternal life ... Adam could have
stood if he wished, seeing that he fell solely by his own will,
but it was because his will was capable of being bent to one
side or the other, and was not given the constancy to perse-
vere, that he fell so easily. Yet, his choice of good and
evil was free, and not that alone, but the highest rectitude
was in his mind and will, and all the organic parts were
rightly composed to obedience, until in destroying himself he
corrupted his own blessings."[5] The proper exercise of the
will in goodness would have resulted in the confirmation of
the self in goodness.

Calvin found the dynamics of the self to be more complicated than was indicated by the philosophers as he understood

them. According to the philosophers, Calvin writes, "the
reason which is located in the mind like a lamp illumines all
counsels, and like a queen governs the will."[6] Yet, the appe-
tite or will, as Calvin preferred to call this aspect of the
self, is located halfway between the reason and the sense.
This "lower impulse," called sense, draws the will off into
error and delusion. The human problem lies in the conflict
between the reason and the lower impulses. For Calvin the
situation after the fall of man was more complicated. The
depravity that resulted from human sin was total in that it
encompassed the whole of human existence. All parts of the
soul were possessed by sin.[7] The understanding was corrupted
as well as the sensual dimensions of existence. The notion
that "man was commonly thought to be corrupted only in his
sensual part and to have a perfectly unblemished reason and a
will also largely unimpaired" was one of the heresies that had
crept into Christian thought. Calvin in contrast insisted
that man was vitiated in every part of his nature and shorn
of supernatural powers.[8] The philosophers knew by experience
that man had difficulty in establishing the rule of reason.
Yet, they remained optimistic. "This is the sum of the opinion of all philosophers: reason which abides in human understanding is a sufficient guide for right conduct; the will,
being subject to it, is indeed incited by the senses to evil
things; but since the will has free choice, it cannot be hin-
dered from following reason as its leader in all things."[9]
But Calvin insisted that the problem is not simply the pull
of the sensual man but also the corruption of the will and
the reason itself.

The criticism can be made that Calvin does not provide
his readers with an exhaustive analysis of the self. This
was not Calvin's purpose. He was concerned to give an account of human self in relation to God, the creator and redeemer. For his purpose Calvin believed that his simple analysis of the soul in terms of the understanding, which included
reason and sense, and the will was adequate.

II

The will for Calvin was a function of the self by which
the self gives unity, direction, intentionality to itself.
It is the self organized toward a goal. In giving conscious
unity and direction to life, the will comes into conflict with
other tendencies in the self and therefore has a negative
function as well as a positive function.[10] Calvin was not

aware as we are today of the various social and biochemical
forces that press in upon the self, but he was well aware that
the will functions in the context of the whole self. While he
spoke of the freedom of the will, he was also aware that "free"
is a quality that must be applied to the total self as the unity
of understanding and will. The role of the will in Calvin's
theology is very similar to Albert Outler's estimate that "the
will is the deepest and strongest bond of unity of the self.
It is in the decisions which man makes for or against God's
offer of love and God's demand of righteousness, that he grows
into unity or falls into disunity."[11] Human action is determined in part by nature and human finiteness, but human action
is also determinable by the self, which is more than a simple
extension of biological processes and the social matrix.
Natural causality never exhausts man's freedom and destiny.
"Will causality is the power to intend a significant project
or end which is immanent and optative. It is the power of an
agent or actor--not an automaton. Once *intended* by the will,
the project's realization enters into and is determined by
the conditions of physical causality in the situation."[12]
Calvin was not as aware of the biological processes from which
the self emerges and the societal matrix in which it lives as
the twentieth-century theologian. This new knowledge illumines the function of the self, but it does not nullify Calvin's concern with unique human acts which at least partially
unify the energies of life in intentionality and purpose.

Calvin's discussion of the will is complicated and somewhat diffused in the context of various theological concerns.
Hence, one way to get a clearer understanding of what Calvin
taught about the will is to isolate the various distinctions
that he made concerning the nature and functioning of the
will.[13]

A. *Free Will As the Power of Choice (Liberum Arbitrium)*

By free will Calvin meant a faculty "to choose one or the
other."[14] This, Calvin recognized, was the popular notion of
free will, "to be master of both his mind and will, able of
his own power to turn himself toward either good or evil."[15]
Free will is here the power of contrary choice, the power to
change the orientation and direction of one's life, "the free
choice equally of good and evil."[16]

Free will as the power of contrary choice has been severely restricted by human sin. Adam had a mutably good will which

could have chosen to love God but which chose to reject God.
After this "original sin" Adam and his descendants no longer
had this choice. In assessing the results of the fall, Calvin
makes a basic distinction between "earthly things and heavenly
things," between matters of political and social life and the
liberal arts on the one hand and matters that have to do with
morality and in particular with God on the other. In "heavenly
things," particularly the power to orient life toward God and
away from self, fallen man cannot reorder life toward God.[17]

Fallen man's understanding and reason still function, distinguishing him from animals, but the reason is distorted by
false images. When the reason has to do with issues that affect the human self and the self in relation to God, then its
judgment has been especially distorted. "Themistius more cor-
rectly teaches that the intellect is very rarely deceived in
general definition or in the essence of the thing, but that it
is illusory when it goes farther, that is, applies the principle to particular cases. In reply to the general question,
every man will affirm that murder is evil. But he who is plotting the death of an enemy contemplates murder as something
good."[18] Calvin likewise argues that the will remains after
the fall, but it no longer chooses the good. "Even though
something of understanding and judgment remains as a residue ...
yet we shall not call a mind whole and sound that is both weak
and plunged into deep darkness .... Similarly the will, because
it is inseparable from man's nature, did not perish, but was
so bound to wicked desires that it cannot strive after right."[19]

While Calvin speaks of the loss of freedom of will in the
sense of contrary choice, a close reading indicates that he
only denies freedom of the will as the power of choice in certain particular situations in which the self is deeply involved
and in particular in the self's relationship to God. The freedom of the self resided both in the understanding and the will,
and some measure of this freedom of choice remains to fallen
man. Calvin is even enthusiastic about the accomplishments of
fallen man in physics, dialectic, mathematics, and other like
disciplines.[20] He also is open to the accomplishments of fallen
men in the political and social ordering of life.[21] The one
point on which Calvin is adamant is that fallen man does not
have the freedom of contrary choice in the relationship to God.
Having rejected God and turned away from him, man by his own
efforts cannot turn back to God. "The way to the Kingdom of
God is open only to him whose mind has been made new by the
illumination of the Holy Spirit."[22] This particular point was
of such primary importance to Calvin that his writings sometimes give the impression that fallen man in no area of his
existence has the freedom which is the power of contrary choice.

Calvin has a pervasive tendency to ascribe everything
to God. Hence, Calvin relates all of the human capacities
for good in civic and social life as well as the arts to the
"general grace of God." "For why is one person more excellent
than another? Is it not to display in common nature God's
special grace, which in passing many by, declares itself bound
to none? Besides this, God inspires many special activities,
in accordance with each man's calling."[23] No person in any
area of human activity ought to boast, for in a fundamental
sense all good things are from God. Yet it is also clear that
Calvin does not deny the reality of the human activity, or the
freedom including the power of choice, that human beings have
at least in partial measure in "earthly" activities. It is
equally clear that Calvin is not especially concerned to affirm the reality and integrity of human activity.

B. The Will As Voluntary

Free will, Calvin acknowledged, can be defined in terms
of the voluntary character of the will. "For Lombard finally
declares that we have free will, not in that we are equally
capable of doing or thinking good and evil, but merely that
we are freed from compulsion .... Man will then be spoken of
as having this sort of free decision, not because he has free
choice equally of good and evil, but because he acts wickedly
by will, not by compulsion."[24] The fall did not destroy the
will and hence its voluntary character. The *voluntary* character of the will is set over against the *compulsion* of the will.
The will is free in the sense that the origin of its actions
is in itself. There is no other necessity for sin than that
which exists in the corruption of the will. Hence, necessity
and free assent exist together. Freedom is part of the nature
of the will, and it cannot possibly be taken away. The compulsion of the will refers to some external hindrance, power
or drug that coerces the will. When the Libertines, a pan-
theistic sect, suggested that man was not responsible, Calvin
replied in as vigorous a defense of the freedom of the will
in this sense as can be found in theological literature. He
pointed out to them "three wretched consequences" of their
doctrine which attributed "to man no free will, any more than
if he were a stone."

> The first of these is that there would no longer
> be any difference between God and the devil: for
> indeed the God which they made for us would be an
> idol, worse than the devil in hell. The second

is that men would no longer have any conscience
to avoid evil, but as beasts would follow their
sensual appetites without any discretion. The
third is that everything would have to be judged
as good, whether it be lechery, murder, or lar-
ceny; and the most wicked crimes that one can
imagine would have to be considered praiseworthy
works.[25]

In the *Institutes,* however, Calvin was concerned not with the
Libertines but with those who wanted to minimize the bondage
to the will's own sinful necessity or to exalt human capacities for good before God. Consequently, he derides those who
wish to label so slight a thing with the proud name of the
freedom of the will. "A noble freedom, indeed--for man not
to be forced to serve sin, yet to be such a willing slave that
his will is bound by the fetters of sin!"[26] Furthermore,
while Calvin did not have a "superstitious dependence on terms,"
he was impressed that the Holy Spirit in Scripture does not
sanction the use of the title free will for the voluntary character of the will.[27]

C. *The Necessity of the Will*

The necessity of the will means that the will must be
itself, that the will cannot escape itself, and that in some
deeply personal areas of life such as the self's relation to
God the will through its own power cannot change its direction
or commitments. An evil will cannot become through its own
efforts a good will. "Simply to will is of man; to will ill,
of a corrupt nature; to will well, of grace."[28] The distinction between the compulsion of the will and the necessity of
the will is very important.

The chief point of this distinction, then, must
be that man, as he was corrupted by the Fall,
sinned willingly, not unwillingly or by compulsion; by the most eager inclination of his heart,
not by forced compulsion; by the prompting of his
own lust, not by compulsion from without. Yet
so depraved is his nature that he can be moved or
impelled only to evil. But if this is true, then
it is clearly expressed that man is surely subject
to the necessity of sinning.[29]

This distinction between *necessity* and the *compulsion* of the will was very important to Calvin and he believed that those who grasped it would not be so appalled by his denial of free will. He quotes with approval Augustine's analysis of the complexity of the human situation.

> Thus the soul, in some strange and evil way,
> under a certain voluntary and wrongly free
> necessity is at the same time enslaved and
> free: enslaved because of necessity; free
> because of will. And what is at once stranger
> and more deplorable, it is guilty because it
> is free, and enslaved because it is guilty,
> and as a consequence enslaved because it is
> free.[30]

The necessity of the will in and of itself is a neutral term. It simply means that the will must be itself, that it cannot escape itself. "Is not God of necessity good? Is not the devil of necessity evil?"[31] God's goodness is not from any violent impulsion but from his boundless goodness. The devil's evil flows out of his own selfhood.

Whenever Calvin denies free will to man, he has reference to the inability of an evil person whose life is directed not to God but turned in upon itself to redirect the course of his life through his own effort. A self-centered person, according to Calvin's teaching, cannot become through his own efforts God-centered. Fallen man does not have this essential freedom.

D. *The Conversion of the Will*

What man cannot do in changing his evil will into a good will, God does for him by his Word and Spirit. Divine grace "corrects and cures the corruption .... God begins his good work in us ... by arousing love and desire and zeal for righteousness in our hearts .... He completes this work, moreover, by confirming us to perseverance."[32] Yet, conversion does not "efface" the will, "not insofar as it is will, for in man's conversion what belongs to his primal nature remains entire. I also say that it is created anew; not meaning that the will now begins to exist, but that it is changed from an evil to a good will."[33] Calvin approves Augustine's statement, "Grace does not destroy the will but rather restores it."[34]

The grace that restores the will respects the personal

integrity of the self. "For who is such a fool as to assert
that God moves man just as we throw a stone? And nothing like
this follows from our teaching."[35]

> God works in his elect in two ways: within,
> through his Spirit; without, through his Word.
> By his Spirit, illuminating their minds and
> forming their hearts to the love and cultiva-
> tion of righteousness, he makes them a new
> creation. By his Word, he arouses them to
> desire, to seek after, and to attain that same
> renewal.[36]

These statements of Calvin mean that grace is a personal cate-
gory, God's gracious presence and the action of God upon the
human self must be understood in terms of personal categories
and analogies. God moves the will in a way that respects the
integrity of the will as will and in such a way that the works
of the converted will are truly the works of the will as well
as the work of God. "Nothing now prevents us from saying that
we ourselves are fitly doing what God's Spirit is doing in us
even if our will contributes nothing of itself distinct from
his grace."[37]

Calvin's primary theological concern in this whole discussion is to give God the glory. "Those who think they have
no power to justify themselves hold to the main point necessary to know for salvation."[38] The great peril to salvation
is in too great a confidence in one's own power.[39] Calvin is
especially concerned to reject all theological strategems that
seem to divide the work of salvation, attributing some to God
and some to man. Everything is from God. This was Calvin's
emphasis. This emphasis and perspective which pervades Calvin's work is the special strength of his theology, but it
creates problems in the light of more ample analysis of the
human self.

Calvin set himself in opposition to every form of syner-
gism or Pelagianism that seeks to divide the work of salvation
between God and man. He was convinced that any faith that
does not rely wholly upon God lives in anxiety about its own
spiritual condition, that if God only acts when we begin to
act, or if he continues to act only if we fulfill certain conditions, our real dependence is upon ourselves, not upon God.
Calvin found peace and confidence in ascribing the whole of
salvation to God. This ascription of the work of salvation
to God belongs with Calvin's emphasis upon God's immediate
governance of the world. While he did distinguish between
general and particular providence, he was uneasy with this

distinction, and he liked to say not a drop of rain falls and no wind arises without the specific command of God.[40] This emphasis and perspective which pervades the whole of Calvin's theology is also a special strength of his theology.

An emphasis upon the immediacy of God's governance creates problems for most contemporary people. For a variety of reasons, especially the findings of physical and social sciences and no doubt also the secularism of society, most modern people ascribe more independence to the order of nature and to the human self than is clear from Calvin's theology. Calvin himself did speak of the importance of second causes, and he could insist that the life and the work of the elect is truly their own work. The modern reader of Calvin is tempted to argue as does a modern Reformed theologian, Karl Barth, that what from one perspective is wholly the work of God is from the historical and psychological perspective wholly the work of man.[41] Yet, Calvin in his particular historical situation did not emphasize this paradox as descriptive of what actually happens in Christian experience. While the contemporary reader can argue that there is a basis in Calvin for such a statement today, it must be clearly noted that this is not Calvin's emphasis.

III

It is instructive to set over against Calvin's doctrine of the will the explication of the human will and divine grace in William Temple's Gifford Lectures, *Nature, Man, and God.* William Temple was Augustinian in his theology, and there is evidence in this discussion that he knew the distinctive Reformed or Calvinist theology on these points.[42] Yet, he writes under the mandate of the Gifford Lectures as a natural theologian subjecting the actual practice of religion to critical review. He wanted to make the Augustinian doctrine of the will and divine grace intelligible to modern man. While it can be convincingly argued that Temple would never have come to his analysis of the human situation if he had not first of all seen the human situation from a Christian perspective, it is nevertheless significant that the human situation is amenable to this analysis.

The will, according to Temple, is "the name for our personality so far as that is integrated."[43] As the agent in moral action it is the organized nature of the person, the personality as a whole. The will does not come ready-made at

creation or birth. Only gradually does the will develop as
the energies and vitalities of life are organized toward a
goal. Indecision and the struggle between conflicting claims
for our attention are not so much indications of a free will
as of an undeveloped will. A strong will is characterized by
"certain splendid incapacities."[44] The fashioning of the
human will is never complete until all the elements of the
human person are fully integrated toward some end. In most
human beings this process of integration falls far short of
full integration. In some instances the will is fashioned
in a powerful way toward evil as well as good ends. Yet, an
evil goal cannot do justice to some elements of human personality. Perhaps in only one instance, that of Jesus, has a
human life been totally integrated in a will directed toward
God.[45]

In the fashioning of the human will it is important to
note that human personality is a self-determining, self-inte-
grating system. "Self-determination is the characteristic of
man as a moral human being, and without it he could never be
called into fellowship with God."[46] This freedom of the self
in its self-determining dimension is more than what Calvin
called the voluntary character of the will. It also has the
power of contrary choice largely through the capacity of mind
to "freely associate ideas."[47] The human mind can, for example, recall the past and anticipate the future and thus free
itself from particular occasions. Human freedom inheres in
the focusing of the attention of the mind. A person grows
under the impulse of his own aspirations. Yet, this freedom
is limited. "For the self which determines cannot carry the
self which is determined beyond its own level."[48]

For this reason Temple concludes that we cannot escape a
doctrine of election in some form.[49]

> What is quite certain is that the self cannot by
> any effort of its own lift itself off its own self
> as centre and resystematise itself about God as
> its centre. Such radical conversion must be the
> act of God, and that too by some process other
> than the gradual self-purification of a self-cen-
> tered soul assisted by the ever-present influence
> of God diffused through nature including human
> nature. It cannot be a process only of enlighten-
> ment. Nothing can suffice but a redemptive act.
> Something impinging upon the self from without
> must deliver it from the freedom which is perfect
> bondage to the bondage which is its only perfect
> freedom.[50]

The power of truth and beauty and goodness in human life
in some measure draws persons from self-centeredness, but the
only power in human experience which can overcome self-centeredness for the whole self is the experience of love. The
power of human love expressed in sacrifice or in doing what
apart from love would not be done is the only power which
evokes the response of love so that when one does the will
of the person who is loved he is very free and yet determined
by the person who is loved.[51]

Temple concludes,

> All is of God; the only thing of my very own
> which I can contribute to my own redemption is
> the sin from which I need to be redeemed. My
> capacity for fellowship with God is God's gift
> in creation; my partial deliverance from self-
> centredness by response to truth, beauty and
> goodness is God's gift through the natural
> world which He sustains in being and the his-
> tory of man which He controls. One thing is
> my own--the self-centredness which leads me to
> find my apparent good in what is other and less
> than the true good. This true good is the di-
> vine love and what flows from it appreciated
> as its expression. In response to that good,
> man finds his only true freedom, for only then
> does the self act as what it truly is and thus
> achieve true self-expression.[52]

Temple states the positive side of predestination and of the
bondage of the will quite as forcefully as Calvin. He leaves
the problem of those who do not respond to God's love an open
question in a way which is quite foreign to Calvin. Yet he
states the positive side of predestination as emphatically.
Nevertheless, Temple's discussion of the bondage of the will
and predestination is very different from Calvin's. The difference can be stated in two ways.

First, Temple was writing as a Gifford Lecturer concerned
to argue his case in the light of an analysis of the human
situation. Calvin's purpose was to proclaim the Christian
faith on the basis of Scripture, though it is very apparent
that a particular experience of Scripture and of faith determined the thrust of his theology. Temple's purpose was to
commend the Christian faith to the human mind and to persuade
the unbeliever. Calvin's purpose was to explicate the divine
revelation as contained in Scripture.

Yet, it is important to note that the theological work which Temple has done so well is not unimportant for Calvin's Biblical theology. Temple's phenomenological analysis of the human situation in the light of Augustinian theology indicates the profundity of Calvin's theology in terms of actual human experience. Apart from this perceived profundity, Calvin's doctrine of the will cannot be sustained except in a religious context that has an intense awareness of the presence and grace of God. In this sense what Temple has done complements Calvin's theology as they both share in the Augustinian tradition.

Secondly, Temple's concern was to demonstrate the intelligibility of the faith, the way it makes sense out of human experience. Yet, the understanding and intelligibility that faith seeks is significantly conditioned by the community in which the believer participates. Faith commitments which are intelligible to believers in a particular community lack intelligibility in other communities. Likewise, the capacity of faith to illuminate and give meaning to human experience is partly determined by the community of faith in which one participates. While Calvin's concern to make the faith intelligible was certainly less explicit than Temple's, this was also a concern of his. He, too, wanted to persuade, as his use of rhetoric and his style of writing fully documents. What constitutes intelligibility in Calvin's context was different from the test of credibility in Temple's post-Enlightenment England.

Yet, the relativity of the test of intelligibility can be exaggerated. The human mind and human experience have a continuity that stretches across cultures and histories. Persons in differing communities ought to be able to share empathetically the criteria of intelligibility in one another. While Calvin's sense of the numinous, of awe in the presence of the majesty of God, is not so cogent in a secular society, it still carries its weight in the community of faith. While modern people are not so easily convinced that they "ought to view God's government of the world, not with impious arrogance, but with devout humility,"[53] this sense of modesty also makes sense to the devout even in a secular culture. Hence, the distinction between Calvin and Temple ought neither to be exaggerated nor overlooked.

Calvin's discussion of the will cannot be understood apart from three peculiar qualities of his theology which contributed to the intelligibility of faith in his particular cultural and religious situation, namely (1) the doxological character of his theology which seeks to give God the glory,

which focuses attention on the immediacy of the divine lord-
ship and grace and minimizes the orders and structures and
energies of human action, (2) his great fear of a false and
dangerous confidence in works,[54] and (3) the modesty and awe
that is the proper human stance in the presence of the majesty
and hiddenness of God.[55] Any failure to note this emphasis
and stance of Calvin is to misread his theology. There is
justification for a dialectical reading of Calvin which sees
the paradox of salvation from one perspective as wholly the
work of God and from another perspective as wholly the work
of man.[56] Calvin himself says as much.[57] Yet Calvin does
not develop the doctrine in this way. Hence, while it is possible to argue that Temple's Augustinian analysis of the human
situation is essentially that of Calvin with a greater emphasis on the human dynamics in the situation, it must likewise
be argued that Temple's statement is very different from Calvin's. It is different because it does not have so pronounced
a doxological character, so great a fear of confidence in
works, and so great a humility that bows before the mysteri-
ousness of God's will.

Two conclusions develop from setting this analysis of
the doctrine of the will in the *Institutes* beside William
Temple's Gifford Lectures that are instructive for us as we
study Calvin today. The first is that theology is historical
and is formulated in terms of the issues, ethos, and the religious or spiritual forces of its time. Hence, theologies
that are expressed differently in particular historical situations may be substantively very much the same. The other
conclusion is complementary. The restatement of a theology
in a new historical situation is never altogether the same.
The three emphases or concerns that have been noted in Calvin's formulation of the doctrine of the will, as well as
his intention to explicate Scripture in his theology, do not
preclude the way William Temple sought to make the Augustinian
doctrine intelligible to Enlightenment man. Indeed, Calvinism
cannot be appropriated for vast numbers of modern people apart
from this concern for actual human experience and its integrity. Yet, when interpreters appropriate Calvin's theology
in a new cultural and religious context they must be aware
that they are saying what Calvin said and also what he did
not say, that the theology is the same and yet different.
On the one hand Calvin's theology may be the clue to the
restatement of Christian faith in our time in a way that sustains with integrity the Reformed tradition, but Calvin's
theology cannot be translated without remainder into the cultural and religious idiom of contemporary life.

NOTES

1. Cf. Will Durant, *The Reformation* (New York: Simon and Schuster, 1957), pp. 463ff. as an example of a failure to understand what Calvin is attempting to say. A more serious study of Calvin that fails to appreciate his theology is R. N. Carew Hunt, *Calvin* (London: Centenary Press, 1933), pp. 118ff.

2. Cf. Langdon Gilkey, *Reaping the Whirlwind* (New York: Seabury Press, 1976), pp. 175ff. Gilkey notes Calvin's differences from Augustine, especially the Biblical character of his theology with less attention to the classical categories of order and nature and also the practical character of his theology with less emphasis on understanding than on living a Christian life of trust and obedience. Cf. Luchesius Smits, *Saint Augustin dans l'oeuvre de Jean Calvin*, Vol. 1 (Paris: Editions Beatrice-Nauwelaerts, 1957), especially pp. 46, 61, 74-75, 83, 114, for documentation of Calvin's extensive use of the writings of Augustine.

3. John Calvin, *Institutes of the Christian Religion*, translated by Ford Lewis Battles (Philadelphia: Westminster Press, 1960), I,xv,6. Future references will be to this translation and will list only book, chapter and section references as here.

4. I,xv,7.

5. I,xv,8.

6. II,ii,2.

7. II,i,9.

8. II,ii,4.

9. II,ii,3.

10. James N. Lapsley, ed., *The Concept of Willing, Outdated Idea or Essential Key to Man's Future* (Nashville: Abingdon Press, 1967), p. 60.

11. Albert C. Outler, *Psychotherapy and the Christian Message* (New York: Harper and Brothers, 1954), p. 91.

12. *Ibid.*, p. 93.

13. The distinction between the necessity of the will and the compulsion of the will, the definition of *liberum arbitrium*, the nature of the will as spontaneous and voluntary are of critical importance for Calvin's thought, as is indicated not only here but also in his tract against Pighius. See *Corpus Reformatorum: Joannis Calvini Opera Quae Supersunt Omnia*, ed. Guilielmus Baum, Eduardus Cunitz, and Eduardus Reuss (Brunswick: C. A. Schwetschke and Son, 1863-1897), Vol. VI, col. 280. A reference to this work is hereafter cited by *CR*, followed by volume and column number.

14. II,ii,4.

15. II,ii,7.

16. II,ii,7.

17. II,ii,12-13.

18. II,ii,23.

19. II,ii,12.

20. II,ii,16.

21. II,ii,13.

22. II,ii,20.

23. II,ii,17.

24. II,ii,6-7.

25. *CR* VII,186. It is interesting to note that Calvin is not as persuasive in defending his own doctrine against these charges in either the *Institutes* II,v,1-5, or the tract against Pighius, *CR* VI,256-257.

26. II,ii,7.

27. *CR* VI,278.

28. II,iii,5.

29. II,iii,5.

30. *Ibid.*

31. *Ibid.*

32. II,iii,6.

33. *Ibid.*

34. II,v,15.

35. II,v,14.

36. II,v,5.

37. II,v,15.

38. II,iv,6.

39. II,ii,10.

40. I,xvi, 5-7.

41. Karl Barth, *Church Dogmatics* (Edinburgh: T. & T. Clark, 1961), Vol. III, Part 3, p. 250.

42. William Temple, *Nature, Man and God* (New York: Macmillan, 1949), pp. 378, 390.

43. *Ibid.,* p. 235.

44. *Ibid.,* pp. 234-236.

45. *Ibid.,* p. 235.

46. *Ibid.,* p. 244.

47. *Ibid.,* pp. 202ff.

48. *Ibid.,* p. 244.

49. *Ibid.,* p. 403.

50. *Ibid.,* p. 397.

51. *Ibid.,* p. 399.

52. *Ibid.,* p. 401.

53. *CR* VI,256.

54. *CR* VI,249.

55. Richard Stauffer in a paper entitled, "Some Unfamiliar Aspects of the Theology of the First Head of Doctrine in the Preaching of John Calvin," and presented to the International Society for Calvin Research meeting in Amsterdam in September, 1978, underscored Calvin's references in his sermons to two kinds of wisdom in God, one revealed to us and one which God possesses in himself which is too deep for our understanding. This emphasis on the mystery of God's wisdom and justice is stated more explicitly in Calvin's sermons than elsewhere in his theology. This would seem to indicate its importance for piety.

56. Cf. Paul Jacobs, *Prädestination and Verantwortlichkeit bei Calvin* (Neukirchen, 1937), pp. 133ff.

57. II,v,14-16. Calvin also appeals to common sense in his development of the doctrine of the will, though he does not develop this line of argument (II,ii,13).

5

THEOLOGY WITHIN THE LIMITS OF PIETY ALONE:

SCHLEIERMACHER AND CALVIN'S DOCTRINE OF GOD

B. A. Gerrish

We shall not say that, properly speaking, God is known where there is no religion or piety.

--Calvin

In one of his most recent publications Ford Lewis Battles gives a sensitive account, illustrated with apt citations, of what John Calvin meant by "piety."[1] Not the sole, but the first aim of the anthology is to furnish a better grasp of the man than one is likely to obtain while plodding through his dogmatic masterpiece. But this, of course, implies no rift between Calvin the man of piety and Calvin the theologian. An anthology illustrative of the spirituality of the Reformer may in fact turn the reader back, with renewed understanding, to the formidable task of mastering the *Institutes*, the contents of which Calvin described precisely as a *summa pietatis*.[2] Similarly, as I hope to show, *failure* to grasp the significance of "piety" in Calvin's dogmatics may account, in part, for some common misrepresentations of his God.

It may be thought odd, even perverse, if at each step of the way reference is made to certain dogmatic principles enunciated by Schleiermacher. Admittedly, the pioneer of liberal Protestant theology is hardly one of the acknowledged doctors of the Reformed church. We have been habituated by neoorthodox historiography to the view that he and Calvin were polar opposites. But no one who has attempted to master *The Christian Faith* (a still more formidable task than mastering the *Institutes*) will begrudge its author the highest praise for at least one thing: an unusually keen insight into the *formal* problems of Christian dogmatics--problems, that is, of

structure and procedure. Possibly Calvin, had he lived four
or five centuries later than he did, would have been as
shocked as Brunner was at the *content* Schleiermacher gave to
many of the traditional Christian themes. He may, besides,
have discovered only fitfully in *The Christian Faith* the ele-
gance of style which, as a humanist, he had learned to admire
and to cultivate. But he could not have failed to notice in
Schleiermacher's dogmatics the presence of at least two formal
characteristics that he regarded highly: conciseness and orderliness.[3] And he would have found Schleiermacher employing
the contrast between piety and speculation--so fundamental to
Calvin himself--as something like a procedural rule.

It is particularly the deliberate striving after order
that invites comparison between these two masters of Protestant dogmatics. When Calvin at last, after many revisions,
expressed his satisfaction with his *Institutes*, the final
arrangement of the work was what he had in mind.[4] Surely he
would have appreciated Schleiermacher's acute perception that
the meaning of a doctrine is in part a function of its place
in the total system.[5] It can further be shown that there is
an affinity between the two systematicians, not only in the
drive for order as such, but also in the actual shape of the
order adopted. Indeed, once undertaken, a comparison of the
two great systems of Protestant dogmatics, the classical and
the liberal, suggests other formal parallels as well, not
least with respect to the dogmatic procedure I wish chiefly
to illustrate: that is, use of the concept of piety to monitor or police the dogmatic system. In both Calvin and
Schleiermacher alike, "piety" functions to exclude inadmis-
sible material and to control the treatment of what is admitted. Each of them in his own way was determined (if we
dare adapt the famous title of one of Kant's works) to do
theology within the limits of piety alone.

There need be no surprise to learn that Schleiermacher,
for his part, commended the *Institutes* as an "invaluable book"
precisely because it never loses contact with the religious
affections, not even in the most intricate material.[6] More
likely to evoke surprise is the fact that he vigorously defended what has sometimes been taken for the regulative theme
of the *Institutes*, the doctrine of election.[7] But the extent
to which he may have been actually dependent on Calvin's
work, as he developed his own system, is a difficult and perhaps insoluble question; for now, it must be set aside. That
there are in fact resemblances (as well as differences) between them, will become clear; so clear that it is tempting
to wonder how far Schleiermacher may have been consciously or
unconsciously appropriating, developing, and correcting in-

sights acquired from his reading of Calvin.[8] But the temptation will be resisted. Bracketing the historical question of possible dependence, I ask only whether certain methodological principles that Schleiermacher keenly formulated can shed light on the order (sec. 1) and the limits (sec. 2) of Calvin's theology, and so can help rectify misapprehensions of his doctrine of God. Finally (sec. 3), some thought will be given to the evident fact that a theology kept within the limits of piety alone poses an embarrassment for Calvin's doctrine of the Trinity, as it does, *mutatis mutandis*, for Schleiermacher's. But it is, of course, my intention to invite--by a purely comparative approach--a reappraisal of the relationship between Calvin and Schleiermacher, and so between Reformation and modern theology.

1

"The doctrine of God, as set forth in the totality of the divine attributes, can only be completed simultaneously with the whole system."[9]

When Schleiermacher immediately adds that *usually* the doctrine of God is treated as a single unit and before any other points of doctrine, our historical curiosity is aroused. But he leaves it ungratified, foregoing any detailed comparison of his own scheme with the scheme prevalent in "our older and newer textbooks and systems." (Would he at this point, one wonders, have included the *Institutes* among the older systems?) "The method here adopted," he explains, "can only be justified by the finished argument itself." He will not be drawn aside into polemics or commend his own approach by subjecting the alternatives to detailed criticism. Still, his objections are plainly, if tersely, stated. One objection concerns us directly: that the "usual arrangement" is apt to conceal the relationship of the doctrine of God to the fundamental facts of the Christian religion, and so gives the impression of a quite independent, speculative theory about God. How, in other words, can you present a Christian view of God before you have specified the works of God in which he is made known? If there is a finished *locus de deo* that virtually introduces the system, must there not be a strong enticement to fill it out with "speculative" materials imported from elsewhere?

Schleiermacher's own arrangement is intended to rectify the defects of the more conventional dogmatic order. His system is divided into two parts, roughly corresponding (though he does not say so) to the double knowledge of God as creator and redeemer in the *Institutes*.[10] But the doctrine of God is

not assigned exclusively to either part alone; it is given in
the system as a whole. And since Part 2 is itself subdivided
(according to the two aspects of the antithesis of sin and
grace), propositions concerning the attributes and operations
of God are distributed throughout the system in *three* clusters. *The Christian Faith* ends with the divine attributes
which relate to redemption (paras, 164-69) and a conclusion
on the Divine Trinity (paras. 170-72). In the strictest
sense, the doctrine of God is only completed simultaneously
with the system as a whole.

In an interesting and highly laudatory essay, Ebeling
has discovered in Schleiermacher's treatment of God his "only
complete departure from the traditional order of [dogmatic]
articles."[11] The originality of Schleiermacher's procedure--
his distribution of the divine attributes over the whole
dogmatic system--is not to be denied. But it must be pointed
out, in qualification of Ebeling's remarks, that the dogmatic
tradition did contain at least a faint adumbration of Schleiermacher's approach: namely, in Calvin's final *Institutio*. And
if Ebeling can affirm that "at the beginning of Schleiermacher's *Glaubenglehre* there is--*cum grano salis*--no doctrine
of God at all,"[12] must we not also affirm, even without the
pinch of salt, that the *Institutes* nowhere *contain* a doctrine
of God but *are* a doctrine of God? There is no *locus de deo*
because the entire work presents the knowledge of God as creator and redeemer.

There is, of course, a difference of opinion among Calvin's interpreters on the extent to which the two fold knowledge of God, as creator and as redeemer, determines the structure of the 1559 *Institutes*. In his classic essay on the form
and content of the *Institutes*, Köstlin argued that Book 1 deals
with God's creation and government of the world in general,
Books 2-4 (collectively) with the historical revelation and
saving activity of God. The fourfold division into books, corresponding to the order of the Apostles' Creed, is thus embraced
within another, twofold scheme, the second part of which is subdivided according to its three distinct aspects: the establishment of salvation through the incarnate Son (Book 2) and the
Spirit's distribution of it to individuals (Book 3) through out-
ward means (Book 4).[13] In the early 1950's, two studies on Calvin's doctrine of the knowledge of God appeared in English almost simultaneously: one agreed with Köstlin's analysis and the
other did not. Arriving independently at Köstlin's conclusion,
Dowey similarly maintained that after Book 1 the "whole remainder" of the *Institutes* represents the revelation of God as redeemer.[14] Parker, on the other hand, concluded that it is Book
2 which presents the knowledge of God the redeemer, whereas
Books 3 and 4 proceed to speak of the one God who has been shown

as both creator and redeemer. The 1559 *Institutio* as a whole, Parker insisted, simply follows what Calvin held to be the four divisions of the Apostles' Creed: It is to be understood as an exposition of the Creed.[15]

My own persuasion is that Parker's criticisms did not invalidate Köstlin's interpretation. It was not quite just, in fact, for him to represent Köstlin as dividing the *Institutio* into two parts *instead* of four:[16] Köstlin spoke rather of the two parts of Calvin's system *in distinction from* the obvious division into four books. But the first of my three reflections on Calvin's doctrine of God--in the light of Schleiermacher's theological method--is relatively independent of the point at issue between Parker and Dowey (or Köstlin). What I wish chiefly to underscore is that, in any case, the doctrine of God in the *Institutes* remains incomplete in Book 1, and that only by a quite arbitrary selection could one presume to complete it from the chapters on predestination in Book 3 (chaps. 21-23). Yet that is exactly how Calvin's doctrine of God has commonly been presented.

Of the Calvin-studies known to me Dowey's, as it happens, comes closest to the point I have in mind, because the complaint he registers in his preface is the exact epistemological counter-part of mine, which is made from the viewpoint of the doctrine of God. According to Dowey, the two major articles on the knowledge of God in Calvin's theology (one by Warfield, the other by Lobstein) both assume that the problem of *knowledge* is done with "when the doctrines of the revelation in creation and in Scripture have been formulated, in the first book of the *Institutes*"; hence in both there is a "lack of a study of Calvin's doctrine of faith."[17] This judgment, clearly, is the epistemological correlate of my own claim that Calvin's doctrine of *God* cannot be derived exclusively from Book 1 of the *Institutes*--or even from Book 1 supplemented with chapters 21-23 of the third book. And his concept of faith, crucial to his thought on *how* we come to know God, will provide us with an important clue to his teaching on *what* we know of God.

In Calvin's own words: "The whole knowledge of God the Creator that we have discussed would be useless unless faith also followed, setting forth for us God our Father in Christ."[18] His reason for so saying is, of course, rooted in his doctrine of sin; the fall of man makes the revelation of God in nature ineffectual, and apart from redemption through Christ there is no unalloyed knowledge of the Creator. But we can just as well make the same point from the perspective of the doctrine

of God: methodologically, it is a mistake to treat Book 1 as
though it were a sufficient source for Calvin's idea of God.
We ought to anticipate at least that what he thinks of God
will become *plainer* when he turns from creation to redemption.
And yet it is a curious fact that many Calvin studies (to say
nothing of *obiter dicta* by non-specialists) fail to operate
out of this expectation, except insofar as Calvin's statements on predestination are extracted from Book 3 to confirm
the chosen statements in Book 1 that they most closely resemble.[19]

The question may certainly be asked whether the tendency
to see Calvin's doctrine of God in the first book of the *Institutes*--or in selected portions of it--is sufficiently explained by the perversity of his readers. Does it perhaps
expose a weakness in Calvin's execution of his task? For if
the dogmatic system as a whole is required for presenting the
knowledge of God, then some concluding effort seems imperative
to state the contents of the entire system, including its
second part, in the actual form of a doctrine of God. Calvin
seems committed by his arrangement of the material at least to
asking in Part 2, on God the Redeemer, a question corresponding to the question of Part 1, "who that God is who founded
and governs the universe."[20] A doctrine of God is surely
something other than a presentation of his works, whether in
nature or in the Incarnation,[21] although it may be only in
his works that he is known.

Schleiermacher tried to solve the problem by drawing up
separate clusters of divine attributes, some pertaining to
creation and others to sin and redemption, so that he gives us
in effect more than one *locus de deo*. The difficulty for
readers of Calvin is that no such *locus*, which many look for
in Book 1, is to be found anywhere at all in the *Institutes*.[22]
As Warfield puts it, everything the Christian needs to know
about the nature and attributes of God is present in the
Institutes "in solution, rather than in precipitate: distributed through the general discussion of the knowledge of God
rather than gathered together into one place and apportioned
to formal rubrics."[23] Nevertheless, Calvin's readers need
not be totally at a loss about where to locate the center of
gravity in all the scattered descriptions of God: Calvin's
concept of piety makes it possible to determine at least *some*
of his priorities.

2

"Dogmatic propositions never make their original
appearance except in trains of thought which have
received their impulse from religious moods of
mind."[24]

Schleiermacher knows very well that this is a prescrip-
tive rather than a descriptive judgment. As he puts it elsewhere: "We *wish* to have nothing to do with any conception of
God reached by way of speculation."[25] In actual fact, the
purely religious springs of an authentic dogmatics have often
enough, throughout the church's history, been muddied by
speculative intrusions. Or, to say it in Schleiermacher's
own words, since the "conglomerate-philosophy" of the Middle
Ages there has been an almost inevitable "confusion of the
speculative with the dogmatic, and consequently a mingling of
the two." And it has been the special concern of Protestantism, so he thinks, to separate out again the two types of prot-
osition—the speculative and the dogmatic—that originally
conveyed quite distinct contents.[26] He writes:

> Our method indeed would seem to be the one
> that will most easily get rid of all traces
> of the Scholastic mode of treatment, by which
> philosophy. . .and real Christian Dogmatics
> were frequently mingled in one and the same
> work.[27]

On a first reading, these striking affirmations of the
purely religious source of dogmatics, accompanied by a firm
exclusion of speculation and scholasticism, sound very like
authentic echoes of Calvin.[28] On closer inspection, however,
it can readily be seen that the concept of piety functions as
a dogmatic limit rather differently in Schleiermacher than in
Calvin. In the first place, Schleiermacher's approach is
rooted strictly in a theory of knowledge and is not, like
Calvin's, simultaneously tied up with a doctrine of sin.
Speculation is to be rigorously excluded, not because it is
perverse, or presumptuous, or futile, but because it arrives
at its talk about God by a quite different route than does
dogmatics. And the concept of piety functions as a dogmatic
limit simply because a specific modification of piety is what
dogmatics is all about: it is "the study of religious affections."[29] The speculative philosopher, too, may—indeed must—
arrive at the concept of God (if he does not start from it);
but exactly because "God" does not for him denote the refer-
ent of piety, it can only lead to methodological confusion if
he tries to combine speculation and dogmatics in a single

system. In short, speculative philosophy is a different, *but equally legitimate* enterprise of the human spirit: it is distinguished from, but not opposed to, dogmatics, which is determined to assert nothing that cannot be derived by reflection from the content of piety.[30] And there is therefore no reason why the theologian himself, when he is off-duty, may not try his hand at speculation and find the results entirely harmonious with his theology. Hence Schleiermacher's own confession on his death-bed: "I feel constrained to think the profoundest speculative thoughts, and they are to me identical with the deepest religious feelings."[31]

In the second place, Schleiermacher's approach to theological studies differentiates dogmatics, not only from philosophical speculation, but also from exegetical theology. The limit imposed by "piety" is established by the understanding of dogmatics as nothing but reflection on the immediate utterances of piety or, more specifically, of evangelical piety. Certainly, an injustice is done to Schleiermacher if one fails to verify (from paras. 128-35 of *The Christian Faith*) that he presents evangelical faith as a consciousness of being under the Word of God. And yet it remains true that he does not offer a biblical (or, as he puts it, "scriptural") theology. Given his essentially descriptive method, the most immediately pertinent texts are the Protestant confessions of faith--employed, of course, not as external authorities, but as indexes to the evangelical religious consciousness. Exegetical theology, in the sense of direct biblical interpretation, is for him not so much a moment in the dogmatic enterprise as a distinct, coordinate theological discipline *alongside* dogmatics.[32]

The contrast with Calvin's procedure is obvious. The piety of the sixteenth-century evangelical is not the datum of his dogmatic enterprise; rather, he has recourse directly to the Scriptures, even though the *Institutes* attempt something other than the commentaries. Indeed, "speculation" has a somewhat different connotation for him precisely because it suggests an arrogant refusal to be limited by what God has chosen to reveal in his Word. In order to test the moderation of faith, God purposely wills some things to remain hidden; speculation is therefore not merely out of place in dogmatics, but wanton, wicked, and hurtful.[33] Writing of the angels, Calvin formulates a general dogmatic rule:

> Let us remember here, as in all religious
> doctrine, that we ought to hold to one
> rule of modesty and sobriety: not to speak,
> or guess, or even seek to know, concern-

> ing obscure matters anything except what has
> been imparted to us by God's Word. Further-
> more, in the reading of Scripture we ought
> ceaselessly to endeavor to seek out and
> meditate upon those things which make for
> edification. Let us not indulge in curiosity
> or in the investigation of unprofitable
> things.[34]

This we may say, if we compare Calvin's warning here with his
introductory remarks on the nature of the knowledge of God
(Book 1, chap. 2), is the *rule of piety*; and it is clear that
his main concern does not entirely coincide with Schleiermacher's. But there is an affinity of concerns, not least in
what is deliberately excluded, and at times Calvin and
Schleiermacher approximate each other's language surprisingly
closely.[35] In particular, the veto on speculation--or the
rule of piety--means for both of them that God is not to be
known in himself, but rather in the totality of his works as
the devout man perceives them.[36]

True, this may seem to bring us not one bit further
than the disconcerting result already reached: nothing less
than the *Institutes* as a whole, it appears once more, can tell
us how Calvin thought of God. In actual fact, however, we
do now have a principle for ordering his priorities--not so
much in our own selection of material as in the perspective
of piety that he himself demands. Selective concentration on
what Calvin says about the providential and electing will of
God has fostered, perhaps even produced, the familiar carica-
ture of his God as a distant and arbitrary despot, who bestows
his favors on a chosen few. He does, to be sure, speak of
God's hidden, inscrutable will, even though he expressly re-
jects the notion of *absolute* will with which his critics frequently confuse it.[37] But if we inquire about the significance of this unknown will for the man of faith, we find that
it drives him--with a shiver of awe--all the more urgently to
the Word, in which everything that is to be *known* of God's
will is revealed.[38] Calvin's remarkable utterances on the
terrifying abyss in the divine will do have their relevance
for piety, but not so much in themselves as in the fact that
they point the believer elsewhere--to the divine benevolence
disclosed in the Gospel. Schleiermacher seems to have understood this very well; at least he insisted, in response to a
Lutheran opponent, that the so-called "unconditioned arbitrari-
ness" of Calvin's deity could not be an occasion for confessional strife, since it lay in the province of the hidden, not
the revealed God.[39] In other words, it is with the revealed
will of God that piety and therefore dogmatics have to do: to

focus on the hidden will would be to confuse the center of piety with the circumference.

Indeed, we can surely take a further step and argue that for Calvin, as for Schleiermacher, the most basic concept of God is nothing other than the correlate of piety itself, so that to understand the meaning of piety is to have a definition of God.[40] Hence the heart, though not the whole, of Calvin's view of God really is, after all, to be found in Book 1 of the *Institutes*--in the introductory reflections on piety, even before the chapters in which his doctrine of God is commonly looked for. Admittedly, his notion of piety is more complex, less elemental than Schleiermacher's. Even here the affinity is unmistakable; and Seeberg, among others, held that "consciousness of absolute dependence on God" was the heart of Calvin's view of religion, transmitted through the Reformed tradition to Schleiermacher.[41] But for Calvin, it must be replied, the divine "Whence" is decisively qualified as source of good (*fons omnium bonorum*) and pious dependence, correspondingly, as thankful and reverential love.[42] From the outset his language is specific and concrete, whereas, at the outset, Schleiermacher speaks abstractly of God as simply the Whence of ourselves and of the finite things on which our dependence is only relative. Calvin can therefore identify as the very first step to piety the recognition that "God is our Father to watch over us, govern and nourish us, until he gather us unto the eternal inheritance of his Kingdom." It follows, in a fallen world, that there is no saving knowledge of God apart from Christ, the Son in whom the infinite Father, as Irenaeus says, becomes finite. Already in Book 2, Calvin thus draws an explicit connection between piety and faith in Christ, although his actual discussion of faith is postponed until the third book.[43] The connection is crucial, because it removes any lingering doubts about what has precedence in his doctrine of God.

The fluidity of Calvin's language about true religion tends to crystallize in a twofold concept of piety as reverence and love, corresponding to a twofold concept of God as Lord and Father. It is remarkable that Warfield, who was by no means innocent of the tendency to equate Calvin's doctrine of God with chapters 10-18 of Book 1,[44] nonetheless--even within the framework of the first book--argued for the precedence of love both in true piety and in the character of God, as Calvin understood them: "His doctrine of God is preeminent among the doctrines of God given expression in the Reformation age in the commanding place it gives to the Divine Fatherhood."[45] If any misgivings remain about the sufficiency of Warfield's argument from the concept of piety (i.e., from Book

1, chap. 2), they must surely be resolved by Calvin's subsequent definition (in Book 3, chap. 2) of the closely-related concept "faith," which denotes the specific form of piety in the context of redemption: *for faith*, God is above all the benevolent Father.[46]

Unquestionably, if we made a similar advance from "piety" to "faith" in Schleiermacher's theology, differences from Calvin would appear. But for Schleiermacher, too, the call of the Christian proclamation was to view the Father in the Son and to receive from the Son power to become children of God.[47] And, like Calvin, he was persuaded that recognition of the divine love "only comes with the efficacious working of redemption, and it comes from Christ."[48] We have the sense of divine love in the consciousness of redemption,[49] and this consciousness is essentially what Schleiermacher meant by "faith."[50]

But now, for both Schleiermacher and Calvin, the rule of piety raises a question about one of the traditional cornerstones of Christian belief. If the limits of piety enable us to assign preeminence to the fatherly goodwill of God (Calvin) or God's disposition of love (Schleiermacher), must they not at the same time rule out the apparently speculative assertion that in the divine essence there are, with the Father, the persons of the Son and the Holy Spirit? In a *summa pietatis* or *Glaubenslehre*, what room can there be for the dogma of the Trinity?

3

"The assumption of an eternal distinction in the Supreme Being is not an utterance concerning the religious consciousness, for there it could never emerge."[51]

The Christian experience of redemption enables us, according to Schleiermacher, to affirm a union of the divine essence (*Wesen*) and human nature in the personality of Christ. With this affirmation the church's doctrine stands or falls. What it affirms, moreover, is nothing other than the essential content of the doctrine of the Trinity, which arose precisely in its defense; significantly, the doctrine of the Trinity is lacking among sects that give deviant interpretations of redemption. Schleiermacher thus represents the notion of the Trinity as the capstone of Christian doctrine--but only insofar as it affirms, on the basis of Christian experience, the union of the divine essence with human nature.

The method of *The Christian Faith* affords Schleiermacher
no means for tracing back the union of human and divine to
distinctions that are in the Godhead antecedently to the union.
Yet that is exactly what the dogma of the Trinity, as ordinari-
ly understood, attempts to do. Now the exegesis by which this
attempt is supported has never, Schleiermacher insists, been
secured against constant attacks. But even if it had been,
and if--on the authority of Christ and the apostles--we accepted the dogma as the assertion of a transcendent fact, it
would make no difference to our living fellowship with Christ.[52]
The doctrine of the Trinity is one of those points at which
the temptation to "speculate" is particularly strong: having
no formula for the being of God in himself, the theologian
could only borrow one from the domain of speculation.[53] To
head off temptation, Schleiermacher takes at least one
preliminary step toward reappraising the doctrine of the Trinity: he assigns it to its proper location at the end of the
system, where its limits as a statement about the Christian
consciousness can be more readily secured.[54]

The attitude of Calvin to the trinitarian dogma has been
the subject of lively historical debate. In the last ten
years of his life he conducted a vigorous literary campaign
against the Italian Antitrinitarians, in whom he saw (somewhat undiscriminatingly) the spiritual kin of Servetus;[55] and
yet, earlier in his career, his own trinitarian orthodoxy had
been placed in doubt. The motives behind his refusal, when
challenged by Caroli, to subscribe to the ancient creeds have
been variously explained, partly because they were in fact
complex.[56] But one thing is clear: throughout all the several
exchanges, Calvin tried to hold fast to his rule of piety,
contrasting (as he sometimes put it) "practical knowledge" and
"otiose speculation."[57] And here again, as before, his approach was both like and unlike Schleiermacher's.

In his chapter on the Trinity (Book 1, chap. 13), the
concern for piety is negatively expressed by Calvin in several
ways: in his direct warning against idle speculation, in his
refusal to follow his mentor Augustine in the quest for psychological analogies of the Trinity, and in his dismissal of the
"silly" notion of an eternal generation of the Son.[58] Posi-
tively, he ends with the claim that his summary will have
satisfied those who impose a limit on their curiosity, if
not those who intemperately delight in speculation.[59] But no
one will fail to notice that his professed zeal for the edi-
fication of the church permits him to say much more than
Schleiermacher; for he has no doubt at all that, albeit God
speaks sparingly of his essence, the Scriptures do inform us
of three hypostases or persons in the divine essence--that is,
of an eternal distinction.[60]

Indeed, it was Calvin's claim that pious experience itself (*ipsa pietatis experientia*) shows us in the divine unity God the Father, his Son, and the Spirit.[61] He even ventured the remarkable assertion: "No one will acknowledge from his heart that Christ is his God unless he first acknowledges a diversity of persons in the unity of essense."[62] Hence the reason why he preserved most of the old trinitarian vocabulary, which Schleiermacher found muddled and obsolete, was because he thought the hallowed terms still served their historical function of defending piety. The doctrine of the Trinity, in Calvin's view, did not transgress the limits of piety: it had its significance for piety chiefly as a *defensive* doctrine. He admitted he would have been happy to see the words "trinity," "person," and "consubstantial" buried--were they not needed for the sake of agreement in faith. And from the very first edition of the *Institutes*, long before he encountered the biblicism of Biandrata, he energetically justified the use of extrabiblical words if they do not add to Scripture but explain its meaning and, by unmasking the deceitfulness of the heretic, defend its truth. Arius said he believed that Christ was God, but he continued to speak of him as created: confronted with the word *homoousios* ("consubstantial"), his craftiness was exposed. Sabellius said he believed the Father was God, the Son was God, and the Spirit was God, but thought he had said no more than if he had described God as strong, just, or wise: with the notion of a *personarum trinitas* (a "trinity of persons") those who had piety at heart shattered his wickedness and fortified themselves against his cunning.[63] These sound like philosophical terms, to be sure. But within carefully-defined limits we may, after all, philosophize in moderation, not speculating further than Scripture raises us but only giving its simple and genuine meaning.[64]

Calvin stood at the confluence of several streams of thought which, between them, moved Christian theology closer to the daily walk of the Christian. Disillusionment with the inherited scholastic style was one respect in which Erasmus, Luther, and Calvin were all at one, despite their differences: they agreed that the logic-chopping and idle speculation of the "sophists" had to yield to study of the earliest Christian documents, the springs of genuine piety. But if they could not follow Castellio in the radical verdict that even the dogma of the Trinity was an *adiaphoron*[65]--a thing of no practical consequence--their reasons for holding back were significantly different.

Even when he gave no indication of seeing much point in ecclesiastical dogmas, Erasmus bowed to the judgment of the church. The reason why he did so was because, for him, "piety" included such deference. "I am not so lacking in piety," he wrote, "as to dissent from the Catholic Church."[66] Luther, by contrast, maintained a sovereign freedom over against the judgments of the church and yet, as has been acutely observed, he managed inwardly to appropriate church doctrines in a manner Erasmus could not comprehend.[67] For his part, Calvin undertook to justify the dogma of the Trinity as a defensive doctrine, whose intent was not to reopen the door to as much speculation as one pleased but to philosophize no further than piety required.

Schleiermacher's methodological principles, though just as much (in their own way) a matter of piety, called for a more thoroughgoing critique of the dogmatic tradition. He held it to have been a defect in the theological program of the Reformers that they made no attempt to revise the trinitarian and christological dogmas, in whose original construction he detected an impassioned polemical zeal that invited error.[68] Others have argued since Schleiermacher that in actual fact a transformation or development of the dogmas was something the Reformation began.[69] Perhaps that says too much. But anyone who, like Schleiermacher, proposes a revision of dogma as part of the unfinished business of the Reformation has enough on his side to make a claim of continuity by no means implausible.

To say nothing here of the other Reformers, Calvin displayed a quite new attitude to the received dogmatic language. Where he felt bound to do so, he rejected hallowed terms (like "eternal generation"); where he accepted the inherited formulas in substance, he refused to be coerced into subscribing to their every letter, arguing that in any case the received language was not uniform.[70] It is hard to see how he could object *in principle*, though he might not approve the results, if another theologian undertook to conform dogmatic language more closely to the Reformation's own courts of appeal: the deliverances of Scripture and the experience of piety. But it must be admitted that *in practice* Calvin was inclined to be suspicious of nonconformists and to suppose that their reticence towards established formulas must cloak a defective faith. Schleiermacher, on the other hand, thought it possible that someone who could not reconcile himself to the difficulties in the trinitarian language might nonetheless have a piety by no means lacking in the specifically Christian stamp.[71] It was this openness, right or wrong, that more than anything else freed mainline Protestantism to think again about the descendents of Calvin's heretics.

NOTES

1. Ford Lewis Battles, trans. and ed., *The Piety of John Calvin: An Anthology Illustrative of the Spirituality of the Reformer,* with music edited by Stanley Tagg (Grand Rapids: Baker Book House, 1978).

2. See the long title of the 1536 edition, which Battles has translated into English as *John Calvin: Institution of the Christian Religion* (Atlanta: John Knox Press, 1975).

3. On Calvin's stylistic ideals see the editorial comments in *Calvin: Institutes of the Christian Religion,* trans. Ford Lewis Battles (from the 1559 Latin ed.) and ed. John T. McNeill, 2 vols., Library of Christian Classics, vols. 20-21 (Philadelphia: Westminster Press, 1960), 1:lxviii-lxxi. Besides the customary citation of the 1559 *Institutes* by book, chapter, and section, I add in parentheses the volume and page of this translation, which I use in my quotations.

4. "John Calvin to the Reader": *Institutes,* 1:3.

5. Friedrich Schleiermacher, *The Christian Faith,* Eng. trans. of the 2d German ed. (1830-31), ed. H. R. Mackintosh and J. S. Stewart (Edinburgh: T. & T. Clark, 1928), 28.2 (p. 120). The citations are by section (or "paragraph"), subsection where appropriate, and the page in the English translation.

6. *An Herrn Oberhofprediger Dr. Ammon über seine Prüfung der Harmsischen Säze* (1818), p. 345. My references are to the text reproduced in *Friedrich Schleiermachers sämmtliche Werke* (hereafter cited as *S.W.*), 31 vols. (Berlin: Georg Reimer, 1834-64), div. 1, vol. 5.

7. Schleiermacher, "Ueber die Lehre von der Erwählung, besonders in Beziehung auf Herrn Dr. Bretschneiders Aphorismen" (1819), reprinted in *S.W.,* div. 1, 2:393-484.

8. The difficulty with supposing a conscious dependence on Calvin's dogmatic *order* is that Schleiermacher apparently wished to claim originality for little else except his arrangement of the material. In the preface to the second edition of

The Christian Faith he writes: "I have invented nothing, so far as I remember, except my order of topics and here or there a descriptive phrase" (Eng. trans., p. viii).

9. Schleiermacher, *Christian Faith,* 31.2 (p. 128).

10. The logical relationship between the two parts seems, in addition, to be similarly understood, since Schleiermacher insists that Christians bear their *entire* consciousness of God as something brought about in them by Christ: *Schleiermachers Sendschreiben über seine Glaubenslehre an Lücke* (1829), ed. Hermann Mulert, Studien zur Geschichte des neueren Protestantismus, Quellenheft 2 (Giessen: Alfred Töpelmann [J. Ricker], 1908), p. 31. Part 1 of *The Christian Faith* does not constitute a natural theology (see 29.2 [p. 124]).

11. Gerhard Ebeling, "Schleiermacher's Doctrine of the Divine Attributes," *Schleiermacher As Contemporary,* ed. Robert W. Funk, *Journal for Theology and the Church,* vol. 7 (New York: Herder and Herder, 1970), pp. 125-62, esp. p. 149; cf. p. 152.

12. *Ibid.,* p. 149.

13. J. [Julius] Köstlin, "Calvin's *Institutio* nach Form und Inhalt, in ihrer geschichtlichen Entwicklung," *Theologische Studien und Kritiken* 41 (1868): 7-62, 410-86, esp. pp. 57-58.

14. Edward A. Dowey, Jr., *The Knowledge of God in Calvin's Theology* (New York: Columbia University Press, 1952), p. 41.

15. T. H. L. Parker, *Calvin's Doctrine of the Knowledge of God,* 2d ed. (Edinburgh: Oliver & Boyd, 1969), pp. 5-11.

16. *Ibid.,* p. 5.

17. *Knowledge of God,* p. vii. On p. viii Dowey describes the aim of his book as "a critical exposition of Calvin's theological epistemology."

18. *Institutes,* 2.6.1 (1:341).

19. Even if it were possible, it would be tedious to attempt here a catalogue of pertinent secondary literature. English readers will find a representative illustration of my point in Reinhold Seeberg, *Text-Book of the History of Doctrines,* trans. Charles E. Hay, 2 vols. (1905; reprint ed., Grand Rapids: Baker Book House, 1952), 2:396-98, cf. pp. 405-8. Later German editions of Seeberg, never translated into

English, are richer and more nuanced in their treatment of
Calvin; but Seeberg continued to hold that, even though the
specifically Christian knowledge of God was sought by Calvin
in redemption and grace, the *fundamental elements* of his
doctrine of God were the divine omnipotence and a consistent
determinism, elements derived from a general metaphysical
framework and filled out from his reading of the Old Testament. Seeberg, *Lehrbuch der Dogmengeschichte,* vol. 4, pt.
2, 3d ed. (1920; reprint ed., Darmstadt: Wissenschaftliche
Buchgesellschaft, 1975), pp. 570-81, esp. p. 578.

20. *Institutes,* 1.6.1 (1:70). Calvin does make a modest
attempt to answer the question of Part 1 in the form of a
cluster of divine attributes: see *ibid.,* 1.10.2 (1:97-98).
The first edition of the *Institutcs,* as is well known, virtually opened with a list of God's attributes: *Institution,* p.
20.

21. For this reason, I am not persuaded when Niesel
claims that no concluding summary is required of him once he
has shown Calvin's pervasive concern with "the God revealed
in flesh": Wilhelm Niesel, *The Theology of Calvin,* trans.
Harold Knight (Philadelphia: Westminster Press, 1956),p.
246.

22. This point, already made by Köstlin ("Calvins
Institutio," pp. 61-62, 423), was emphasized by Muller: P. J.
Muller, *De godsleer van Calvijn uit religieus oogpunt beschouwd
en gewaardeerd* (Groningen: J. B. Wolters, 1881), pp. 10-11,
26, 38, 46.

23. Benjamin B. Warfield, "Calvin's Doctrine of God,"
Princeton Theological Review 7 (1909): 381-436, esp. p. 391.

24. Schleiermacher, *Christian Faith,* 16, Postscript (p.
82).

25. *Ibid.,* 167.1 (p. 730); my emphasis.

26. *Ibid.,* 16, Postscript (pp. 82-83).

27. *Ibid.,* 28.3 (p. 122).

28. I have in mind, of course, the introductory segment
of the *Institutes* (Book 1, chaps. 1-2), from which my initial
epigram is taken: *Institutes,* 1.2.1 (1:39).

29. *Christian Faith,* 16, Postscript (p. 83). Cf. the
more specific definition of *Christian* doctrines in Proposition

15: "Christian doctrines are accounts of the Christian religious affections set forth in speech" (p. 76). It is this methodological principle that led Schleiermacher to prefer the term *Glaubenslehre* ("doctrine of faith") to *Dogmatik:* his aim was to unfold the contents of Christian faith. Interestingly, the German translation of Calvin's *summa pietatis* (the first edition of the *Institutes*) titled it *Christliche Glaubenslehre:* see *Institution*, p. i.

30. See esp. *Christian Faith*, 4.4 (p. 17), 16, Postscript (p. 81), 28.2-3 (pp. 121-22), 33.3 and Postscript (pp. 136-37).

31. Quoted from his wife's reminiscences in *The Life of Schleiermacher as Unfolded in His Autobiography and Letters*, trans. Frederica Rowan, 2 vols. (London: Smith, Elder and Co., 1860), 2:337. Admittedly, he was under the sedative effects of opium when he said it, but the sentiment was not out of keeping with the principles and practice of his life.

32. *Christian Faith*, 19, Postscript (pp. 92-93), 27.1-4 (pp. 112-17).

33. *Institutes*, 1.14.1 (1:160). Calvin's demand that theology should be immediately conducive to piety, and not just about piety, is reflected in his description of speculation as "frigid" (e.g., *ibid.*, 1.2.2 [1:41], where the English translation has "idle" for *frigidis*).

34. *Ibid.*, 1.14.4 (1:164). It will be noted that the rule is implicitly twofold: it both excludes some things and regulates the approach to what is included.

35. So, for example, Schleiermacher, too, can insist that philosophizing will not *generate* piety (*Christian Faith*, 33.3 [p. 136]); and Calvin occasionally echoes Luther's view that philosophy is unobjectionable *in suo loco* (e.g., *Institutes*, Book 2, chap. 2).

36. Calvin, *Institutes*, 1.2.2 (1:41), 1.5.10 (1:63); Schleiermacher, *Christian Faith*, 169.1 (p. 735), Proposition 54 (p. 211), 172.1 (p. 748).

37. *Institutes*, 1.17.2 (1:214), 3.23.2 (2:950). The scholastic "absolute will" Calvin finds impious because it separates God's justice from his power.

38. This ought to have been plain enough from what Calvin actually says in the favorite chapters extracted from Books 1 and 3. He takes particular care to confine the doctrine of

election within the limits of piety alone. For specific references and a fuller discussion see B. A. Gerrish, "'To the Unknown God': Luther and Calvin on the Hiddenness of God," *Journal of Religion* 53 (1973): 263-92, esp. pp. 279-86.

39. *An Ammon,* p. 377.

40. Schleiermacher, *Christian Faith,* 4.4 (pp. 16-18).

41. *Dogmengeschichte,* 4^2:561 and note.

42. *Institutes,* 1.2.1 (1:40-41). Cf. Schleiermacher, *Christian Faith,* 4.3-4 (pp. 15-18).

43. *Institutes,* 2.6.4 (1:347); cf. 2.6.1 (1:341). These references are to the second part of the *Institutes,* on God the Redeemer; but it should be noted that an association of *pietas* with *paterna cura* appears already in 1.2.1 (1:41).

44. Warfield identifies Book 1, chap. 10, as "the opening of [Calvin's] discussion of the doctrine of God" ("Calvin's Doctrine of God," p. 412), and his attempted reconstruction of Calvin's (implicit) definition of God is documented overwhelmingly from Book 1 (*ibid., p. 416-19).

45. *Ibid.,* p. 425; see also p. 423.

46. *Institutes,* 3.2.16. Notice that already in 1.2.2 (1:42) the genuine, pious knowledge of God includes *fiducia,* which, of course, Calvin closely links with *fides* (see, e.g., *ibid.,* 3.2.15 [1:561], where the terms, though they may be used synonymously, are differentiated by speaking of *fides* as the source of *fiducia*).

47. Schleiermacher, *Predigten in Bezug auf die Feier der Uebergabe der Augsburgischen Confession* (1831), reprinted in *Friedrich Schleiermacher: Kleine Schriften und Predigten,* ed. Hayo Gerdes and Emanuel Hirsch, 3 vols. (Berlin: Walter de Gruyter and Co., 1969-70), 3:135.

48. *Christian Faith,* 166.2 (p. 729). God's "love" Schleiermacher understands to mean the disposition in God that corresponds with the desire of a person for union with an other: *ibid.,* 165.1 (pp. 726-27).

49. *Ibid.,* 167.2 (p. 732).

50. Faith is inward assurance of Christ's redeeming power. It is brought about by the Word, but the Word viewed less as

the declaration of a divine promise than as the protrayal of Christ--and so the instrument of his continuing activity, influence, and presence: see *Christian Faith*, 14:1 (pp. 68-69), 105.1 (p. 467), 108.1 (p. 483), 108.5 (pp. 490-92). That this way, too, of relating Word and faith answers to one side of Calvin's thinking in his chapter on faith, needs no detailed proof.

51. Schleiermacher, *Christian Faith*, 170.2 (p. 739).

52. In these two paragraphs I have condensed the argument in *Christian Faith*, 170 (pp. 738-42); but I have not, for the present purposes, taken account of the union of human and divine that Schleiermacher postulates in the "common spirit of the church." On the twofold appeal to Scripture and facts of experience, cf. *ibid.*, 170, Postscript (p. 741).

53. *Ibid.*, 172.1 (p. 748).

54. *Ibid.*, 172.3 (pp. 749-50).

55. See Antonio Rotondò, *Calvin and the Italian Anti-Trinitarians*, trans. John and Anne Tedeschi, Reformation Essays and Studies, no. 2 (St. Louis: Foundation for Reformation Research, 1968), pp. 11-12, 17-19. Calvin does sometimes note differences between Servetus and the Antitrinitarians: see, e.g., *Institutes*, 1.13.23 (1:149). But it was the kinship that impressed him.

56. My chief debts on this theme are to Warfield, Koopmans, and Nijenhuis: Benjamin B. Warfield, "Calvin's Doctrine of the Trinity," *Princeton Theological Review* 7 (1909): 553-652; Jan Koopmans, *Das altkirchliche Dogma in der Reformation*, trans. from the Dutch (1938) by H. Quistorp, Beiträge zur evangelischen Theologie, vol. 22 (Munich: Chr. Kaiser Verlag, 1955); W. Nijenhuis, "Calvin's Attitude towards the Symbols of the Early Church during the Conflict with Caroli," *Ecclesia Reformata: Studies on the Reformation*, Kerkhistorische Bijdragen, no. 3 (Leiden: E. J. Brill, 1972), pp. 73-96 (first published in Dutch in the *Nederlands Theologisch Tijdschrift* 15 [1960-61]: 24-47).

57. *Adversus P. Caroli calumnias* (1545): *Ioannis Calvini opera quae supersunt omnia* (hereafter cited as *C.O.*), ed. Wilhelm Baum, Edward Cunitz, and Edward Reuss, 59 vols., Corpus Reformatorum, vols. 29-87 (Brunswick: C. A. Schwetschke and Son [M. Bruhn], 1863-1900), 7:312-13; cf. *Institutes*, 1.13.13 (1:138).

58. *Institutes*, 1.13.19 (1:144); 1.13.18 (1:142), 1.15.4 (1:190); 1.13.29 (1:159).

59. *Ibid.*, 1.13.29 (1:159).

60. *Ibid.*, 1.13.1 (1:121), 13.20 (1:144), 13.17 (1:141-42).

61. *Catechismus* (1538): *C.O.* 5:337. Cf. the French *Catéchisme* (1537): *C.O.* 22:52. The name "God" is empty unless we grasp the three persons: *Institutes*, 1.13.2 (1:122).

62. *Ad quaestiones Blandratae responsum* (1557 or 1558): *C.O.* 9:331, trans. Joseph Tylenda, "The Warning That Went Unheeded: John Calvin on Giorgio Biandrata," *Calvin Theological Journal* 12 (1977):24-62, esp. p. 61.

63. *Institutes*, 1.13.3-5 (1:123-28).

64. *Ibid.*, 1.13.21 (1:146); *Ad quaestiones Blandratae responsum*, *C.O.* 9:331, trans. Tylenda, p. 61. In substance, Calvin is not far removed here from Schleiermacher's views on the formal use of philosophical concepts: *Christian Faith*, 16, Postscript (pp. 81-83).

65. Rotondò, *Anti-Trinitarians*, p. 28.

66. Erasmus to Lorenzo Campeggio, 6 Dec. 1520: *Opus epistolarum Des. Erasmi Roterodami*, ed. P. S. Allen, H. M. Allen, and H. W. Garrod, 12 vols. (Oxford: Clarendon Press, 1906-58), 4:410.

67. Karl Zickendraht, *Der Streit zwischen Erasmus and Luther über die Willensfreiheit* (Leipzig: J. C. Hinrichs, 1909), pp. 63-65.

68. *Christian Faith*, 96.3 (p. 396), 172.2 (p. 748).

69. See Warfield's remarks on F. C. Baur and I. A. Dorner: "Calvin's Doctrine of the Trinity," pp. 557-59, 583 n. 48.

70. *Institutes*, 1.13.5 (1:126-27), 13.19 (1:143-44); cf. *Ad quaestiones Blandratae responsum*, *C.O.* 9:332, trans. Tylenda, p. 62.

71. *Christian Faith*, 172.2 (p. 749).

PART TWO: THE REFORMATION

6.

"A WAY TO WYN THEM"

ECCLESIOLOGY AND RELIGION
IN THE ENGLISH REFORMATION

Robert S. Paul

I. *An Act of State*

One often has the impression that those who write about
the English Reformation are half apologizing for it: the
leadership and motives seem mundane compared with the continental Titans and their heroic spiritual struggle against
ecclesiastical and imperial reaction. How can one compare
Cranmer or Thomas Cromwell with Luther, Zwingli or Calvin,
or even with Melanchthon and Bullinger? Nor can we even set
the motives of 'bluff King Hal' side-by-side with the blunt
honesty of Frederick the Wise of Saxony, although we admit
that Philip of Hesse seems to have shared some of Henry's
weaknesses. Those who write the text books of English
church history seem to state flatly that the causes of the
Reformation in England were almost entirely political, as if
to say, 'We're sorry it happened that way, but that is the
way it was.'

The impression that we move on a lower plane religiously
and theologically in the English Reformation is strengthened
when we look at the basic documents. There is nothing in
Luther's moral outrage in any of the Acts of Parliament or
Royal Proclamations which established Protestantism in England, and little of the quality of 'Here I stand' about the
career of Cranmer--except perhaps at the stake, when after
seven recantations he realized that nothing could save him.[1]

T. H. L. Parker may well be right in insisting that there was
more support for the Protestant faith in England than many
historians have allowed.[2] He has argued persuasively that only
more widespread acceptance of Protestant views can explain the
eventual acquiescence of the people at the time of the Elizabethan Settlement or the generally Protestant character of the
Elizabethan church despite the Queen's known prejudices. On
the other hand, we shall be arguing that there were other
significant reasons for the English people's acceptance of
the Elizabethan church, and we can hardly escape the conclusion that, despite any religious sentiments latent among the
population, the material causes of England's Protestant
settlement *were* political--first, Henry VIII's desire for a
male heir and his determination to marry Anne Boleyn, and
secondly, the accident that Elizabeth was the product of that
questionable union and was therefore forced to support Protestantism in order to maintain any semblance of legitimacy.

The Continental Reformation produced some of the great
doctrinal classics of Protestantism--Luther's magnificent
treatises of 1520, Calvin's *Institutes* and commentaries, the
Augsburg and Heidelburg Confessions, to cite but a few. The
English produced no great redefinitions of Christian Faith to
compare with these, and the classics it did produce--the Book
of Common Prayer and the Authorized Version of the Bible
(King James' Version)--were more the expressions of corporate
English piety than creative attempts to re-state Protestant
faith theologically. For the rest, the writings of the English churchmen of the period do not appear to be very inven-
tive or novel. They repeat ideas and insights borrowed from
European thinkers which the continental Reformers had expressed earlier more radically and with more force.

This becomes almost monotonously clear as one reads
through the original works in the numerous volumes of the
Parker Society publications: the native pungency of illus-
trations from the preacher, Hugh Latimer, continues to stir
us, and the essential reasonableness and moderation of Cranmer impress us, but on the whole nothing really new was contributed to the understanding of Christian doctrine by the
English Reformers. After all, the principles of Justification
by Faith, *sola scriptura*, and the Priesthood of all Believers
had already been laid down by Luther, the sacramental issue
had been thoroughly worked-over by the Continental Reformers
from every possible point of view, while Calvin had already
produced in the *Institutes* the most logically integrated and
comprehensive statement of Christian doctrine on the basis of
the new biblical principles.

II. *The Significance of Ecclesiology*

On the other hand, although the feeling of *déjà vu* may
be justified if one expects to discover a similar approach in
England to that which we find in the continental reformers,
it is not justified if we examine the English Reformation in
the context of English history. I suggest that the treatment
of the English Reformation, not least by those who have
sought to do it justice, has been too narrow, overly concentrated on discovering signs of originality in doctrines for
which the German and Swiss Reformers had already provided the
basic Protestant insights.

The original contribution of the English Reformation, I
suggest, was in the doctrine of the Church,[3] which in the context of English history, from the accession of Elizabeth I
(1558) to the Restoration in 1660, was probably explored more
deeply and experimented with more comprehensively than anywhere
else in Europe. The starting-point of the Reformation may
have been Henry VIII's break with Rome in the early 1530's,
and certainly, during the reign of Edward VI, the English
Reformation inherited the insights of the Continental Reformers
in all essential doctrines of the faith (as the Second Prayer
Book of 1552 illustrates), but the situation in England did
not become stabilized until 1558, and by that time the peculiar
quirks of English history already showed signs of producing
significant differences and considerable variety in the field
of ecclesiology.

Perhaps it was precisely the curiously personal reasons
for Henry VIII's break with the papacy, and the ecclesiastical
legacy that he therefore handed on to his children, that made
this exploration in ecclesiology possible and even inevitable.
In the other countries the Reform movement was dominated by
theologians. Although the authority of the princes had to be
invoked at the political level, rulers did not interfere with
theology to the extent of determining the detailed form that
the Church should take:[4] they might react to specific ideas
and force their views upon the Reformers--as the city fathers
in Zurich did on the matter of Baptism, or as the Genevan
Syndics did to some of Calvin's proposals--but they looked
primarily to the theological leaders to provide them with the
blue-print of a reformed church.

It was different in England. There was no prophetic
voice like Luther, Zwingli, or Calvin to take the lead and
sweep the people into new courses by intensity of conviction,
strength of personality or consistency of argument. The break

with Rome came simply because the king wanted it, and the
ecclesiastical pattern that would take the place of the
medieval church would simply be what Henry VIII was prepared
to tolerate and would enforce.

III. *The Problem of a Basic Authority*

This could not go unchallenged by those who dissented.
Roman Catholics continued to assert the supreme authority of
the Papacy, while Puritans of different shades advanced the
alternative authority of the scriptures and the restoration
of the New Testament church. Moreover, although conforming
Puritans and nonconforming Separatists agreed on the absolute
authority of the scriptural pattern, they could not agree on
its interpretation or on their rival forms of the church:
Presbyterians, Congregationalists and Baptists showed that
their answer to the problem of authority was by no means as
simple as they often assumed in their writings against Roman
Catholics and Anglicans, or against each other. With the
later appearance of'the Quakers, they found themselves having
to reconcile the absolute authority they accorded to scripture with the on-going authority of the Holy Spirit in the
experience of the individual Christian, and as the seventeenth
century progressed they would also have to take some account
of the place of human reason in their understanding of the
scriptures: the problem of the primary spiritual authority
was much more complicated than any of the churches and sects
of the seventeenth century was prepared to recognize.

As I have argued elsewhere, this problem of an ultimate
theological authority is at the heart of the ecclesiological
problem, for there can be no doctrine of the Church itself
until we can clearly state what form the Church should take,
and *why*.[5] If any 'church' is to be regarded as the Church of
Jesus Christ, the reasons for its structure, forms of worship
and government must rest on a revelation more obviously divine
than that of anyone's personal whim, prejudices or ecclesiastical pragmatism. Whatever shortcomings the English Puritans
and Separatists of the sixteenth and seventeenth centuries
may have had, they recognized that truth, and this was the
basis of their opposition to the authority of the crown.

Furthermore, from the time of Elizabeth's accession, the
crown could never muster sufficient political strength or
popular support to win over or subdue completely either the
Catholics or the Puritans, although a succession of able and
vigorous prelates--John Whitgift, Richard Bancroft and finally

William Laud—actively pursued that end. As a result, the
countries of the British Isles and the English colonies in
America developed a religious pluralism that few Englishmen
of the time wanted to permit or to recognize.

Apart from a few Separatists such as Roger Williams,
most English Protestants in the sixteenth and early seventeenth centuries inherited the conviction that there is only
one true Church, and a medieval conviction about the unity of
church and state.[6] The ecclesiological disputes were a search
for that one true Church. Everything else claiming to be the
Church was in error—and no politically responsible person
could permit error of that kind to go unchecked when eternal
salvation depended on the acceptance and endorsement of God's
revealed truth. Until the outbreak of the Civil War in the
1640's it is doubtful if any reputable religious group would
have defended religious pluralism as a permanent solution to
the ecclesiastical differences, or would be less than reluctant to concede toleration to others. Yet the *de facto* pluralism that became inevitable through the sheer extent of
America became inevitable also in Britain through pressures
of civil war. By the fortunes of circumstance and history at
this point in time, the Anglo-Saxon peoples were able to ex-
periment with the doctrine of the Church more radically and
more extensively than any other country in the western world.

IV. *The Classic Struggle*

The tendency to relegate the ecclesiological issue to
the periphery of the sixteenth and seventeenth centuries may
cause historians to overlook a significant clue for understanding the period and the people who participated in it.
Seen from the point of view of what was happening in the
Church rather than from the perspective of what was happening
in civil society, the period from the death of Edward VI
(1553) to the Great Ejectment of 1662 was dominated by a
classic struggle between four major systems of church government, each of which believed it was the true Church of Jesus
Christ by Divine Right and was prepared to promote its supremacy by all political and theological means that were to hand.

Roman Catholic (papal), Anglican (episcopal), Presbyterian and Congregational polities were all engaged in this
struggle, and during a century of activity there were periods
when each was successful and looked as if it would win complete control. The dominance of the Anglican establishment
under the Tudors and Stuarts and its political success in
1660 should not obscure the significance of the struggle

itself. The Roman Catholic Church re-established itself
during the reign of Mary (1553-58) and came within an ace of
winning everything back under James II (1685-88); the Presbyterians were in control as a result of the Westminster Assembly and during the days of the Commonwealth (1643-52); and if
Congregationalism was not actually established in the British
Isles during Cromwell's Protectorate (1653-58),[7] its theology
and leaders dominated the ecclesiastical system set up by the
Protector[8] and it became supreme in New England.[9]

Furthermore, although the Anglican form gained social
and political predominance through its success in England
after the Civil War, that predominance could never be made
absolute throughout the whole of the British territories,
and each of its ecclesiastical rivals was able to carve a
geographical niche for itself within which it became the majority church and, *de facto* if not *de jure*, the Establishment.
So although the episcopal form re-asserted itself as the
established Church of England and maintained its control in
Virginia, Presbyterianism was adopted by the Church of Scotland, Roman Catholicism retained the overwhelming allegiance
of the Irish people, and Congregationalism strengthened its
hold over the New England colonies. Whenever an attempt was
made to impose episcopacy on the English pattern over any of
these areas outside England itself there was bitterness and
often bloodshed, as during the Covenanting wars in Scotland,
throughout the running sore of Irish troubles, and in the
attempt to introduce an 'American' episcopate to the colonies--
a major reason why the Puritan clergy of New England were
prepared to make common cause with the radical gentry of the
South in the eighteenth century struggle for Independence.[10]

Yet control by the majority church in none of these
areas was so absolute that others could be entirely excluded.
The lesson of the period seems to be that because of the conditions imposed by British history, religious pluralism had
come to stay and each church would have something to contribute to the development of Anglo-Saxon society: in areas
of British influence no one church was able to snatch the
whole cake, although each managed to get its hands on a
slice.[11]

V. *The Significance of the Elizabethan Settlement*

In the face of problems at home and abroad Elizabeth's
political priority had been a unified country, and in the
sixteenth century this would have been impossible without a
unified national church and the support of its leaders. The

shape that the Church of England assumed under the Elizabethan
settlement reflects the queen's situation: in the eyes of
Rome she was illegitimate, and to maintain any claim to legitimacy she therefore had to be a Protestant. On the other hand
she was religiously conservative like her father, and she
would certainly use the power of appointing trusted advisers
to the episcopal bench. Perhaps even more significantly for
national unity, by retaining as much as possible of the traditional form and worship of the Church, Elizabeth stood a
chance of winning over the great mass of Catholic or at least
conservative opinion that had readily conformed to or ap-
plauded the religious policy of her Catholic half-sister, Mary
I. As Sir John Neale has said about the Queen's attitude on
religious matters, "The Church, if Elizabeth could manage it,
was at any rate to look old-fashioned and decorous."[12] So
Elizabeth endorsed a liturgical form for the Church's worship,
insisted on priestly vestments, and permitted vestiges of
popular medieval piety such as bowing at the name of Jesus,
using the sign of the cross in baptism, and kneeling at the
altar. These things would not offend (or hoodwink) the sophisticated, but they could be of very great importance in
winning the allegiance of a simple, devoutly conservative people who were only just emerging from superstition and feudal-
ism, and whose religion was still largely what it had been for
a thousand years.

Furthermore, although she gave in to the concerns that
led the Act of Supremacy to describe her as 'supreme governor'
of the Church of England, whereas her father, Henry VIII, had
not scrupled to designate himself its 'supreme head', she
showed that she did not intend to lose one whit of the control
he exercised over the churchmen. This is illustrated in the
rather pathetic career of Edmund Grindall, whom she had appointed Archbishop of Canterbury in 1576, but whom she de-
prived a year later for his support of the Puritan 'proph-
esyings'.[13] He was reinstated after abject apologies in 1582,
a year before his death, but Elizabeth did not make the mistake of appointing a person of such questionable fidelity
again. In John Whitgift she discovered a prelate after her
own heart--one who had not been contaminated by foreign radi-
cals, a convinced episcopalian, an enthusiastic supporter of
everything she liked in traditional churchmanship from
Prayer Book to vestments, and a celibate into the bargain.
Elizabeth was committed to her ecclesiastical program both by
personal preference and the needs of public policy.

* * * * * * *

It is almost impossible to arrive at any accurate estimate of the relative strength of Protestant and Catholic
opinion at the time of the Elizabethan Settlement. The Count
de Feria, Spanish ambassador at the time of the Queen's accession, reputedly estimated that almost two thirds of the
population may have been at heart Catholic,[14] while another
foreign observer reported that:

> Although the latter [the Protestants] in-
> crease in number, they are not so power-
> ful as the Catholics, who comprise all the
> chief personages of the kingdom, with very
> great command of their estates, having also
> many followers; and the greater part of the
> common people out of London, in the sev-
> eral provinces, are much attached to the
> Roman Catholic religion.[15]

Returned Protestant exiles such as Richard Cox, the newly
appointed Bishop of Ely, and John Jewell, soon to be appointed
Bishop of Salisbury, complained about the overwhelming Catholic sentiment among the clergy and the lack of headway that
the new opinions were having in the universities.[16] It looks
as if the Count de Feria's educated guess in 1559 may not have
been far short of the mark; and yet within a little over a
hundred years the sympathies and prejudices of the population
were Protestant enough to depose the Catholic James II, and
Anglican enough "to burn [Dissenting] Meeting Houses or
Popish Chapels according to the political requirements of the
hour."[17] How did this happen?

Although Henry VIII had caused the decisive break with
Rome, he "continued to abhor and persecuted Protestants, and
if he had not done so he might have lost his throne in the
then state of opinion."[18] It is also clear that the Edwardian
shift in a more decidedly Protestant direction was generally
unpopular, although some of the unrest had as much to do with
the rapacity of Edward's advisers as it had to do with religious convictions. It was clearly an overwhelming weight
of public sentiment that swept the Dudleys from power in 1553
and set Mary, an acknowledged Catholic, on the throne, and
popular opinion does not seem to have been outraged by the
prospect of returning to papal obedience.

On the other hand it has been pointed out that we need
not impugn the sincerity of the many monks and friars who had
joined the ranks of Protestant clergy during Edward VI's
reign.[19] Furthermore, there was general revulsion at the
burning of Protestants under Mary,[20] and an intense fear of

the increasing influence of Spain in England's affairs.[21]
The public joy at the accession of Elizabeth in 1558 seems to
have been genuine;[22] and yet it must have been clear that if
Mary had carried the English Church back to Rome, Elizabeth
was just as likely to revert to Protestantism.[23]

If we ignore the sincere believers on both sides who
were prepared to be exiled or martyred for their faith, we
get the impression that the greater number of the English
people was not deeply committed to one side or the other;
but the population was intensely patriotic, insular, agrarian
and religiously conservative in its prejudices. It was not
likely to protest against a break with Rome that brought
the Church of England under a Tudor Queen, but it might protest very loudly if the worship and shape of that church
strayed too far from what the nation had known traditionally.
This suggests that the Englishman of that time was not too
much bothered by Elizabeth's being declared 'supreme governor'
of the Church of England but by whether he would continue to
enjoy the ministrations of the same parish priest, and whether
his priest would conduct weddings, baptisms and funerals in
much the same way as in the past. The things that influenced
the ordinary subject most in religion were practical and
visual.

Everything--Elizabeth's birth, her personal prejudices,
the conservatism of the English people and the situation at
home and abroad--conspired politically to make the Elizabethan
Settlement what it became. Of Elizabeth it has been said that
"it is evident from her words and attitude that she was not a
zealous Protestant":[24] she was temperamentally a Catholic
like her father, she liked the orderliness of a fixed
liturgy, she was probably more Catholic than Protestant in her
view of the eucharist, she never hid her distaste for married
clergy,[25] and, she liked a hierarchy of which she was the
unquestioned head. Perhaps most importantly, she needed a
united national church to assist her in bringing about a
united nation. On the one hand, only Protestantism could
allow her legitimacy, but on the other hand she needed a form
of the Church that offered some hope of winning that great
mass of conservative, semi-feudal sentiment in the shires.[26]
Once all these factors are put together, the shape of the
Elizabethan settlement in religion is seen to have been inevitable.

The Queen also seems to have been very well informed as
to the men who would serve her best on the episcopal bench.
Whenever possible, her bishops were chosen from clergymen who
had been close to the crown under Edward VI and who had managed

to keep their Protestant sympathies under wraps during the
Marian persecution, but failing such men she turned especially to those who had championed the Prayer Book while in
exile.[27] The disputes on that issue at Frankfurt in 1554-56
had been very instructive in this respect. She could rely on
these men because they had already demonstrated their loyalty
to the principle of royal supremacy in religion and to a
fixed liturgy, and because in them she found a form of churchmanship that modified the rigour of the Reformed churches at
large and stopped short of the older Catholicism "with a maxi-
mum blurring of the dividing line between the two."[28] Under
this kind of leadership the Church of England could be expected
to make a determined bid to win the great mass of traditional
sentiment that was at the heart of the nation.

* * * * * * * *

The Stuarts heartily endorsed this policy, for once the
factors governing the Church of England's unique shape are
recognized, the episcopal structure, the traditional vestments
and ritual, and even the growing opposition to Puritanism make
a good deal of political sense. If the objective was a *national* church, then the traditionalist heart of conservative
'middle England' had to be captured, and this seems to be admitted in a tract that has been attributed to Richard Bancroft.
The writer observed that Puritan arguments were more likely to
repel Catholics than to convert them, and declared it "is in
deede rather a way to wyn them, when they shall not onelie
see in vs, the lawfull practise of suche thinges, as they had
supersticiouslye abused [,] but also a most charitable inten-
c̄on, and meaninge to beare what wee maye, and to reiect, mislike or alter nothinge, which hath longe tyme bene contynued
in the Churche without most vrgent and necessarie causes."[29]

It was a policy of becoming 'all things to all men' that
they might by any means save some for the national church,
and it was brilliantly successful. Through the hundred years
that followed Elizabeth's accession, the Church of England
succeeded in assimilating the greater part of this conservative
opinion and was able to bring it into formal relationship to
its services and ordinances.[30] If national unity was still to
be measured in terms of medieval uniformity, the policy was
probably as successful as it could expect to be; but it had
two inevitable effects on the character of the national church
that were not to be foreseen by those who followed it.

In the first place, it led to a general lowering of the
spiritual vitality of the Church, for how religiously committed could we expect many of the new converts to be?

From 1530-1560 the parish priest and his parishioners had
to survive no less than four major changes and several minor
shifts in religion--from the original Catholic orthodoxy which
won Henry the papal title 'Defender of the Faith' to his break
with Rome, through the remaining years of the Henrican church,
veering sometimes in a Protestant direction (during the negotiations for the hand of Ann of Cleves) and sometimes to
Catholicism (the Act of Six Articles); then the changes of
Edward VI's reign (1547-1553) and the forms of worship governed by the two editions of the Prayer Book of 1549 and 1552;
this in turn was followed by reversion to papal allegiance
under Mary (1553-1558), and finally by the Protestant settlement of Elizabeth.

Yet there was never any evidence of a mass exodus from
the national church through these changes, and it appears
that the great majority of both priests and people accepted
each ecclesiastical change with relative equanimity, tending
if anything to become rather more restive during the extremes
of Protestantism in the reign of Edward and of Catholicism in
the time of Mary, but ready to acquiesce in an orthdox and
conservative expression of national independence. The population seems to have been conventionally orthodox in most
doctrinal matters, but none too willing to risk martyrdom and
none too happy with those whose zeal made martyrs of others.

We find similar attitudes and a similar succession of
changes in the Church of England at the beginning of the
eighteenth century (ca. 1680-1715), which was amusingly
satirized in the popular song, 'The Vicar of Bray'.[31] A majority of the English clergy after the Great Ejectment of
Puritans in 1662 became Anglican Tories, acquiescent in the
changes imposed upon them but generally reluctant to relinquish the security of a good living for the uncertainties of
persecution or exile.[32] This provided the government of that
time with a loyal ecclesiastical civil service, but it did
not give the nation any deeply committed spiritual leadership,
and this lowering of the religious temperature undoubtedly
communicated itself to the population at large.[33] The result
for the national Church was a huge credibility gap, for
thoughtful people--and, during the Evangelical Revival, religiously intense people--could not help asking how a church
of this temper compared with the apostolic church of the New
Testament.

In the second place, the assimilation of such a large
block of conservative opinion in the sixteenth and seventeenth
centuries inevitably pushed the Church of England in a more
'Catholic' direction: the *via media* between Rome and Geneva

became a much more consciously held stance in Laud and the
Caroline divines than it had been when the Thirty-Nine Articles were being formulated or when English clergymen were representing their church at the Synod of Dort.

Of course, there is a sense in which the English, however
conservative by inclination, had to reconcile themselves to
the separation from Rome if they remained within the national
church. Here nationalism played a part. A series of events
strengthened national unity and the determination to resist
all foreign interference in church and state, because each of
these events had sinister overtones—the plots against Elizabeth that led to the execution of Mary Queen of Scots in 1587,
the threat of invasion by the Spanish Armada in 1588, the War
of Dutch Independence, the Gunpowder Plot of 1605, the outbreak of the Thirty Years War in 1618 and the sufferings of
the Elector Palatine, the unpopularity of Charles I's French
Queen, and rumours of the widespread massacre of Protestants
by the Catholic Irish in 1641[34]—all these events helped the
English to become decidedly anti-papist.

This does not mean that the nation lost its conservative
preference for the form and ritual of the old order. Those
committed Protestants who embraced Puritanism abhorred everything that had the least reminder of Rome, but they represented
a minority. The rest, centered in the towns and villages of
rural England, probably had neither time, talent nor inclination seriously to question church practice: they simply
wanted the Church to continue to perform the offices it had
always performed and in the way it had always performed them.

The most attractive aspect of this policy of comprehen-
sion, which nonetheless also illustrates its essential appeal
to the conservatism of the English people, is seen in the
bookish physician, Sir Thomas Browne, who admitted that he
adhered to "that reformed and new-cast Religion, wherein I
mislike nothing but the name", but which, he maintained, was
"of the same beliefe our Saviour taught, the Apostles dissem-
inated, the Fathers authorized, and the Martyrs confirmed."
It is attractive because Browne refused to un-church Roman
Catholics, however misguided he thought them to be; but "I am,
I confesse", he went on to say, "naturally inclined to that,
which misguided zeale termes superstition", and despite the
new cast to his reformed faith,

> yet at my devotion I love to use the civility
> of my knee, my hat, and hand, with all those
> outward and sensible motions, which may ex-
> presse, or promote my invisible devotion. I

should violate my owne arme rather than a
Church, nor willingly deface the memory of
Saint or Martyr. At the sight of a Crosse
or Crucifix, I can dispence with my hat, but
scarce with the thought and memory of my
Saviour. . .I could never heare the *Ave Marie*
Bell without an elevation, or thinke it sufficient warrent, because they erred in one
circumstance, for me to erre in all, that is
in silence and dumbe contempt.[35]

At its best, despite the circumstances of its own history and
despite the way in which it was enforced, this English experi-
ment pointed towards catholicity.

* * * * * * * *

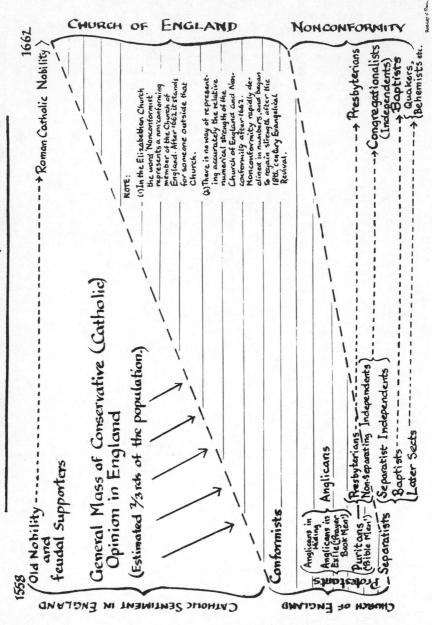

The reader is referred to the diagram facing this page, which illustrates the tendency of the Church of England through the reigns of Elizabeth I to that of Charles II to move in a more Catholic direction. The left hand of the diagram shows the constituency at the time of Elizabeth's accession, and the right hand represents the same constituency after the English Church had sloughed off its more intransigent Protestants and absorbed the great number of clergy and laity that was conformist by nature and catholic by inclination.

This process of assimilation was well advanced by the time the Civil War broke out, and it was only temporarily halted by that conflict. We suggest that by absorbing such a large body of relatively conservative sentiment the Church of England could not avoid being influenced theologically and ecclesiastically, and that it was a major factor in the Church's movement to a more Catholic position.

It should be remembered that after the débâcle at the Hampton Court Conference of 1603, many clergymen of Puritan views had conformed,[36] and that up to the outbreak of the Civil War in 1642 Puritanism was not separate from the national Church. Throughout the reign of James I (1603-1625) the dominant theology of the Church was Calvinist,[37] and the Church of England had been officially represented at the Synod of Dort. During the next few decades that theological stance changed very rapidly. Certainly the war itself, the social morality imposed by Cromwell's Major-Generals, the excesses of the sects, and sheer weariness with the ecclesiastical bickering were all contributory factors in persuading people to identify themselves with the more traditional form of the national Church after 1660. Many people who had been otherwise indifferent to religion must have welcomed the episcopal form and liturgy as a long-lost friend after the uncertainties of the Interregnum; but it was the *traditional* form that was attractive. This had been given to the Church already in the Elizabethan Settlement, and its causes were to be found in the Queen's own situation. Granted that, the episcopal Church of England was already set on the *via media* that became its logical destiny.

But if the Elizabethan Settlement determined the nature of the episcopal Church in England, it also produced dissenting protests from the right and from the left and helped to crystalize the form of Catholic opposition in Ireland, Presbyterian opposition in Scotland, and Congregationalist opposition in New England. The form that the Church took in England, and the way in which it was established by royal *fiat*, forced the ecclesiological issue into the forefront of all

the lands where the King or Queen of England ruled, and unwittingly encouraged those dissenting churches to define their
own positions more precisely. For that reason it provided a
matrix from which the ecclesiastical pluralism of America began to arise.

NOTES

1. The continuation of the Lollard tradition in England
and the fidelity of Hugh Latimer and the others who suffered
martyrdom for their Protestant convictions must not be down-
graded. But these men did not occupy positions of effective
political leadership in the nation. Latimer himself had
gained his reputation more as a preacher and popular bishop
than as an original theologian or as a political figure.

2. T. H. L. Parker in his Introduction to *The English
Reformers*, (Vol. XVI of *The Library of Christian Classics;*
Philadelphia, Westminster Press, 1966), pp. xv-xix.

3. This is illustrated even in T. H. L. Parker's selection of English Reformation writings in *The English Reformers*,
(1966). The one work that the editor includes which could
lay some claim to originality is John Jewell's, *An Apologie
of the Church of England*--a work on the doctrine of the Church
that arose directly out of England's ecclesiastical settlement.
    The Scottish situation, insofar as it was intimately re-
lated to what was happening in England, is also instructive.
Although the Scottish National 'Covenant' of 1557 and the
Scots Confession of 1560 are far closer to the work on the
Continent than anything produced in England--just as John
Knox was closer to the Continental Reformers than his English
counterparts--the originality of their thought centers in the
doctrine of the Church. Cf. chapter XVIII on 'The Notes by
Which the True Kirk Shall Be Determined From the False, and
Who Shall Be Judge of Doctrine', in *The Scots Confession*.

4. Luther had to make a strong appeal to persuade the
princes to intervene when the ecclesiastical situation in Germany appeared to be dissolving into chaos. See his Preface to
'Instructions for the Visitors of Parish Pastors in Electoral

Saxony,' *Luther's Works*, (Philadelphia, Muhlenberg Press, 1958, etc.), XL. 269ff. *W.A.* (Weimar Ausgabe) XXVI, 195ff.

5. The issue of theological authority in relationship to the ecclesiological problem has been explored more fully in *The Church in Search of Its Self* (Grand Rapids, Wm. B. Eerdmans Publishing Co., 1972).

6. It was the recognition of this that enabled Perry Miller to open a new era in Puritan studies in his book, *Orthodoxy in Massachusetts* (Cambridge, Mass., Harvard University Press, 1933), particularly chapters I-IV.

7. It is interesting to note that Cromwell used a kind of 'royal prerogative' in matters of religion to broaden the religious liberties of the subject during his rule. Cf. his speech to the 1st Parliament of the Protectorate, 12th September, 1654, *Writings and Speeches of Oliver Cromwell*, edited by Wilbur Cortez Abbott, (Cambridge, Mass., Harvard University Press, 1937-47, 4 vols.), III, p. 459.

8. Cf. Richard Baxter, *Reliquiae Baxterianae*, edited by Matthew Sylvester, 1696, I. §99, p. 64; II. §§50-55, pp. 197ff.

9. Cf. Perry Miller, *Orthodoxy in Massachusetts*.

10. See Carl Bridenbaugh, *Mitre and Sceptre* (New York, O.U.P., 1962).

11. The appearance of Peter Milward's *Religious Controversies of the Elizabethan Age* (Lincoln, Nebraska, University of Nebraska Press, 1977) suggests that there is beginning to be some interest in the sources of Anglo-Saxon pluralism within the Tudor and Stuart period. Fr. Milward promises us a companion volume on *Religious Controversies of the Jacobean Age*.

12. J. E. Neale, *Elizabeth I and her Parliaments, 1559-1581* (1958: New York, W. W. Norton & Co., 1966) p. 79.

13. Edmund Grindall (1519?-1583) had been a Fellow of Pembroke Hall, Cambridge, where he seems to have caught the attention of Nicholas Ridley, a member of the same college and later to become Bishop of London and a martyr in Mary's reign. Grindall had also been a royal chaplain in Edward VI's reign, but when Mary came to the throne, he escaped to the continent. He seems to have settled in Strasbourg and then went to Frankfurt, where he took part in the dispute regarding the prayer book on the side of Richard Cox against John Knox.

In *A Brief Discourse of the Troubles at Frankfort* (sometimes attributed to William Whittingham, and published in
1675) Grindall appears as one of ten signatories of a letter
to John Calvin justifying what had been done. Of the ten
signatories, no less than five were later bishops under
Elizabeth; *Op. cit.*, edited by Edward Arber (London, 1908)
pp. 78-80; cf. also C. H. Garrett, *The Marian Exiles* (Cambridge, Cambridge University Press, 1938) pp. 167-9. Returning to England in 1558, he was appointed Bishop of London
and master of Pembroke Hall (1558-1561), and then successively
Archbishop of York (1570-75) and Archbishop of Canterbury in
1576.

Although Grindall sympathized with the Puritans, it can be
seen that from the time of his appointment as a royal chaplain,
he had impeccable credentials for high office under Elizabeth.

14. "I am sure that religion will not fall, because the
Catholic party is two-thirds larger than the other." To the
King, 19th March, 1558/9, *Calendar of Letters and State Papers
relating to English affairs, preserved principally in. . .
Simancas,* edited by Martin A. D. Hume (London : Public Record
Office, 1892) Vol. 1 (Elizabeth 1558-1567) p. 39. [The Calen-
dars of State Papers are hereafter referred to as *Cal. S. P.*]
If we take de Feria's estimate at face value, (and it is the
only estimate we have), this would imply that over 60 per
cent of the population was still Catholic in sympathy.

15. Il Schifanoya to Ottaviano Vivaldino, Mantuan Ambassador at Brussels, March 21, 1559. *Cal. S. P.* (Venetian),
Vol. VII (1558-1580), p. 52 [No. 45].

16. In a letter to Wolfgang Weidner, Cox confessed that
although there had been some success among the nobility and
with 'vast numbers of people' he could discern none among the
clergy, while Jewell informed Heinrich Bullinger that 'at
Oxford there are scarcely two individuals who think with us'
and could not recommend that Bullinger should send any of his
students to study there. Cox to Weidner, May 20th, 1559;
Jewell to Bullinger, May 22nd, 1559, *Zurich Letters* (Parker
Society, Cambridge, C.U.P., 1842) I. pp. 27, 33.

17. A. M Trevelyan, *English Social History* (London, Longmans, Green & Co., 1944), p. 331.

18. *Ibid.,* p. 101.

19. *Ibid.,* p. 105.

20. "The level of English callousness to suffering had been a crucial factor. The Tudor English were revoltingly callous by the standards of their descendants, but they were tender-hearted by the standards of their own Christendom. Where the Netherlands endured without resistance for a decade a rate of burning from five to ten times that of the Marian persecution, where the French with a taste for blood rather than flame were prepared to indulge in the wild massacre of thousands in a week, and where the Spaniards witnessed with grim approval and no scruple of pity the routine proceedings of the *auto da fe*, the English found Mary's hundred victims too much for their stomachs. The persecution had been at a higher rate than England would continue to permit, and it had been at too low a rate to put an end to Protestantism, and there was no way of bridging the gap between the two requirements." James A. Williamson, *The Tudor Age.*(London, Longmans, Green & Co., 1953), pp. 249f.

21. This may well have been the initial cause of 'the Black Legend'. Cf. *The Black Legend in England: The development of anti-Spanish sentiment,* by William S. Maltby (Durham, N. Carolina, Duke University Press, 1971).

22. Williamson, *The Tudor Age,* p. 247ff.

23. Mary's policy was dictated by her own strong Catholic convictions, by her Spanish marriage, but even more by her loyalty to her mother's memory and as a protest against the divorce. Elizabeth, on the other hand, although she shared many of the Catholic preferences and even prejudices of her half-sister, was forced to move in a Protestant direction.

24. James A. Williamson, *op. cit.*, p. 250.

25. Cf. *The Other Face: Catholic Life under Elizabeth I,* Collected and Edited by Philip Caraman, (New York, Sheed & Ward, 1960) pp. 64-71, especially p. 68.

26. Cf. K. R. Clark, *Elizabethan Recusancy in Cheshire,* (Totowa, N.J., Rowman & Littlefield, 1972), Dom Hugh Aveling, *Post Reformation Catholicism in East Yorkshire, 1558-1790,* (York, E. Yorks, Local History Soc., 1960); William Raleigh Trimble, *The Catholic Laity in Elizabethan England, 1558-1603,* (Cambridge, Mass., Belknap Press, 1964). Cf. also the review of this last book by Patrick Collinson, who urges the dependence of Catholic recusancy on the landed gentry, *Renaissance News,* Vol. XVIII, No. 3 (Autumn 1965), p. 241.

27.   Cf. *supra* p. 107, note 13 on Edmund Grindall. In the disputes at Frankfurt we meet a number of other future Elizabethan bishops siding with Richard Cox in the quarrel with John Knox:

Richard Cox had been royal almoner and tutor to Edward VI, and he had been one of the Commissioners on the Liturgy 1548-50. He became Bishop of Norwich in 1559 and was almost immediately translated to the see of Ely.

Robert Horne had been Dean of Durham under Edward VI, and had helped with the preparation of the 45 Articles of Religion. In 1560 he became Bishop of Winchester.

John Jewell became Bishop of Salisbury in 1560.

John Parkhurst became Bishop of Norwich in 1560.

James Pilkington assisted with the 1558 revision of the B.C.P., and became Bishop of Durham in 1561.

John Scory had been Bishop of Rochester (1551) and then of Chichester (1552) under Edward VI. Before leaving England he had briefly recanted, but went into exile and on returning after Elizabeth's accession became Bishop of Hereford.

Edwin Sandys had supported Lady Jane Grey, but under Elizabeth became Bishop of Worcester (1559), then of London (1570), and finally Archbishop of York (1576).

It is worth noting that Matthew Parker, who became Elizabeth's first Archbishop of Canterbury (1559), had earlier been chaplain to her mother, Anne Boleyn, and had lived in hiding after surviving the fall of Lady Jane Grey and the Dudleys.

The man who perhaps most embodied Elizabeth's churchmanship, however, was John Whitgift, who had remained at Peterhouse, Cambridge, during Mary's reign under the protection of the Master, Dr. Pearne. After Elizabeth's accession he became chaplain to Richard Cox at Ely (1560) and then Bishop of Worcester (1577) and eventually Archbishop of Canterbury after the death of Grindall (1583). [For Whitgift's life at Cambridge during the Marian persecution under the care of Dr. Pearne, the Master of Peterhouse, see Sir George Paule's *The Life of John Whitgift*, London, 1612, pp. 1-8].

It is interesting also to note that at least two men who had been bishops under Edward VI (John Bale of Ossory, and Miles Coverdale of Exeter) did not take sees in the Elizabethan church, although Bale accepted a prebend at Canterbury.

28.   James A. Williamson, *The Tudor Age*, p. 250.

29.   *Tracts Ascribed to Richard Bancroft*, edited by Albert A. Peel (Cambridge, C.U.P., 1953), p. 157.

30.   Perhaps the most distinguished convert at this time was the poet priest, John Donne (1573-1631), who had been

raised as a Roman Catholic by his mother. According to Isaac
Walton he was persuaded by James I to take orders in the
Church of England (1615), and was eventually appointed Dean of
St. Paul's in 1621. Cf. Isaac Walton's *The Life of Dr. John
Donne*.

31. The song satirizes an incumbent who manages to trim
his position and thus hold on to his ecclesiastical living
through the religious changes of Charles II (Divine Right
Anglican), James II (Roman Catholic), William and Mary (Low
Church Whig), Anne (High Church Tory), and George I (Latitu-
dinarian). Its sentiment may be gathered from the refrain to
be sung after each verse:

> And this is the law that I'll maintain
> Until my dying day, sir,
> That whatsoever king may reign,
> Still I'll be the Vicar of Bray, sir.

32. The one significant exception was the small number of
Non-jurors who had left the Church because of their loyalty to
the Stuarts and the Divine Right of monarchy in 1688.

33. Cf. Trevelyan, *English Social History*, chapters X-
XIII.

34. Clarendon estimated that between 40 and 50,000
Protestants had been killed, but the more generally accepted
figure was 200,000! This is the figure that was believed by
such normally restrained writers as Lucy Hutchinson and
Richard Baxter. Cf. Robert S. Paul, *The Lord Protector*,
(London, Lutterworth, 1955), p. 52 and notes.

35. Sir Thomas Browne, *Religio Medici* (1642, 1643;
edited by Jean-Jacques Denonain, Cambridge, C.U.P., 1954, pp.
6-8) Pt. I, §§2, 3.

36. For example, Samuel Ward, who was later to become
Lady Margaret Professor of Divinity at Cambridge, Master of
Sidney Sussex College, and one of the representatives at the
Synod of Dort. Cf. M. M. Knappen, *Two Puritan Diaries* (Chica-
go, American Soc. of Church History, 1933).

37. The earlier Church of England theologians appear to
have had a distinctly Reformed soteriology in contrast to
the later Caroline Divines. Cf. C. Fitzsimons Allison, *The
Rise of Moralism*, (New York, Seabury Press, 1966).

7

SCOTTISH CALVINISM
AND THE PRINCIPLE OF INTOLERANCE*

James K. Cameron

In some popular historical writings Calvin is often depicted as the 'dictator of Geneva', 'the arch-inquisitor' of
Protestantism, and branded, along with his colleagues Farel
and Beza, and his disciple Knox, as a 'persecutor' - indeed
as the one who 'brought Protestant persecution to a head'.[1]
Together they are held responsible for impressing upon Reformed Protestantism a character which, for the larger part of
two centuries, is held to have discoloured its Christian witness in those areas where it held sway. As a result, Calvinism for some cannot be painted in too dark a hue nor its
adherents too severely condemned. This almost universal popular antipathy, particularly among 'lay' writers, has not gone
without challenge, or at least modification, from serious
students of Calvinism and from a number of ecclesiastical
historians who, in the post-war period, have added significantly to 16th century studies.

'Calvinism', as J. T. McNeill remarked in his preface to
The History and Character of Calvinism, 'has usually been discussed in an atmosphere of controversy and has often been
judged even by academicians with slender reference to evidence'.[2] But with the publication of hitherto unedited source
material and with new and elaborately annotated editions of
some standard works, it may be that Calvinism, as Calvin himself requested in the prefatory letter to the first edition of

*Based on a paper originally read at an Oxford Conference
of the Commission Internationale d'Histoire Ecclésiastique
Comparée.

The Institutes, can still hope to be accorded a full impartial inquiry, and particularly in the area of toleration.

The accusation of intolerance is often popularly based on the treatment of Michael Servetus in Geneva in 1553, which has been described as 'one of the most famous controversies of modern times about religious freedom'.[3] Calvin, as the leading preacher of the city and as the one who assisted in the denunciation of the Spanish scholar to the civil authorities, has been held supremely responsible. It is of particular interest that one execution by burning at the stake in a century in which the death penalty for trivial offences was so common, and in which so many hundreds in all religious groupings suffered the extreme terrors of persecution, should subsequently be singled out, almost isolated, as the 'peak of religious intolerance' in an age in which, as Professor Bainton has justly remarked, 'we incinerate whole cities for the saving of democracy'.[4]

The Servetus incident need not be discussed in detail. In recent years it has been the subject of a number of important studies, particularly by R. H. Bainton in his *Michel Servet Heretique et Martyr* published in Geneva in 1953, and we now have in the second volume of *Registres de la Compagnie des Pasteurs de Genève au tempes de Calvin 1553-1564*, the 'Accusation et Procès de Michel Servet', edited by J. -F. Bergier.[5] Here are brought together an authoritative collection of texts hitherto unedited, of considerable historical and theological importance. Any future study of toleration in the Reformed Churches must take into account this invaluable additional source material.

For our purpose only the main points of the incident need be recalled. Calvin accepted full responsibility for bringing the accusation against Servetus before the civil magistrates. Along with his fellow ministers, he produced as evidence of heresy extracts from Servetus' writings which the accused was permitted to discuss with Calvin and his ministerial colleagues. No doubt about Servetus' theological ideas and his persistent attachment to them to the end can have remained in the minds even of the most sympathetic onlooker. That he rejected what were then regarded as fundamental doctrines of the Christian Church long universally accepted by the orthodox, was considered abundantly clear. That he had thereby committed an offence against the civil code of the empire accepted as legally binding on Geneva, and rendered himself guilty and subject to criminal punishment, has not, however, always been stressed.[6]

The dividing line between religious belief and acceptable moral behaviour in accordance with the Law, which in the 20th century is taken for granted, and the removal of matters of dogma to a special compartment of life outwith the concern of the state, was not entertained as politically acceptable in the minds of the vast majority of both the ruled and the rulers. The Peace of Augsburg with its principle *cuius regio eius religio* two years later, made this clear within the empire. From the point of view of those in authority in Geneva, that principle was in the Servetus case already being effected. Further, this decision accorded with Calvin's politico-ecclesiastical understanding. Western society was based on the historic Christian faith, and although there may have been radical disagreement about 'recent innovations' or 'novelties', there was no disagreement on the doctrine of God. Further, the doctrine of natural individual rights to modify or reject or ignore or in any way qualify its acceptance of that religious basis had no place in reformed thinking.

The conclusion seems fairly clear, the accusation of intolerance is grounded on the fact that Calvin, by upholding the accepted basis of society and in seeking the punishment of one whom he, along with his contemporaries, both Catholic and Protestant, regarded not merely as having divergent religious beliefs, but as an offender against the criminal code and as hostile to society, did not rise above his contemporaries. He did not plead for toleration because toleration with regard to the fundamentals of society would have been politically irresponsible and, secondly, an affront to God the sovereign Ruler of creation. That he did not rise above his contemporaries and advocate for Servetus and others that the precise formulation of religious beliefs should be left to individuals, has been regretted by many Calvin scholars, but that in seeking the condemnation of Servetus with support from other Swiss cities and reformers he believed he was acting in accordance with both the law of God and the law of the state as a responsible citizen of the day, has perhaps been all too easily ignored. He was the leader among intransigent upholders of a society that had on the whole not yet come to conceive of the possibility of tolerating private religious opinions.

Calvin's stand, and the defences which both he and Beza set out, mark the early development of the struggle between the advocates of intolerance and those of toleration in Reformed protestantism. Much has been done, particularly in the post-war period, in setting out the views of Calvin's opponents. Professor Bainton has given us, amongst many other valuable works, his translation of Castellio's treatise[7] and more recently Dr. Uwe Plath has published his important Basel doctoral thesis *Calvin und Basel,*[8] so that little more need be

added at this point to the continental aspects of this study.
But what of the history of intolerance and intransigence in
other areas of Calvinist influence? The purpose of this
paper is to examine some aspects of this topic in the history
of the Reformed Church in Scotland.

It is generally held that among the countries influenced
by Calvinism Scotland takes a leading place. Scotland, at
first affected by Lutheranism, gave way to the rising tide of
Reformed teaching in the late 1540's, which culminated in the
activity of John Knox, especially from 1560 onwards, Knox
is generally regarded as one of the most outstanding of Calvin's disciples; he had spent the years immediately before
his return to his native country in Geneva. His high regard
for that city and its discipline has often been quoted.[9] The
leading role often ascribed to Knox in the Scottish Reformation has, however, been challenged by Professor Gordon Donaldson, who tends to regard his position as much less dominant
than that hitherto generally accepted.[10] But, be that as it
may, Calvin's teaching, largely mediated through Knox, has
deeply coloured Scottish religious life. Scotland's basic
reformation documents are all strongly Calvinist. In the
Scots Confession of 1560, the First and Second Books of Discipline, and the Book of Common Order can be traced the para-
mount influence of Geneva.

As a pupil of Calvin, Knox fully absorbed his teaching on
the limits of religious toleration as in almost every other
area. His fundamental theological ideas were already firmly
established before he returned to Scotland in May 1560 and
were soon to appear in print from the press of John Crispin
in Geneva in a work written in English which Knox's 19th
century editor David Laing described as his 'most elaborate
production'.[11] This work, on predestination, comprised an
answer to a treatise in English of an anabaptist, anonymous
but known to Knox, who had attacked the doctrine of predestination and other tenets of Calvinism. Its unidentified writer
had drawn on the publications of Sebastian Castellio and had
in the course of the discussion referred to the reformers as
'persecutors, on whom the blood of Servetus cried a vengeance',
and accused them of setting forth books affirming it to be
lawful to persecute and to put to death such as dissent from
them in controversies of religion as 'blasphemers of God'.[12]

This attack upon Geneva and its reformers, and in particular the reference to Servetus, called forth from Knox, in all
probability at the request of English and Genevan friends, a
spirited, indeed vehement defence. Geneva is praised for its
discipline; there'the sword of God's vengeance shall strike

the murderer, the blasphemer, and such others as God by his Word commandeth to die'.[13] The penalty for blasphemy had been set out in God's Word, that 'God had appointed death by his law without mercy, to be executed upon the blasphemers is evident by that which is written, Leviticus 24'.[14] Knox goes even further and argues that those who defend murderers and blasphemers are themselves guilty of the same offence and ought to suffer the same death penalty. Indeed, he warns his 'Adversary', that his purpose is 'to lay the same charge against him, and that he will so act if I shall apprehend thee in any commonwealth where justice against blasphemers may be ministered as God's Word requireth'.[15] This man's 'manifest defection from God' and his 'open blasphemy spoken against his eternal truth' broke 'all familiarity' which had existed between them; and Knox goes so far as to assert 'although thou were my natural brother I durst not conceal thy iniquity in this case'.[16]

Obviously the definition of blasphemy is important, for it was, Knox held, as 'an abominable blasphemer against God' that Servetus had been condemned.[17] Blasphemy, according to Knox, is comprised under six points. To speak blasphemy or blaspheme God is (1) not only to deny that there is a God but also lightly to esteem the power of the eternal God; (2) to spread abroad such opinions of his Majesty as to make his Godhead to be doubted; (3) to depart from the true honouring and religion of God to the imagination of man's inventions; (4) obstinately to maintain and defend doctrine and diabolical opinions plainly repugning to God's truth; (5) to judge those things which God judgeth necessary for our salvation not to be necessary; (6) and, finally, to persecute the truth of God and members of Christ's body.

In seeking to prove that Servetus was guilty of these offences Knox listed twelve 'erroneous opinions' which he ascribes to him and appealed to Castellio to say if the propositions cited do not contain blasphemy - among them the well known accusation 'that Christ Jesus is not the eternal son of the eternal Father'. Further, Knox stresses that these opinions were obstinately maintained.

In thus defending and supporting the action of the Genevan reformers and those who shared their point of view, Knox made clear the policy which he would wish to have effected in Scotland. To live according to the Word of God entailed both the upholding of the validity for Christians of the Old Testament law and the responsibility of seeking from those who exercised the civil sword their full co-operation and compliance. Knox, of course, was aware that some claimed that Christians lived

under a new dispensation, for whom the rigour of the Levitical
law had passed away. His answer to them is characteristically
blunt. 'If ye claim any privilege by the coming of the Lord
Jesus, himself will answer "that he is not come to break nor
destroy the law of his heavenly Father"'.[18]

The uncompromising position of the Scottish reformer is,
however, not consistently embodied in the *First Book of Discipline*, of which he was one of the authors and in which the
leading reformers set out at the request of those in authority
their requirements for the establishment of a reformed Church.
Here heresy is defined as 'pernicious doctrine plainly taught
and openly defended against the foundations and principles of
our faith':[19] and such a crime we learn is, in the case of a
minister, deemed to deserve 'perpetual deposition from the
ministry'. 'For', the authors continue, 'most dangerous we
know it to be to commit the flock to a man infected with the
pestilence of heresy'. True, a way is still left open for the
advocates of extreme punishment; the death penalty was requested elsewhere in the book for blasphemy, adultery, murder,
and perjury.[20] But punishment of such offences it was held
'ought not properly to fall under censure of the Church because all such open transgressors of God's laws ought to be
taken away by the civil sword', as indeed Calvin maintained in
his commentary on Deuteronomy 13 'in a well constituted polity
profane men are by no means to be tolerated by whom religion
is subverted'. But if the civil power failed, the Church in
such cases could do more than resort to excommunication.

The principle is thus affirmed by the Scottish reformers:
those guilty of crimes which, according to scripture carry
the death penalty, should be so punished. Nevertheless, we
are given to understand that there was little hope of this
principle being put into practise. The Book, in fact, makes
generous provision if such offenders are not punished by the
State. After excommunication they could even be received
back into the fellowship of the Church. Although the Book of
Discipline sought the death penalty for adultery, its authors
were prepared to concede that if the adulterer was spared by
the civil authority and the 'fruit of repentance' appeared he
may not only be restored to the fellowship of the Church, but
may even be allowed to remarry.[21] Still the reformers did not,
in principle, modify their basic demand that the law of the
land should be brought into accord with the Levitical law.

An interesting but scarcely noticed section of the First
Book of Discipline at this point invites attention. In the
final section in which request is made 'for the punishment of
those that profane the sacraments and condemn the Word of God
and dare to administer them not being thereto lawfully called',

reference is made to those who 'dare counterfeit in their houses that which the true ministers do in open congregations' and the request is made that without delay strict laws be made against such persons. The penalty of death is affirmed on the following grounds. 'If he who doth falsify the seal, subscription, or coin of a king is judged worthy of death what shall we think of him who plainly doth falsify the seals of Christ Jesus, prince of the king of the earth.'[22] This passage is clearly reminiscent of St. Thomas Aquinas' argument 'it is far more serious to pervert the faith which ensures the life of the soul than to counterfeit money which is only necessary for our temporal needs'.[23] In the Book of Discipline, however, it is also supported also by a reference to Ezra 6, vv. 11, 12, in which the death penalty is decreed for those who hinder the rebuilding of the temple. Those who hinder the rebuilding of the temple of God, which is the souls and bodies of the elect, are, it is asserted, likewise guilty of a capital offence. In this passage we have one of the very few references to sectaries to whom Ninian Winzet alluded when he upbraided the reformers for contending 'tooth and nail' with some of the Lords and Gentlemen who had administered the sacraments in times passed in their own households.[24]

As is well known, the Book of Discipline, unlike the Scots Confession, failed to gain the support of the civil rulers in 1560. Nevertheless, the reformers continued to seek ratification for it from Parliament and repeatedly called for the inflicting of the death penalty on blasphemers to be embodied in the statute law. For example, in May 1562 the General Assembly petitioned for the punishment of 'horrible vices' including blasphemy, contempt of God and of his word and sacraments, and claimed the supreme authority of scriptures. 'If any object that punishments cannot be commanded to be executed without a Parliament, we answer that the eternal God in his Parliament has pronounced death to be the punishment for adultery and for blasphemy; whose acts if ye put not to execution (seeing that kings are but his lieutenants having no power to give life, where he commands death), as that he will repute you and all others that foster vice, patrons of impiety, so will he not fail to punish you for neglecting his judgments'.[25] Again, in 1565, a similar petition was made for an act of parliament, but no act inflicting the death penalty for blasphemy was passed,[26] and the General Assembly had to be content as late as 1589 with its own enactment that 'blasphemers of God are ordained to be tried and censured by particular sessions of the parish and (those) who shall be convicted of these offences shall be denied the benefits of the church with further censure as the word of God will allow'.[27]

In their efforts to have the statute law brought into
line with scripture, the Scottish Reformers met with no conspicuous success even though as act making adultery a capital
offence was passed. They had secured the acceptance of their
statement of the faith; they had worked hard to have the Reformed Church organization set up throughout the land, but
Knox's intention to have the law brought into line with the
severity of the Levitical law and to make heresy and blasphemy
of the type he had attacked in his treatise on predestination
punishable by death, was not realised until well into the next
century.[28] It is not without justice that King James VI could
boast that he was no persecutor of men for their religious
opinions.[29] Indeed, although there were in 16th century
Scotland, in certain areas, rigorous attempts to exercise a
strict moral discipline by kirk sessions and Church courts
generally, and a perpetual fear of the activity of Roman Catholics which called for the signing of such documents as the
Negative Confession, the persecution of individuals for their
religious beliefs is with few exceptions remarkably absent.
There are no heretical burnings and those who do suffer do so
as enemies of the State. It is not until the religio-political
struggle of the next century that suffering for one's religious
loyalties on any scale that may be called grand, became a
prominent feature of Scottish life among protestants. The conflict between the Crown and the Church, between Episcopacy and
Presbytery, and the various conflicts among Presbyterians
themselves in the 17th century form no part of this paper, nor
do the attempts to suppress Roman Catholics. My purpose is
rather to restrict attention to the efforts directed towards
making heresy a criminal offence and to the outcome of those
efforts in the final decade of the century.

A new period in the religious history of Scotland opened
with the Restoration - a period which, strange as it may seem,
was to make blasphemy and the denial of the Trinity a criminal
offence punishable by death.

During the Commonwealth sectarians had made their appearance in Scotland. George Fox had in fact visited the country,
but had not found it 'a congenial soil' for the advancement of
his religious ideas.[30] Nevertheless, the strength of sectar-
ianism appears to have been sufficient for parliament in
January 1661 to pass an act prohibiting the meetings of
'Quaikers, Anabaptists and fyft monarchie men', and requiring
that offenders be punished as 'enemies to all lawful authority
and government who upon specious and religious pretences at
unlawful times and places keep frequent meetings and conventi-
cles together'.[31] Some offenders were in fact put in prison
and in 1667 the council went so far as to have children taken

from parents who were Quakers in order that they may be
brought up in the orthodox faith.[32] During the greater part
of the reign of Charles II, the Privy Council regarded the
suppression of Quakers as 'a national concern'. But the penal
measures which were taken were 'impotent to effect their end'.
The Quakers continued 'to perturb the Council as a dangerous
and implacable section of his Majesty's subjects'.[33]

It was probably in order to show its determination to
root out sectarians and to allay any fear that might have
existed over the kingdom's loyalty to Protestantism in the
face of the restoration of episcopacy, that, in May 1661 and
before the reestablishment of the Privy Council, Parliament
passed an act making blasphemy a crime punishable by death.
The act is short and may be quoted *in extenso:*

> 'Our sovereign the Lord and Estates of
> Parliament considering that hitherto there
> has been no law in this kingdom against
> the horrible crime of blasphemy. There-
> fore his Majesty with advice of his said
> Estates, doth hereby statute and ordain
> that whosoever hereafter not being dis-
> tracted in his wits shall rail upon or
> curse God or any of the persons of the
> blessed Trinity shall be processed before
> the chief justice; and being found guilty
> shall be punished with death. . .that
> whoever hereafter shall deny God or any of
> the persons of the blessed Trinity and
> obstinately continue therein shall be
> processed and being found guilty that they
> be punished with death.'[34]

The act was to have retroactive effect.

> 'All persons who have committed the foresaid
> crimes since the 17th day of February, 1649,
> shall be proceeded against according to this
> act.'

Further, all past decrees and judicial proceedings
against any persons who had committed such crimes since 1649,
and who had been found guilty, were ratified; and those who
had pronounced such sentences, it was decreed, could not have
their decisions called in question. In effect the act was to
be held as having been in force since 1649.

This remarkable statute which after a lapse of 100 years
had put into effect Knox's desire - the punishment of blasphemy

according to the Levitical law by death - appears out of
keeping with Restoration policy. Was it, perhaps, in the
Scottish scene a political concession to religious extremism?[35]
To a large extent it remained a dead letter; no proceedings in
a civil court in which it was invoked have come to my knowledge.

It is worth noting at this point that this act was not
invoked in 1678 when Hector Allan, 'a skipper of Leith' who
'taught several eroneous heretical and blasphemous tenets',
and on occasions 'set himself up to interrupt the services of
accredited ministers', was, after he had been imprisoned,
finally brought before the Privy Council by the Lord Advocate
merely on a 'charge of breaking the peace', and fined 2000
marks. On this occasion the statute cited was the Act of
James VI's eleventh Parliament against creating a disturbance
during a divine service.[36] Indeed, there appears to have been
no resolute desire to put the act of 1661 into operation. It
is also interesting to note that, despite certain attempts to
suppress Quakers by brief imprisonments, a Quaker meeting
house was built and opened at Urie in Kincardine and continued
for more than 100 years to be the headquarters of the Friends
in the North of Scotland.[37] Renewed short imprisonments of
David Barclay (one of the leaders of Quakers in Scotland), at
the instigation of the clergy of Aberdeen, were powerless to
shake his constancy. His son, Robert Barclay, the Quaker
apologist, succeeded to the barony in 1686 and on several
occasions presided at the baron court. In his justly celebrated work *An Apology for True Christian Divinity*, published
ten years earlier, he had in the preface appealed to Charles
II for toleration on behalf of himself and his coreligionists;
and although he himself suffered prison, the extreme rigour of
the law was never invoked against him.[38]

The Revolution settlement in 1688, the establishment of
Presbyterianism and the permitting of the continued existence
of an Episcopal Church, and at the same time the rising influence of the new philosophical and theological ideas along
with the king's avowed desire for 'moderation' would, one
might have expected, have opened up the way for granting of a
measure of toleration. It is therefore somewhat surprising,
indeed strange, to find Parliament as late as June 1695
ratifying and confirming the act against blasphemy of 1661 in
all its parts, and further ordaining that it was 'to be put to
new and punctual execution'. It was now ordained that "who-
ever hereafter shall in their writings or discourse deny im-
pugne or quarrell, argue or reason against the being of God,
or any of the persons of the blessed Trinity, or the providence of God in the government of the world shall for the
first fault be punished with imprisonment, until they give

public satisfaction to the congregation within which the scandal was committed'. For the second fault the delinquent was
to be fined, and for the third fault he was to 'be punished
by death as an obstinate blasphemer'.39 This act in fact
was one of a number passed by this Parliament in favour of
religion and a stricter observance of religious life in the
country. But it did permit of less severe action being
taken against blasphemers than the one which it confirmed.

Toward the end of the same year similar zeal for orthodoxy, reflecting the current climate of theological discussion
and the emerging opposition to new philosophical movements,
is seen in the passing by the General Assembly of the Church
of an act against Quakers. It was decreed that all proper
means should be used for reclaiming them and only in all
cases of obstinacy should they be proceeded against 'with
the censures of the church'.40 Early in the following year
the celebrated act against Deists was passed; only after they
had been remonstrated with were they to be proceeded against
'as scandalous and heretical apostates used to be'.41

These acts of Parliament and General Assembly, reflecting
hardening theological tendencies, may be regarded as evidence
of a last stand by the State and the Church against the slowly
rising tide of toleration. The 16th and early 17th centuries
had seen much religious intolerance in Scotland, but in in-
quiring into the individual's theological understanding of
his faith, extreme persecution had had no real part. The
second half of the 17th century had, as we have seen, brought
blasphemy and heresy closely together and in two acts of
Parliament made them criminal offences punishable by death.
But as yet no-one had felt the full force of these lamentable
laws, and in this way the century might have closed had it
not been for the outspoken rashness of a young student of 18
years.

The case of Thomas Aikenhead has been described as 'a
painful incident in the history of intolerance', but 'the last
of the kind which happened in our country'.42 It is probably
known today only to specialists, apart from the readers of
Macaulay, who spared nothing in recounting it.43 Macaulay's
graphic, if somewhat overdrawn account occasioned considerable interest at the time in the press, notably the evangelical
papers *The Witness, The Scotsman,* and the then *Daily Express,*
and led to the publication of several pamphlets. The case
was argued on both sides with considerable fervour, but since
then no new light has illumined this dark episode of which it
is necessary only to recall the briefest details.44

A young student 'was indicted before the Court of Justiciary for the crime of blasphemy or railing and cursing against God or the persons of the Holy Trinity'. He was found guilty, condemned to death on 24th December, 1696, and publicly executed on 8th January, 1697. Both the State, in the person of the Privy Council and the Lord Advocate, and the Church, as represented by the ministers of Edinburgh, must bear responsibility. During the course of the trial, Aikenhead was not allowed the help of counsel. After he had been condemned two or three ministers made 'a feeble show of intercession'. One of the most merciful of them preached a sermon before the judges in which there was not one word in favour of mercy, the accused was not mentioned, but this minister, along with one other, sought a reprieve at the last possible moment.[45]

The General Assembly meeting at the same time made no direct reference to what was taking place, but one cannot escape noticing that its reply to the King's letter, read and passed on January 6th, two days before the execution, these words, 'We cannot but lament the abounding impiety and profanity in this land, so we must acknowledge your Majesty's Christian care in enacting good laws for suppressing the same, the rigorous execution of which we humbly beg.'[46] Further, in the same Assembly on January 11th as 'Act against Profaneness' was decreed in which are found words recalling 'the many laudable Christian laws of this nation and the Acts of the General Assemblies of this church against all impiety and profaneness', and lamenting that even now 'the open outbreakings of wickedness are not restrained but God is daily dishonoured and provoked. . .by the abounding scandals of profane and idle swearing, cursing,. . .mocking of piety and religion,. . .Deism, the blasphemy and other gross abominable sins'.[47] The act also refers to the act of the General Assembly of 1694 recommending ministers and kirk sessions to apply to the magistrates for putting the acts of Parliament against profaneness into execution, and stresses that it is incumbent upon ministers and church judicatories faithfully to use all 'suitable means' in dealing with the consciences of offenders in order to bring them to repentance and reformation. Further, ministers and kirk sessions from a true zeal for God are 'to hold hand to delating, informing against and punishing of all profane transgressors without respect to persons by civil punishments conform to the Acts of Parliament made in that behalf'.[48] There is, however, detectable in this act evidence that ministers had not always been as diligent as the General Assembly would have liked, and that the same fault was also to be found in magistrates. Where this had happened it was decreed that the magistrates should be pursued before the Lords of Council or Session. So seriously did the General Assembly take this

125

matter that this act was to be read in all churches twice a year from the pulpit. Clearly, the Assembly approved of the action of the State in the enforcing of the law in January 1697.

In the last decade of the 17th century, Church and State in Scotland, in their exercise of their co-ordinate powers, were seeking to effect a policy of intolerance unknown in its severity in the second half of the 16th century, in their efforts to establish what they both regarded as a 'Christian society'. It may never be possible fully to understand how these laws came at so late a date to mar the Statute book, and the records of criminal proceeding. We can only be thankful that those in authority succeeded in bringing a single case only before the courts in which the full force of the law was applied. One case, however, was one too many. The time was ripe for the age of 'moderatism', and with it in time toleration.

NOTES

1. See for example, R. H. Bainton, *The Travail of Religions Liberty*, (Lutterworth, London 1953), p. 53.

2. J. T. McNeill, *History and Character of Calvinism*, (O.U.P., 1967), p. vii.

3. J. Lecler, *Toleration and the Reformation*, (Longmans, London), vol. 1, p. 325.

4. R. H. Bainton, *The Travail of Religions Liberty*, p. 92.

5. R. M. Kingdon and J. -F. Bergier, *Registres de la compagnie des pasteurs de Genève au temps de Calvin*, (Droz, Geneva 1962), vol. 2, 1553-1563.

6. Calvin published in January 1554 his *Declaratio orthodoxae fidei, Calvini opera (Corpus Reformatorum*, 1870), vol. VIII, pp. 453-644. See further É. Doumergue, *Jean Calvin, Les hommes et les choses de son temps*, (Lausanne 1899-1928), vol. 6, pp. 411ff.; also Lecler, *Toleration and Reformation*, vol. 2,

pp. 333ff.; Beza, *De haereticis a civili magistratu puniendis*, (Geneva 1554); See further P.-F. Geisendorf, *Théodore de Bèze*, (Geneva 1967), and Lecler, vol. 1, pp. 237ff.

7. R. H. Bainton, *Concerning heretics. . .An anonymous work attributed to Sebastian Castellio*, (Octagon Books Inc., New York 1965).

8. *Calvin und Basel in den Jahren 1552-1556*, Theologischer Verlag Zürich, 1974. Dr. Plath has appended to his book an extensive bibliography of both unpublished and published sources.

9. D. Laing, editor, *The Works of John Knox*, (Edinburgh 1855), vol. 4, p. 240; see also vol. 5, pp. 211ff.

10. Gordon Donaldson, *The Scottish Reformation*, (Cambridge 1960), and *Scotland, Church and Nation through Sixteen Centuries* (Scottish Academic Press 1972), pp. 55-79.

11. Laing, *Works of John Knox*, vol. 5, p. 9.

12. Vol. 5, pp. 207f.

13. Vol. 5, p. 212.

14. Vol. 5, p. 224.

15. Vol. 5, pp. 222f.

16. Vol. 5, p. 225.

17. Vol. 5, pp. 226ff.

18. Vol. 5, p. 229.

19. J. K. Cameron, editor, *The First Book of Discipline*, (St. Andrew Press, Edinburgh 1972), p. 177.

20. *First Book of Discipline*, pp. 165ff.

21. *First Book of Discipline*, pp. 165, 197f.; see also p. 33.

22. *First Book of Discipline*, pp. 204ff.

23. S. Thomas Aquinas, *Summa Theologica*, II, ii, Quae. IX *De haeresi*, art. iii: 'If forgers of money and other evildoers are forthwith condemned to death by the secular authority,

much more reason is there for heretics, as soon as they are convicted of heresy, to be not only excommunicated but even put to death.'

24. *First Book of Discipline*, p. 205.

25. *Acts and Proceedings of the General Assemblies of the Kirk of Scotland from the year MDLX*, (Maitland Club, 1839), vol. 1, p. 21; W. C. Dickinson, editor, *John Knox's History of the Reformation in Scotland*, vol. 2, p. 49.

26. *Acts. . .of the General Assemblies*, vol. 1, p. 60.

27. *Acts. . .of the General Assemblies*, vol. 2, p. 746; see also pp. 750ff.

28. See for references, *First Book of Discipline*, pp. 165, 196.

29. See D. H. Wilson, *King James VI and I*, (London 1956), pp. 217ff.

30. *The Register of the Privy Council of Scotland*, Third Series, vol. 1, p. 368.

31. *The Acts of the Parliament of Scotland (1127-1707)*, vol. 7, p. 16.

32. *R. P. C. Scotland*, vol. 2, p. xxi, and pp. 312f. This treatment was also meted out to the children of Catholic parents, see pp. xxiii, 94, 370f.

33. *R. P. C. Scotland* Third Series, vol. 1, p. xxvii.

34. *A. P. S.*, vol. 7, pp. 202f.

35. The theological background can be found in James Durham, *Treatise concerning Scandal*, (London 1659), pp. 161f. For this reference I am indebted to Mr. E. K. Cameron's unpublished Stanhope Prize Essay (University of Oxford 1978), entitled 'The Scottish Covenanters'.

36. *R. P. C. Scotland*, vol. 5, pp. xix, 477f.

37. D. G. Barron, editor, *The Court Book of the Barony of Urie in Kincardineshire*, (Scottish History Society, 1892) pp. xxviff.

38. *Court Book of. . .Urie*, pp. xxxff.

39. *A. P. S.*, vol. 9, pp. 386f.

40. *Acts of the General Assembly of the Church of Scotland 1638-1842*, (Edinburgh 1843), p. 248.

41. *Acts of the General Assembly*, p. 253.

42. J. Cunningham, *The Church History of Scotland*, (2nd edition, Edinburgh 1882), vol. 2, p. 198.

43. *The History of England*, (London 1889), vol. 2, pp. 620ff.

44. See J. Gordon, *Thomas Aikenhead: A historical review in relation to Mr. Macaulay and The Witness*, (London 1856).

45. Gordon, *Thomas Aikenhead: a Supplement*, (Edinburgh 1856).

46. *Acts of the General Assembly*, p. 258.

47. *Acts of the General Assembly*, pp. 261f.

48. *Acts of the General Assembly*, p. 262.

8

THE POLISH-LITHUANIAN CALVIN

DURING THE "SUPERINTENDENCY" OF

JOHN ŁASKI, 1556-60

George Huntston Williams

Historians can be interested either in John Calvin's attitude toward and influence in the Polish-Lithuanian Commonwealth
stretching from Cracow well beyond Kiev, the biggest state in
Europe in the sixteenth century; or in the attitude of the Reformed leaders in the Commonwealth toward Calvin amidst their
quite distinctive organizational and theological problems; or
in both points of view--the stance of the present article. For
periodization, the first phase begins with Calvin's initial
contact with the Poles in his dedication of his *Commentary on
Hebrews*, 18 May 1549, to King Sigismund II Augustus (1548-72),
with an exhortation to him to promote the reformation of the
Commonwealth.[1] The second phase is quite distinct. The
direction of the church by John Łaski (1499-1560), who was regarded by Calvin and the Swiss Reformers as the distinguished
and experienced representative of the pan-Reformed movement,
was a decisive period of less than four full years (1556-60).[2]
The third phase extends from the death of Łaski to the death
of Calvin himself in 1564, another short four years.

The purpose of concentrating on the middle phase is to
trace the inter-connections between Geneva and the Commonwealth during a period when the emerging problems were so
great that if Calvin and his Swiss colleagues had been more
observant, attentive, and responsive, the Reformed Church of
the Commonwealth might have emerged from organizational and
doctrinal controversy as a major and abiding entity.[3] Instead
they relied largely on the somewhat Erasmian Łaski. The
nephew of the sometime Primate namesake and himself once bishop
of Veszprém in Hungary had more of the strengths of an administrator than of a theologian, which the local situation surely
required.

We cannot start with the day of Łaski's arrival to take command. In 1553 the King sent his former tutor and his mother's Franciscan confessor, Professor Dr. Francis Lismanino (1504-66) on a book-buying mission abroad to stock the royal library. Between 1550 and 1553 Lismanino had read to Sigismund from the *Institutes* twice a week after supper. Thus Lismanino was no doubt on a second, undeclared mission, to obtain first-hand information about the reformers and their churches. From November 1554 till February 1555 Lismanino resided in Geneva, followed Calvin's lectures, and married a Huguenot, publicly breaking with the Catholic Church. He urged Calvin to promote the Reformed cause in the Commonwealth.[4] Accordingly, already on 9 December 1554 Calvin exhorted the King to put an end to papal domination of his Kingdom.[5]

In the meantime Nicholas Oleśnicki, owner of Pińczów in Little Poland organized the first Reformed church in the Commonwealth in 1550 with the Mantuan Hebraist Francis Stancaro (1501-74), author of the MS "L Canones" on Reformation, as the first pastor, while in the very year of Lismanino's departure abroad, 1553, Nicholas IV Radziwiłł the Black (1515-65), palatine of Vilna, had been won to the Reformed position. His capital would remain the center of Calvinism in the Grand Duchy of Lithuania, united with Poland in the Commonwealth. In Little Poland Felix Cruciger (Krzyżak), a bachelor of arts from the Jagiellonian University in Cracow, was elected superintendent of the still very few Reformed congregations in Little Poland in 1554. He and Stancaro attended the synod of Słomniki, four miles from Cracow. There, "because of the name" of the author (who had become bitterly involved in the controversy over the Mediator with Andrew Osiander at the University of Königsberg),[6] the now printed *Canones* (Frankfurt on the Oder, 1552) were not immediately, but eventually adopted at the end as the basis of the rites for "the whole church."[7]

In a letter to John Łaski in Frankfurt on the Main of 26 January 1555[8] Calvin explained (on the basis of a lost reply of the Polish King to Calvin) that, although Sigismund wished the Church to be in good order, he seemed to be beset by scruples as to whether to undertake such a task. Calvin suggested that Łaski, as nephew of a former Primate and an experienced reformer, write to Sigismund and promised, for his part, to write in similar fashion to several Commonwealth lords.

Henry Bullinger had received ecclesiastical questions of polity from Sigismund through the good offices of Lismanino, sojourning in Zurich, and also the astounding news that the King was soon to undertake the reformation of his Church. He relayed this information to Calvin in a letter of 18 January

1555 and urged him to respond.[9] Instead, counting on Łaski's direct appeal to the King, Calvin wrote to two nobles whom Lismanino had suggested as being influential at court: Nicholas Radziwiłł (brother of the King's late beloved Queen Barbara) and Palatine Spytek Jordan of Sandomierz. In the letter to Radziwiłł, 13 February 1555,[10] Calvin told him that Lismanino had recounted the interest of the Palatine in "true doctrine" and encouraged him therein, appealing to him in his turn--in response to the suggestion of Bullinger--to exhort the King to reform the Church.

The Reformed in Little Poland were in the meantime being much attracted by the regional reorganization of the Czech Brethren in Great Poland and discussed the desirability of union with them in two small synods in March, in Krcziecice, then Gołuchów. In Gołuchów in Great Poland, 28 March 1555, Cruciger, now calling himself "Superintendent of the Reformed churches in [all] Poland," wrote urging the Czech Brethren to make common cause with them.[11]

At a synod in Pińczów, 1 May 1555, the delegates received from the hand of Stanislas Budziński (destined to become the first historian of Polish Unitarianism) a letter from Lismanino in which the former Franciscan recounted his conversion to the Reformation. Budziński was expected to convey the books Lismanino had purchased to the King. In the name of the synod, Cruciger urged Lismanino to return to Poland and give leadership to reform in the land he knew so well.[12]

Church Reform was, indeed, very much on the minds of the King, the Senators, and the Deputies who at the Diet of Piotrków convened in Great Poland, 3 May to 15 June 1555, dealt with four articles on the agenda. Article 1 considered the principle of religious toleration and the exemption of the lay Senators and the Deputies from the control of the Bishops in matters the lords temporal regarded as non-ecclesiastical. The article also sought a decision concerning the next ecumenical council (which would turn out to be Trent, Period III) as to whether laymen should be represented as well as prelates, and whether in the meantime the King might not call a national-synod-council for immediate reform.[13]

Pending the royal implementation of their hopes, Albert Marszewski presented to the King what a contemporary account called the Augsburg Confession in Polish. In fact it was a Confession in twenty-four articles revised by Stanislas Lutomirski, who had once studied in Wittenberg, of a content roughly midway between Lutheranism and Helvetic views, with phrases from Stancaro and Martin Bucer and an article on the eucharist drawn from the Wittenberg Concord of 1536.[14] This

document did not have any synodal backing, although it served
as a rallying point for Protestant-minded lords. Lord Jacob
Ostoróg presented the somewhat Lutheranized Confession of the
Czech Brethren in Great Poland, a document which would be presently worked over by the Reformed of Little Poland.

On 7 May 1555, out of Article 1 of the opening agenda, a
Polish Interim was further refined. It was agreed that until
an ecumenical or a national council could be convened (1) the
King would be regarded as Lord and common Father in matters of
religion, (2) the Interim arrangement would be followed until
an ecumenical or national council, (3) during the Interim the
jurisdictional authority of the bishops over laymen in non-
ecclesiastical matters would be suspended, and (4) during the
Interim there would be freedom for the Word of God as interpreted by the conscience of each. A copy of the Augsburg Interim of 1548 was present during the debates in the two houses
(Senators and Deputies). Finally, the Diet, the King consent-
ing, actually called for a national reform council over the
protest of, and even with the threat of resort to arms by, the
bishops led by Andrew Zebrzydowski of Cracow. It was foreseen
by the most ardent promoters that such a council *eventuel*
would adopt five propositions: (1) that the Word of God be
preached freely, as by Christ and the apostles, (2) that evangelical preachers should be unmolested by the bishops, (3)
that the Mass might be celebrated in Polish, (4) that communion might be received under both kinds by all who so desired,
and (5) that clerics who so wished might take wives.[15]

There were three spinoffs of the almost cyclonic Diet of
Piotrków. The first was the decision of the King to send an
ambassador to Rome with a public and a private message, hoping
to gain papal support for a national reform council. The
second was a perfunctory synod of bishops at Piotrków, June
1555, so poorly attended that it had to be postponed. The
third was a succession of two Reformed synods that would not
seek to implement within the context of their separated Church
what some of the Senators and especially Deputies had called
for at the Diet. We shall presently take up these synods.

In the meantime, correspondence continued between Calvin
and certain Poles. Radziwiłł responded to Calvin's letter
(above at n. 10) with warmth and admiration on 13 June 1555.[16]
Grand Treasurer Jordan wrote him on 20 August 1555.[17] It
would appear that Budziński carried Cruciger's letter from
the synod of Pińczów of 1 May (above at n. 12), letters of the
King to Conrad Gesner, Bullinger, and Calvin, all presumably
written in haste during the Diet of Piotrków, and the aforementioned response of Radziwiłł.[18] Calvin, at the prompting
of Lismanino, wrote Jordan on 13 September 1555,[19] without

having yet received the above mentioned letter, exhorting him to remain constant in the faith and asking him to urge the King to undertake the reform.

The Swiss, it should be remarked at this point, never seemed to take into consideration the largest Church of the Commonwealth, which was under the Metropolitan of Kiev and remotely under the Patriarch isolated in Istanbul. This Church dominant in the eastern two thirds of the Commonwealth had a vernacular liturgy (with a creed without the *Filioque*), communion in both kinds, a married priesthood, lay brotherhoods strongly complementing the powers of the mostly ill-educated bishops, and above all a claim to apostolicity. Similarly the Czech Brethren, especially of Great Poland, with their still medieval usages and high doctrine of the eucharist, with an episcopal tradition that derived from the Waldensians and with their earlier established contact with the patriarchs of Alexandria and Constantinople, seemed to many of the Reformed minded Poles alluringly apostolic and scriptural.

In any case, the Reformed of Little Poland, in order to make of themselves a strong force for a pan-Protestant and pan-Commonwealth alternative to even a reformed Catholicism, negotiated, under Cruciger, the union of the Calvinists and the Czech Brethren at the first fully joint synod of Koźminek in Great Poland, 24 August to 2 September 1555.[20] A synod of the Reformed alone met at Pińczów, 21 September 1555,[21] while Alexander Witrelin informed Lismanino of the situation in Poland, Pińczów, 15 September 1555.[22]

Lismanino, who had received the urgent summons from the earlier synod of Pińczów, replied on 11 November from Zurich that he was prepared to serve the Little Poland Church.[23] Stimulated by his prospects, Lismanino, in an undated memorandum for Calvin,[24] lists those in the Commonwealth to whom he should write, apparently spurred by suggestions in the aforementioned letter of Witrelin. These included: the King (again); Radziwiłł; Lord John Tarnowski, castellan of Cracow, the first personage of the Realm after the King; Lord Stanislas Teczyński, the second after the King and already appointed by him lay legate to Trent; Cruciger, elected "superintendent at the convocation of Pińczów [presumably of 1 May 1555]"; and even Bishop Jacob Uchański. Calvin would presently write to most of these, except Uchański, and to others.

In the letter of Witrelin embedded in the memorandum to Calvin is a list of five problems agitating the Church which was still in formation: (1) the view of Andrew Musculus of the Brandenburg University of Frankfurt as to Christ's passion in two natures; (2) the view of Osiander on essential (experi-

ential) justification through the divine nature of Christ;
(3) the corrective view of Philip Melanchthon in response to
Osiander, Stancaro, and Musculus that Christ in his Person and
by his office mediated in both natures; (4) the rise of some
who denied that the Son according to his humanity ought to be
said to be natural (with reference to the celestial flesh
taught by Caspar Schwenckfeld and Menno Simons, both with followers, especially in Silesia and the Lower Vistula); and (5)
the error of Michael Servetus which was attracting some.

Without specific reference to the foregoing problems,
Calvin proceeded to follow up the suggestion of Lismanino,
stimulated by Cruciger and Witrelin, to write to the King, 24
December 1555,[25] and in rapid succession to John Boner of
Cracow,[26] in whose home the Reformed met for worship, Lord
Ivan Karninski,[27] Lady Agnes Dłuska of Iwanowice,[28] Stanislas
Lassocki,[29] Nicholas Myszkowski,[30] again Radziwiłł,[31] John
Tarnowski,[32] Andrew Trzecieski,[33] and Spytek Jordan.[34]

On the Eve of Christmas 1555 Calvin, taking note of Sigismund's earlier call for a national reform council (of Catholics and Protestants), made his last effort to bestir the
King, pointing out that the "true religion" had begun to
emerge in Poland and calling upon him to join it in the name
of the King of kings. After referring to his earlier letter
of 5 December 1554, Calvin magisterially continues: "Therefore, I, whom the Supreme King has appointed preacher of his
Gospel and minister of his Church, since true religion has now
begun in Poland to emerge from the baneful darkness of the
papacy. . ., appeal to your Majesty in God's name to perform
this duty in preference to all others." Calvin asks whether
"kings should delay whom God has raised to such a height that
from it they [the Polish Reformed] might give light to all
nations?" Among the letters of December 1555 addressed to almost all the personages suggested by Lismanino and to some
others, Calvin made his most substantive proposal, apart from
that to the King, to the polyglot scholar, Trzecieski, namely,
that he should undertake the translation of the Bible into
Polish--and urged Boner to provide the money.

On 31 December 1555 Łaski, as Calvin had earlier urged,
wrote three spirited letters. One was addressed to the King,
to whom he dedicated his Church Order of London as just printed
at Frankfurt on the Main. Another was addressed to the Protestant lords temporal, and the third to the lesser lords and
pastors of evangelical persuasion.[35] In the letter to the
King he exhorted Sigismund to be an active and energetic *rex*
in the work of the reformation, while he as an experienced
reformer in Frisia, London, and elsewhere would serve as *sacer-
dos* and *propheta*, appealing to the Erasmian threefold office

of Christ, first formulated by the Dutch humanist in his Commentary on Psalm 2.[36]

At the beginning of 1556 Sigismund was, despite Catholic reluctance or opposition, indeed ready to call a national council. With the Czech Brethren and Calvinists not yet fully united, both bodies met together at the Reformed synod of Secemin 21-29 January 1555.[37] Cruciger was elected presiding officer. After Trzecieski read the Czech *Confessio* in Polish with the approval of its contents by all hearing it,[38] there was much consternation when on the second day Dr. Peter of Goniądz (Gonesius), an alumnus of Padua and an acquaintance of the Servetian jurisconsult Matthew Gribaldi, presented a second confession. Purportedly initiated by Nicholas Radziwiłł, it asserted the divinity of the Father alone, denying the acceptability of the very term "Trinity." In six points, based allegedly on Irenaeus, Gonesius argued "that the Logos was the invisible immortal Word which in its time became flesh in the womb of the Virgin" as "the seed of the Son incarnate." (The impending schism of 1563 in the Reformed Church, over the doctrine of the Trinity, cast its shadow before.)[39]

The Brethren and the Reformed sketched at Secemin their outline of what they would propose for the national reform council, (1) that the King himself preside (on the model of Constantine), (2) that outside royal and princely arbiters be summoned to assess the arguments of the Catholic bishops and the Protestant professors, (3) that bishops and *periti* should not be arbiters, since they with the Protestant professors would be equal parties, (4) that Scripture alone be normative, (5) that Calvin, Melanchthon, Theodore Beza, and Nicholas du Quesnoy (Quercetanus), a professor of philosophy at Lausanne, should be invited together as the Protestant professors, and (6) that a confession of faith be put together.[40]

The next Reformed synod was that of Pińczów, 24 April to 1 May 1556,[41] held jointly with the superintendent and major leaders of the Czech Brethren. The fundamental concern was still to shape a comprehensive common policy with respect to the impending, as they trusted, national reform council promised by the King. The letters from the divines of the German, Savoyard, and Swiss churches were brought by Lord Stanislas Karniński and received "with tremendous joy" on 30 April 1556. There is nothing extant from Calvin but he sent a (lost) *memoriale* with Lismanino (on whom, see below at n. 47). We therefore take note of the views of Beza *et al.* in the Lausanne reply to the five propositions in the Lismanino letter aforementioned.[42] The Western Reformed respondents denied that Christ in his divine nature could suffer or die. They refuted Osiander's position by asserting that Christ's humanity

was important in individual justification. It was agreed
that Christ was a Mediator in both natures because to be the
Mediator between God and man, Christ had to partake of both
natures. The office of soteriological (as distinguished from
cosmological) Mediator belonged to the Person of Christ and
not the human *natura*. The synod of Pińczów decided that indeed Calvin, Beza, and Quesnoy ought to be called to Poland
and invitations were sent. Beza's reputation as a biblical
scholar had been carried to Poland by Lismanino, who had briefly visited his Academy in Lausanne. The letter of invitation
to Calvin on 2 May was signed by the most important ministers
and by ten prominent nobles.[43] The Polish authors explained
that the piety of Calvin, his spirited battle with the Roman
Antichrist, and his hatred of heresy of all kinds were well
known to them through Lismanino. Therefore, they made bold to
ask him to come to Poland. At the same time, Superintendent
Cruciger and four other pastors wrote to the Geneva council
asking them to allow Calvin to come to Poland for a few
months.[44] The letter to Beza and one to Bullinger also were
sent by Cruciger alone the next day.[45]

To step back a couple of weeks, Lismanino had, urged on
by the synodal summons from Cruciger and with a farewell letter from Calvin,[46] arrived secretly in the environs of Cracow
at the beginning of March, living in various manorial homes.
He could not know how his former royal tutee would take his
conversion and marriage. He kept away from synodal gatherings
and, under the influence of the episcopacy, was actually
placed under an edict of banishment in May. As early as 15
April 1556, he had written from Aleksandrowice to Calvin, beg-
ging him to speed the departure from Lausanne of Peter Statorius suggested by him as a teacher for Pińczów. On 2 May,
after the synod of Pińczów, Cruciger headed a delegation of
seven ministers (not including Lismanino) and seven laymen who
urged Calvin to come to Poland to help them, mentioning the
memoriale on the issue of Stancaro brought to them by Lismanino with letters.[47] In June of 1556 Calvin wrote that Statorius would soon be on his way.[48]

Three nobles replied to Calvin in May and June.[49] In
July Castellan Tarnowski of Cracow, to whom Calvin had written
(though remaining a Catholic, yet eager for reform), responded
to three letters from Lismanino, expressing doubt as to
whether the King had personally approved of the edict of banishment.[50] In August there was a letter from Stanislas
Szarczowski of Iwnowice, describing in halting Latin the Catholic counter-offensive;[51] another, from Lady Dłuska,[52] in
whose house the Lismaninos were sheltered, thanked Calvin for
his earlier letter.

From 6 to 11 September 1556 the postponed national "reform" synod resumed at Łowicz under the presidency of Papal Legate Aloysius Lippomano. This strong Catholic action had not been foreseen by the most eager of the lay Senators and the Reform-minded Deputies at the Diet of Piotrków of 1555. Bishop Stanislas Hosius of Warmia[53] was a major factor in restraining Bishop Uchański from doing anything that would even suggest concessions to the most moderate of Erasmian Catholics, not to say Protestants.

The once seemingly bright promise of Piotrków was thus dashed by the time Łaski could reach his native land, having departed from Frankfurt on the Main in the company of John Utenhove, Łaski's former collaborator in the Strangers' Church of London. Łaski arrived in Poland by way of Breslau in December 1556.

Ministers gathered at Iwanowice 28 December 1556 to 1 January 1557.[54] Present for the first time since his full adherence to the Reform was Lismanino, listed first, along with *inter alios* Cruciger, pastor in Secemin. Pastor Israel Bohemus of Ostoróg was the only Czech Brother present. Stanislas Sarnicki, pastor in Niedźwiedź, Alexander Witrelin, pastor in Pińczów, and John Siekierzyński, pastor for the Reformed in and around Iwanowice were also present. On the first day of January Łaski also made his first appearance in a Polish Reformed clerical assembly. Before his arrival, the Bohemian *Confessio*, which had already been accepted in principle at Secemin (21 January 1556), was read again and more revisions were suggested with a view to presenting it at the next Diet.

On 19 February 1557, Utenhove sent Calvin news from Cracow both of Legate Lippomano's chilling influence on the King and Łaski's efforts to rewarm him to his former optimism as to reform, with a paragraph from Łaski himself on how busy he was.[55] Calvin had not even responded to the invitation from the synod of Pińczów (above at n. 40, item 5) until nearly a year after it came. On 8 March 1557[56] he turned down the request, blaming his conspicuous delay in response on difficulty in finding a letter carrier. In any case, he added, the Genevan Council would not permit him to leave. Surely his presence, he continued, was no longer urgent now that Łaski, "a most faithful interpreter," had arrived.

Whether or not he was "a faithful interpreter," Łaski had found himself cast by providence in the role of reformer of the Commonwealth or at least as the organizer of a pan-Commonwealth Protestant Church which could embrace the Czech Brethren, the Lutherans, and the Reformed. He no doubt felt that the Reformed under Cruciger had yielded too much to the Czech

Brethren. With his comprehensive plan, Łaski had already set
out from Cracow on 25 February 1557 for Vilna, where he arrived
17 March to have an audience with the King and to confer with
Palatine Radziwiłł. The King could only consent to a private
colloquy, and in this setting Łaski was emboldened to express
himself fully on a general reformation. The King, temporizing
but friendly, expressed the hope that something could be done.

While Sigismund continued to show sympathy for the Protestant Reformation (except for his having yielded to Catholic
advisors with respect to Lismanino), he never allowed that ill-
defined proclivity permanently to impair his religious ties
with the national episcopate and the Pope. From the point of
view of many theologically confused Reformed Poles, the on-
going involvement of Calvin or Beza or both, on the scene,
could have made the decisive difference in their confessional
development and in their constitutional status in the Commonwealth. Łaski was more the politician and organizer at a
moment when no other Reformed Church had to consider so directly the reformation of high doctrines in the face of five
highly trained and so divergently oriented doctors. Four were
specialists in theology or canon law, two in medicine: Dr.
Lismanino, Dr. Osiander, Dr. Stancaro (both theology and medicine), Dr. George Biandrata,[57] and Dr. Gonesius. In addition,
reforms were to be enacted amidst what must have been a latent
rivalry for leadership. That rivalry was between the locally
faithful leader, Cruciger, the first superintendent as of
1554, and the internationally renowned and locally prestigious
major Polish Reformer, Łaski now back in his native land, impelled to carry out comprehensive plans.

Having mentioned the organizational and theological
dramatis personae polonicae italicaeque, we do well at this
juncture to state the two theological issues uppermost in the
minds of several of the foregoing and their followers. The
one issue has been mentioned—the countervailing impulses (1)
to form a powerful Reformed Church on the model of that of
each Swiss canton, but in the case of the Commonwealth a con-
geries of churches under powerful lay patrons and (2) to move
toward intra-Protestant ecumenism, with perhaps some support
from the Greek Orthodox lords, possibly involving a federalist
compromise but surely with mutual toleration as regards rites
and the less important doctrinal formulations. The other
issue flared up first in Königsberg over the mediatorship of
Christ as between Osiander and the newly arrived Stancaro,
eventually drawing in Musculus and then Melanchthon. At first
the controversy was intra-Lutheran; it became cyclonic within
the Polish Reformed Church and divided the Reformed Church
during the leadership of Łaski; and by his death the outlines

of three emerging separate Reformed synods will be discerned.

It is important to say a further generalizing word, since no country faced the organizational problem and the theological issue of Christ the Mediator in such complexity and intensity as precisely the land of Łaski. The Augsburg Confession of 1530, *Pars I, articulus iii, De Filio Dei,* had been traditional in stating that "the Word, i.e., the Son of God took unto him human nature. . .so that there are two natures in unity of Person." There is no mention of Christ the Mediator. But once the eucharist had ceased to be for Lutherans, as presently it would be for Calvinists as well, a repetition of the once-for-all sacrificial Atonement of Christ on Calvary, then the problem of Christ the Mediator of salvation and the relationship of that office to the eternal intra-deical decrees was bound to become a new problem. A millennium after the Council of Chalcedon the Reformers tended to think of Persons in the Triune Godhead, not as Hypostases in the sense of the ancient conciliar creeds from Chalcedon through Constantinople II to Constantinople III, but as personages or persons in the modern sense. Stancaro could have accepted the aforementioned Augsburg article, but he insisted, with the three aforementioned creeds, the citations of many Fathers, and the clear formulation of Peter Lombard, that "Christ can be called Mediator only according to his humanity, not according to his divinity."[58] For a long time Stancaro truly believed that Melanchthon, Bullinger, and Beza would, of course, agree with him. But after a thousand years of Christian thought they had come to use "Christ" when they meant the eternally begotten Son, just as the Fathers had read the philosophically long defined hypostatic Logos behind their more scriptural "only begotten Son." Stancaro was acutely aware that by the very etymology of the term the Son could become the *Anointed One* only in historic time. Though Melanchthon and Calvin sought to be careful with their terms, they were not so well versed, as was he, in the post-Chalcedonian conciliar clarifications that had led to the "asymmetric Christology"[59] of antiquity.

In contrast to the Lombardian position of Stancaro stood Biandrata, whose view came to be pilloried by Calvin as "tritheist," although it purported to be simply non-philosophical like the Apostles' Creed, which he preferred, and the Scripture, holding--though he never said this expressly--that the unity of the Godhead was voluntarist rather than ontological. He would prefer the scriptural adverb *unum* with respect to the wills of the Three Persons to the Nicene adjective *consubstantialis* with respect to the common essence.

It was the fate of Łaski to have the problem of the Mediator and with it the clarification of both Triadology and Christology crest in Poland during his leadership, for he, like Biandrata and then Lismanino and Gonesius, would prefer to remain with the Reformation principle of *sola scriptura*, systematized in the Apostles' Creed.

In the synodal assembly at Włodzisław, 15-18 June 1557,[60] Peter Statorius was appointed the headmaster of the Pińczów school. (In 1558 he would be joined by John Thénaud, a former student of Calvin.) The synod of Włodzisław was important for the reason that Łaski alone was mentioned by name at the head of the acts, along with "ministerial elders." Cruciger, though present, was not formally mentioned at the beginning of the protocol, though in annexed letters from the synod he signs as superintendent. Fresh provisions were made for a translation of the Bible into Polish, for the establishment of a printing press for this and other publications, and for the ministerial elders to elect lay elders (*seniores*) from among the nobility. On 17 June two ministerial *seniores* of the Church of the Czech Brethren presented themselves at the assembly. This was an unexpected and pleasant surprise, but it is clear that the Brethren in Great Poland, who up to this time had been dealing with the Little Poland Reformed Church, were ultimately dependent upon the Mother Church in Bohemia. The somewhat authoritarian chain of command seemed to the Poles to entail some subordination to an external hierarchy with customs stemming from the fifteenth century. The "legation" in fact expressed some anxiety, for its part, about the sense in which the Polish Reformed understood the intended union. The synod accordingly authorized Cruciger and Łaski to write to the "Bishop" of the Czech Brethren to clarify matters. They did so on the day following the close of the assembly wherein they had amiably shown their desire for both unity and spiritual freedom in accordance with Scripture (2 Cor. 3:17).

Another synodal assembly took place in Pińczów, 5-6 July 1557,[61] Łaski being mentioned at the head of otherwise unnamed ministers present. Here among ten actions it was agreed that the Genevan *Catechismus* of 1545 should be adopted without alteration as a counterpoise to the Bohemian *Confessio*, that excommunication should be practiced according to the usage of the Church of Geneva, and that plans should be made for a general synod of representatives from Great and Little Poland, Lithuania, and Ruthenia. This took place in Pińczów, 10-17 August 1557,[62] where further organizational and confessional discussion prevailed. Of interest is the insistence on the part of the elected noble *seniores* that they have the right to approve the final version of the *Confessio*, derived from the

Czech Brethren but undergoing adaptation in successive Reformed synods. Of more interest was the question of Lord Jerome Ossoliński as to whether it was permissible to attend mass where there was no evangelical congregation. To this latter point Łaski replied promptly in the negative, citing 1 Cor. 10:21. Łaski had been simply accepted as the chief ecclesiastic without his relationship to Cruciger or the lords being clarified.

At the synod in Pińczów, 8-9 September 1557,[63] the union of the Czech Brethren and the Reformed was still being held up over more questions (nine) than had previously come into the open. The Czech Brethren were distrustful of the Calvinian conception of lay elders and especially the Polish Reformed adaptation thereof. This consisted of electing noblemen who, with their ownership of the very villages in which the congregations met, could exercise power in spiritual as well as temporal matters. Another concern of the Polish Reformed was that the (Czech) Unity, as latter-day Hussites, might uphold too high a view of the eucharist together with liturgical customs related to its observance. There was another gathering in Pińczów, 18-22 October, at which more work was done on the Bohemian *Confessio*.

Cruciger (among several Poles) wrote to Calvin presenting the issues raised at Włodzisław already in June between the Brethren and the Reformed and asking his advice about the Czech *Confessio* as revised. The letter was in this case carried by Budziński, and Calvin responded, 25 October 1557,[64] to all the signatories in detail, concentrating on the eucharistic problem. It happened that on this very day by chance in Tomice near Poznań Lismanino, who was more disposed to the Czechs than Łaski, was engaged in a colloquy with them.[65] Calvin, as was characteristic of the Swiss, thought of the Czech Brethren in Bohemia and in Great Poland as Waldensians and regularly called them by this name. This usage was based on the success of the French Swiss Reformed in bringing the Waldensians of "Savoy" and elsewhere into the Reformed fold at the synod of Cianforan in the Cottian Alps, 12 September 1532. In any case, Calvin urged the Poles to remain in close contact with their leaders in order to present a common front, but he did find their doctrine of the bread and wine, after consecration as the veritable body and blood of Christ, papist. He also took occasion to present again his own view that Christ according to his body remains in heaven, descending "with the wonderful virtue of his spirit to us" and "lifting us up at the same time to himself." This was his effort to show the Czech Brethren that the Reformed in Switzerland believed that the body and blood of Christ were truly mediated in faith through the eucharistic symbols, and he averred that the Augsburg Confession could be understood in this sense by the Reformed. In all events, he urged that the two bodies, by now so close, not speculate on or quarrel over doctrine.

In an undated letter to Utenhove in October 1557,[66] Calvin expressed his gratification that the King had lifted the ban on Lismanino but he expressed reservations about what he had heard of the "austerity" of Łaski toward the Czech Brethren in pursuit of a pan-Protestant front. The Polish Reformed had chosen ministerial and lay delegates but none showed up at the gathering of Czech Brethren at Gołuchów in Great Poland, 16 October 1557. Instead they met by themselves at Pińczów, 18-22 October, under the leadership of Łaski, and again at Włodzisław, 21 December 1557 and 14 January 1558. The first meeting dealt with matters of moral discipline and the second was largely concerned with constitutional difficulties in the Czech *Confessio*.[67] About this time (early 1558) Łaski would write out his strictures respecting several articles of the Czech Confession (Wittenberg, 1538), his *Adnotata*.[68]

To resolve outstanding confessional differences, it was argued that the Polish Reformed and the Czech Brethren would meet, as earlier agreed upon, at Gołuchów. Łaski, however, was still turning his thoughts to Königsberg with a view to shaping a pan-Protestant grouping with the support of the Duke and to outflanking the efforts of Peter Paul Vergerio both to gain the Czech Brethren for the Lutheran camp and to denigrate the work of Łaski in the eyes of the Swiss Reformed. Łaski left Cracow at the end of February 1558, arriving in Königsberg by April.

One cannot pass by a letter of Calvin to Prince Radziwiłł of 24 May 1558 in which the Reformer asked the Palatine of Vilna to intervene with Duke Cosimo de Medici to help the Sozzini family regain their lost properties, among whom Calvin was most concerned for Laelius Socinus![69]

After a synod in Książ on 26 July 1558, at which he was not present, Utenhove wrote urgently to Calvin on 30 July 1558 to become further involved in Polish affairs.[70] Łaski also wrote to Calvin from Ociec on 5 August 1558,[71] about how Zebrzydowski of Cracow was harassing Boner. From 4 to 15 September[72] there was a major synod in Włodzisław, with Łaski at the head, which closed with an affirmation of the three Creeds—of the Apostles, of Nicaea, and of Athanasius—and condemned especially the followers of Servetus, Gonesius, and the ancient Cerinthus (less as a Gnostic than as an Adoptionist). During the synod Utenhove wrote again to Calvin, 12 September, urging him in the difficult religio-political circumstances to write

Castellan Tarnowski. He included the names of three more sympathetic lords in a letter of 18 September, directed to all the ministers of Geneva.[73] Bullinger undertook to write Bishop Uchański, 28 November 1558, urging him openly to take the side of the Reformed.[74] Calvin had already written to Uchański on 19 November, as also to Tarnowski and Ostoróg.[75] He had also written in a different vein to Lismanino, mostly about Biandrata.[76]

Biandrata, a former physician to the King's mother, Bona Sforza (d. 1557), returned to Poland (from Geneva to Pińczów) in the fall of 1558 and presented his confession of faith to Łaski on 7 November. Programmatically concealing the extent to which he was on bad terms with Calvin, Biandrata perhaps descried in the unsettled situation in the Commonwealth the possibility of helping to give birth to a national Reformed Church by playing the role of moderate physician in both his medical and theological capacity.[77] But in the Genevan's letter to Lismanino there was ample warning of Biandrata's "cunning tricks. . .which entangle simple minds." Lismanino, now living in Pińczów and in frequent contact with the courtly fellow "Italian", questioned the physician-theologian closely, no doubt in their common tongue, but allegedly he could not elicit anything unorthodox, although Biandrata admitted to certain "scruples" concerning Triadology and Christology, preferring, like Łaski, to refer to the Three Persons in exclusively scriptural terms and those of the Apostles' Creed.

In the meantime things had moved so far that a delegation of Polish Reformed, headed by Lord Jerome Filipowski and a Reformed superintendent *eventuel*, Stanislas Sarnicki, had held a colloquium with the leaders of the Czech Mother Church in Lipnik in Moravia on 25 October 1558.[78]

On 27 January 1559[79] Utenhove wrote Calvin that Senator Tarnowski had recently proposed at the Diet of Piotrków (5 December 1558 to 18 February 1559) the elimination of bishops from the Senate because of their loyalty to. the Pope rather than to the King, also that Radziwiłł had urged that the Reformed in the Grand Duchy and the rest of the Commonwealth conform in faith and ceremonies and meet annually in synod in different convenient centers.

Biandrata, destined to influence the Palatine, had already influenced Lismanino and Statorius favorably as can be guaged from the latter's letter to Calvin, 1 February 1559.[80] Although Statorius professed to defend Calvin against the charges of being proud and disputatious, he was also critical of him. And Statorius pled with Calvin to effect a reconcili-

ation, since inadvertently, no doubt, Calvin had wronged him.
The Genevan should take the initiative since "There is no one
who can move him [Biandrata] as effectively. . .He is accus-
tomed to calling you *his* apostle and has acknowledged that a
single sentence of yours can change his mind more quickly
than six hundred books written by others." He continues:

> Therefore, by the bowels of God the Father, I
> implore you and by the blood of Christ I beg you,
> to write a letter, directing it to me, so that
> you can recall him, if possible, to that pris-
> tine peace between you.

Statorius so angered Calvin that he did not answer the appeal.

In June 1559 Biandrata was sent by Sigismund to attend
his ailing sister, Queen Isabelle, in Transylvania until her
death, 15 September.[81] Stancaro had departed for Transylvania
at about the time of the arrival of Łaski in Poland in 1556.

The trinitarian and christological problems Stancaro had
created seemed virtually to have subsided in Poland, when now
three years later, in late May 1559, he returned from Transylvania. Then in September Biandrata also returned. Controversy was thus again inflamed by the presence of the two
Italian doctors.

There were many synods and synodal assemblies during the
year 1559,[82] to which we now return. Back on 13 March 1559 at
Pińczów Łaski had opened the synod with a report on his con-
versations with His Majesty. The King could do nothing about
Reformed councils or episcopal or national synods but he
looked with favor upon the Reformed synods and ministerial
gatherings. They were, however, to confine themselves to pro-
moting "the glory of God and the advance of the Church of the
Lord." He also deplored what seemed to him the spoliation of
the properties of the Old Church under the pretext of religion
at the same time it was reported that, presumably with royal
approval, the Vice Chancellor of the Realm was prepared to
invite Łaski and other pastors to a colloquium with the episcopal adversaries. In preparation for this they should diligently study the *Confessio fidei Catholicae* (1553; 5th ed.
1559) of Bishop Hosius, for which task of providing an evangelical response Łaski, Lismanino, Cruciger, Gregory Paul (an
incipient Unitarian), Stanislas Lutomirski (husband of Barbara
Łaska), and Sarnicki were named and day and place set nearby.
Among the nine points of the agenda the last was a reproof of
the teachers of the school of Pińczów for having made changes
in their Polish translation of the *Epistola* annexed to the Genevan *Catechism* adopted earlier (above at n. 61). Statorius

was ordered to undo the changes. We know more about the entry
of this renowned Catholic *Confessio* into the Reformed discussions from a letter of Lismanino to Rudolph Gualter, written
on 10 March 1559.[83] The Response of the synod to the *Confessio* was essentially the work of Łaski, *Brevis ac compendaria
responsio* (Pińczów, 1559).

There followed another synod in Pińczów, 25 April,[84]
where among eight items or acts on the agenda, the second item
dealt with eight uppermost problems, from the definition of
the doctrine of the Trinity to that of the office of pastor,
which were to be taken up systematically at the next synod
(Włodzisław). The three teachers of Pińczów were commissioned
to translate the Bible into Polish: Statorius (the incipient
Biandratist), Thénaud, and Gregorv Orsatius (the incipient
Stancarist). On the problem of the baptism of infants
offered by peasants on the estates, themselves fearful
of their Catholic priests, it was agreed that a Reformed owner
of the estate could stand in the capacity of patron as god-
parent of the *baptizandi*. The following synod in Pińczów, 13
June, confirmed the foregoing in different words and dealt
also with (Catholic) baptisms in homes, from which it was advised that the Reformed refrain, since such domestic ceremonies were attended by drinking and revelry.

The synod of Włodzisław, 26-28 June 1559,[85] had to forego
the discussion of the eight theological and other problems re-
manded to it (at n. 84) and became in fact much worried about
disputations, clerical disorders, the problem of the poor. We
take note only of the fact that they censured Orsatius and his
printer for having published the *Collatio doctrinae Arii et. . .
Melanchtonis. . .et Francisci Davidis* (12 pages), written by
Stancaro (Cracow, 1559).[86] The Unitarian Bishop of Transylvania *eventuel* was a Lutheran at the time of Stancaro's comparison of him and Melanchthon with Arius. Stancaro argued
that both Lutherans held that Christ (and hence the Son) was
in his office of Mediator in both natures *ipso facto* inferior
to the Father.

Then came the synodal assembly of Pińczów of 7 August
1559,[87] at which Stancaro was present "in his own interest."
Łaski, who presided, stated that the synodal assembly had been
called to refute once and for all the doctrine of Stancaro,
which he in the name of all pastors condemned. Stancaro was
guilty of "the crime of *lèse majesté*, because he "with Nestorius openly denies that the only begotten Son of God is Mediator in his divine nature but only in his human nature." Łaski
called for the publication of an orthodox statement on the
Mediator. It appeared, 10 August 1559 at Pińczów, as *Confessio*

de Mediatore generis humani Jesu Christo Deo et homine.[88] It
is a compact, critically worded document, organized around the
Erasmian-Łaskian *triplex munus Christi,* with Jesus Christ assigned the office as Mediator in the following order: as
Prophet, Priest, and King. It states the emerging Protestant
position, which had moved from the *theory of the satisfaction
of God's honor* (Anselm and Lombard) to a more fully scriptural
(Pauline) *penal theory of the innocent Second Adam's assumption* of the punishment due all the progeny of the First Adam.
It had shifted thus because of Luther's stress on justification to the relative neglect of the act of Redemption on Calvary (except to insist on its once-for-all effectiveness),
and also because of Calvin's stress on the birth, life, teaching, as well as the death of Christ as together the salvific
action. Perhaps most of even the leading participants were
not fully aware of the extent of the shift (also apparent
among many Catholics) in the conceptualization of this central
transaction in Christian theology. The Pińczów *Confessio* affirms with scriptural backing that the Mediator had to share
the nature of God and that of man. It reiterates the Church's
belief in the deity of Christ and his equality with the Father.
By understanding Christ as Prophet, eternal High Priest, and
King "from the beginning and without end," the *Confessio* made
Christ almost eternally a Mediator and thus, as to that office
and as Person in that office, inferior to God the Father.

The synod of Pińczów, having adopted a Polish *Confessio
de Mediatore* which was directed in large part against Stancaro
yet so formulated as to avoid certain allegedly subordination-
ist phrases respecting the Mediator in Calvin and Bullinger,
also requested the owner of Pińczów, Lord Oleśnicki, to prevent Stancaro from staying any longer in the very town where
he had formed the first Reformed congregation in Poland.
Stancaro betook himself to Lord Nicholas Stadnicki at Dubiecko
in Ruthenia. Castellan Drohojowski of Przemyśl, Lord Ossoliński of Goslice, and Lord Zborowski remained supporters of
Stancaro, as did also some national Catholic lords. Lismanino
informed the Zurich divines of all this in a letter of 1
September 1559.[89]

Bullinger would later inform Calvin that the Polish *De
Mediatore* was completely acceptable to himself and to the
other ministers of Zurich.[90] With *De Mediatore* finished,
Statorius wrote a second letter to Calvin, 20 August 1559,[91]
about Biandrata and about the achievements in clarifying the
Reformed position in the Commonwealth against Stancaro. Yet
strangely, his first concern was still about vindicating Biandrata, as yet unnamed in the correspondence. Insisting on

Biandrata's integrity, he told Calvin of the physician's growing influence in the Church, especially of Little Poland. He
said that because of his excellent character, Biandrata had
easily convinced many that Calvin indeed had done him a grave
injustice. Statorius said that even Łaski tended to accept
this assessment, which is not surprising in that Łaski, too,
wished to keep all doctrinal formulations consonant with
Scripture and the Apostles' Creed. Statorius therefore for a
second time implored Calvin to heal the breach with Biandrata
before it should damage the Polish-Helvetic Church: "I have
no other purpose in mind than that I desire especially *that
your reputation among us remain unsullied.*"

Interestingly, Laelius Socinus was in Vilna during the
summer and reported to Calvin from Zurich, 22 August 1559,[92]
that "the struggle for the Kingdom of Christ" in the Commonwealth was being made difficult by the theological confusion,
the admixture of greed for earthly goods on all sides, and the
disposition of the King to remain on good terms with the
bishops who might prove to be decisive in Rome in establishing
his hereditary right to the county of Bari through his mother
Bona Sforza (d. 1557).

Back in the Commonwealth an assembly of elders in Pińczów,
20 November 1559,[93] decided on the publication of *De Mediatore,*
Lismanino being commended for his work on it. But another act
of business was to hear complaints against Statorius for having opposed the invocation of the Holy Spirit. After acknowl-
edging the charge, explaining that it seemed "absurd" to in-
voke the Spirit instead of the Father as "fount of all goods,"
Statorius proceeded to set forth an accepted profession of
faith on this and related points and to denounce any and every
"heretical blasphemy" whether "the Arian, the Servetian, the
Eunomian, or the Stancarist, or the Papal," a profession, however, which was already Biandratan in that Statorius recognized the equality and distinction of God the Father, the Son ,
and the Holy Spirit according to "prophetic and apostolic
doctrine" and "the truth of Holy Scripture."

After a long silence, during which Calvin received still
a lost third letter from Statorius in behalf of Biandrata,
Calvin finally on 15 November 1559 answered his former pupil:

> Since you exhort me in both letters, and not
> without threatening denunciation, that I should
> reconcile myself with George Biandrata, I beg
> you, my Peter, reconsider a little, by what right
> you suggest that this is necessary for me? I do
> not think that I am bound to your authority that I
> should consent to be governed by your judgment.[94]

There followed a continuation of the synod at Pińczów 22 November 1559,[95] at which both Biandrata and even Stancaro were present, and at which there was more discussion about the mediatorial view of Stancaro. At this assembly a formal statement was received of Lord Remigian Chełmski, which appears to have been written by Gregory Paweł, and in which Remigian also had opposed the invocation of the Holy Spirit. The synod's defense of that invocation was signed (it would appear not wholeheartedly by all) by Cruciger, by Paweł himself who was at the time pastor in Chełm (a village close to Cracow), by Jacob Sylvius, and by Lismanino.

On 7 January 1560 Łaski died at Pińczów. A succession of synods and ministerial gatherings took place in the face of the crisis of leadership and the theological crisis heading toward the schisms of the Reformed in the Commonwealth. The synod at Pińczów 13 to 16 January 1560[96] received a letter from Lord Stadnicki, asking for a pastor to replace Stanislas Sarnicki at Niedźwiedź, and dealt with Orsatius and Christopher Przechadzka Leopolitanus (of Lwów) who had together composed a Stancarist confession of faith, while two others expressed doubts about the *De Mediatore* of the majority.

Łaski was buried in Pińczów "in the parish church," where the major east altar had been located, and addresses were delivered by Sarnicki, Statorius, and Cruciger. This was all in the context of a general synod 29 January to 1 February 1560.[97] On the second day, Orsatius, "follower of the Nestorian heresy, Stancarism," said that the lips of Łaski in the coffin had been sealed as a divine sign of disapprobation of his opposition to Stancaro. The consternation was such that the coffin had to be opened to demonstrate the falsity of the charge.

Lismanino, 10 February 1560,[98] informed the Zurich divines of the death of Łaski through whose life *Deus Optimus Maximus* had accomplished much for the Church in the Commonwealth. Three days later, John Łużyński,[99] the first Reformed pastor in Iwanwice in Cujavia, as no doubt one among many, informed Calvin of Łaski's death and asked Calvin to prepare something "more ample" against Stancaro than what he had recently written (lost), to the bookseller Sebastian Pech, since Stancaro, with the support of two patrons in Ruthenia was bent upon organizing a rival Church "between ours and that of the Papists."

Cruciger wrote to both Geneva and Zurich, again summarizing Stancaro's views and asked for a further refutation. In letters of 18 March 1560 to Zurich[100] and Geneva,[101] Cruciger explained that Stancaro disturbed the congregations by accusing their pastors of Arianism because they held (following

Melanchthon, Calvin, and Bullinger) that Christ was the Mediator in both natures: "For he [Stancaro] says, if he is a Mediator in his divinity, it is proper that he is less than he
to whom he mediates: if he intercedes, he pleads as God,
[therefore] he is less, he says, than he to whom he pleads."
In Scripture, Cruciger, in rebuttal on his own, observed that a
mediator did not demean himself as a supplicant to another.
Or: "Stancaro says that the man Christ mediates to the Trinity."

From 5 to 9 May a synod convened at Pińczów.[102] Because
of its expected importance in reorganizing the Reformed Church,
the King had named Lismanino and Biandrata as his personal representatives. The purpose of the synod was to set a date and
place for a truly constitutional general synod--at Książ in
September. There was a strong sentiment that the Reformed
Churches of Lithuania and Poland be regarded as a single entity. In the meantime, Biandrata was commissioned to ask Palatine Radziwiłł for financial assistance for Lismanino.
Christopher Trecy,[103] at the request of Radziwiłł, asked approval and arrangements for a Polish Bible translation, now at
the expense of the prince. The synod dealt with Gonesius, who
was to be expelled from the synod unless he suspended his
propagation of "Arianism" in secret, and with Martin of Lublin.
The latter, though charged with the view of Stancaro on the
Mediator, said that because of the furor and personal rancor
against Stancaro which prevented the issue from being discussed on the merits, he would let it stand that: "I indeed
hold with Bullinger and Calvin and Beza concerning the Mediator." Herein he perhaps reflected Stancaro's conviction that
the Swiss divines could not possibly differ from Augustine,
Anselm, Lombard, and himself. Orsatius persisted in his Stancarist position, and the synod commissioned Biandrata to persuade Lord Olésnicki to get rid of him and ordered that the
faithful should avoid him. Orsatius presently joined Stancaro
at Dubiecko. The synod ordered Palatine Nicholas Sienawski
of Ruthenia, captain of Halicz, and his pastors at (another)
Niedźwiedź that they should take precautions against the con-
tamination of the flock with the error of Gonesius. After the
synod Biandrata, as commissioned, went to Vilna to gain the
financial support of Palatine Radziwiłł for the Polish Bible
and at once gained also his confidence and friendship.

Important interventions of Calvin lie ahead, but we must
close this story. What has been rapidly unfolded here is a
compacted account of the correspondence, synods, and other
events connected with the "superintendency" of Łaski. In conclusion, we are constrained to point out that when Łaski returned to his fatherland, a union of the Czech Brethren of

Great Poland and the Reformed of Little Poland had been virtually consummated under Cruciger at Koźminek. It would not
be until 1570 that anything like that union would be accomplished in the federation of Czech Brethren, Lutherans, and
the Reformed by the Consensus of Sandomierz. When Łaski arrived, Palatine Radziwiłł of Vilna (who would die in 1565,
virtually a Unitarian) was emerging as foremost in seeking a
pan-Commonwealth *Reformed* Church with annual synods of the
whole Commonwealth of "the Two Peoples." At his death, the
"fatherly" leadership of Łaski scarcely extended beyond Little
Poland and Ruthenia with courtesy contacts with the Reformed
of Great Poland and of the Grand Duchy. When Łaski arrived,
the controversy over the Mediator was primarily an intra-
Lutheran dispute involving Osiander, Musculus, Melanchthon--
all upset by Stancaro. By Łaski's death the countervailing
effect of the incipient voluntarist "tritheism" of Biandrata
(locally much esteemed) and the near "Sabellianism" of Lombardian Stancaro (locally, for the most part, much disliked),
the human nature mediating with an almost undifferentiated
Trinity, had laid the basis for *two* schisms in the Reformed
Church. The first would be that of the Stancarist Reformed
Synod (1561-70), its school and seminary with five teachers
and three hundred students in Dubieko.[104] This group represented a position also fostered by Poland's greatest publicist
of the century, Andrew Frycz Modrzewski, who would write three
libelli, *De Mediatore*, the first in December 1560. (The
ministers of the Stancarist Synod would submit at Sandomierz
in 1570). The second Reformed schism is better known, that of
the Minor Church of the Unitarian, eventually immersionist
Polish Brethren--following Lismanino, Biandrata, Peter Gonesius,
and Gregory Paweł (1563-1660).[105] The Calvinist Synod of
Cruciger was to be headed by Sarnicki and Sylvius.

We already know what Calvin thought of Biandrata! After
learning of the death of Łaski he remarked that, alas, the Pole
had taken pleasure in Biandrata and, for his part, he was
ashamed that Łaski would have called a synod to discuss his own
family affairs. Of Lismanino in the same paragraph of assessment he would speak as "that Graeculus who sings Biandrata."[106]
He would at least twice remark to Polish correspondents that
he really did not like their race (*gentem*).[107]

If Calvin had better understood the strengths and weaknesses of Łaski and his people and also more swiftly perceived
the theological agony and confusion of the Poles pulled between
two Italian doctors, Biandrata and Stancaro (of a race widely
regarded as perhaps the most intellectually prodigious and
prestigious of the age), and if he had shown half the interest
in the Commonwealth that he did in his native Catholic-Huguenot

France, European history would have taken a fundamentally different course, whether for good or ill.

NOTES

1. Johannis Calvini *Opera omnia* (henceforth: *OC*), XIV, no. 1195.

2. The authority here is Halina Kowalska, *Działalność Reformatorska Jana Łaskiego w Polsce 1556-1560* (Wrocław, etc., 1969), which completes the account of the late Oskar Bartel, *Jan Łaski, część I, 1499-1556* (Warsaw, 1955). Łaski was never called "superintendent."

3. Nancy Conradt in her unpublished dissertation, "John Calvin, Theodore Beza and the Reformation in Poland," Madison, Wisconsin, 1974, sets forth as a major thesis that Calvin's relative neglect of the Poles during Łaski's superintendency was responsible for the final failure of the promising beginnings of the Reformed Church in the Commonwealth. I am much indebted to her at many points. In my own "Erasmianism in Poland 1518-1605," *Polish Review*, XXII (1977), pp. 3-50, slightly changed in *Renaissance East and West*, ed. by Cyriac Pullapilly (New Rochelle, N. Y.: Caratyas Brothers, 1980), ch. 1, I have tried to show that Łaski remained a pupil of Erasmus, whose library he purchased while a student in his home, 1524-25, that he stressed Scripture alone without recourse to the conciliar creeds, only the Apostles' Creed, and that he identified the visible Reformed Church with the elect, not being drawn into speculation about an invisible Church of the elect.

4. Henryk Barycz, "Meandry Lismaninowskie," *Odrodzenie i Reformacja w Polsce* (henceforth: OiRwP), XVI (1971), pp. 37-67; Theodor Wotschke, "Francesco Lismanino," *Zeitschrift der Historischen Gesellschaft für die Provinz Posen*, XXVIII (1910), pp. 213-332; Lorenz Hein, *Italienische Protestanten und ihr Einfluss auf die Reformation in Polen* [to 1570] (Leiden, 1974), chs. 2, 5.

5. *OC*, XV, no. 2057.

6. On Stancaro, see most recently, Hein, *op. cit.*, ch. 3.

152

7. Maria Sipayłło, *Akta Synodów Różnowerczych w Polsce*, 2 vols. (Warsaw, 1966/1972), I, pp. 2f.

8. *OC*, XV, no. 2070, col. 360.

9. *OC*, XV, no. 2090, col. 392.

10. *OC*, XV, no. 2113.

11. Sipayłło, *Akta*, I, pp. 16f.

12. The letter is undated except for the year 1555. Stanislas Lubieniecki, *Historia Reformationis Polonicae* (Amsterdam, 1665; facsimile ed., Warsaw, 1971). pp. 50-58, preserves considerable detail derived from the lost MS History of Stanislas Budziński, a principal. Maria Sipayłło, "W sprawie synodu pińczowskiego z 1. V. 1555 r.,"*OiRwP* X (1965), defends the existence of this contested synod and many of the details preserved by Lubieniecki and others and assigns to it the synodal letter of Cruciger to Lismanino, which Theodor Wotschke, *Der Briefwechsel der Schweizer mit den Polen* (Leipzig, 1908), cites as no. 26. This *Briefwechsel* is invaluable in calendaring the correspondence, citing *OC* (but beware of occasional faulty numbering) and printing letters not therein contained or elsewhere readily accessible. It is in fact he who prints Cruciger's Letter "ex convocatione Pinczoviensi 1555" elsewhere and asigns it a later date, 21 September. Sipayłło is convincing in her article, but she only lists this earlier Pińczów synod in her Table of Synods in *Akta*, I, without assigning to it a page in its own right with bibliographical information, as she does in other cases where the records have been lost.

13. For the King's efforts to have a national reform council, see Czesław Frankiewicz, "Starania Zygmunta Augusta w Rzymie o Sobór Narodowy," *Reformacja w Polsce* II (1922), pp. 266-71.

14. Ludwik Finkel, "Konfessya podana przez posłów na Sejmie piotrowskim w r. 1555," *Kwartalnik Historyczny*, X (1896), pp. 257-85, which gives a general account of the Diet. See also Theodor Wotschke, "Stanislas Lutomirski," with appendices, *Archiv für Reformationsgeschichte* III (1908), pp. 105-71; *idem*, succinctly in context, *Geschichte der Reformation in Polen* (Leipzig, 1911), pp. 126-30.

15. See items in n. 14 and for the four points of the Interim, see also Christian A. Salig, *Vollständige Historie der Augsburgischen Confession*, 3 vols. (Halle, 1730-31), II, p. 597.

16. *OC*, XV, no. 2227. The Palatine mentions that Calvin's letter to him had been brought by Budziński.

17. *OC*, XV, n. 2276

18. The evidence for letters from the King to the three Swiss is in Lubieniecki, *Historia*, p. 58. Only a fragment of that to Bullinger survives, Wotschke, *Briefwechsel*, no. 27, who refers to the Diet in progress as his excuse for brevity. Sipayłło, "W sprawie," makes a good case for the synod of Pińczów of 1 May 1555 (n. 12) and for the recalendaring of the letters here involved over against Wotschke, observing that Budziński returned to Switzerland in the middle of August, taking the letters mentioned but not Jordan's. This new sequence explains why Lismanino's response to Cruciger would be 11 September, from Zurich.

19. Wotschke, *Briefwechsel*, no. 2276.

20. Sipayłło, *Akta*, I, pp. 18-43. The Reformed yielded to the Czech Brethren on most matters, although in time they were to come to realize that the Czechs of Great Poland were themselves subject to the Mother Church and that the Polish Reformed were, unless they debated further, to be subjected to the control of bishops from outside their country, scarcely an improvement over what they thought they were doing over against the Catholic Church. Hence more and more issues will be raised on both sides in the course of the subsequent synods.

21. Sipayłło, *Akta*, I, p. 2.

22. Wotschke, *Briefwechsel*, no. 28.

23. Wotschke, *Briefwechsel*, no. 28.

24. *OC*, XV, no. 2350, cols. 868-71. (In the *Briefwechsel* this no. is assigned to Alexander Witrelin, whose five problems might well be only incorporated into the memorandum.)

25. Wotschke, *Briefwechsel*, no. 33.

26. *Ibid.*, no. 34.

27. *Ibid.*, no. 35.

28. *Ibid.*, no. 36.

29. *Ibid.*, no. 37.

154

30. *Ibid.*, no. 38.

31. *Ibid.*, no. 39.

32. *Ibid.*, no. 40.

33. *Ibid.*, no. 41.

34. *Ibid.*, no. 42.

35. Abrahm Kuyper, *Opera tam edita quam inedita*, 2 vols. (Amsterdam, 1866), I, pp. 247-388.

36. It is commonly thought that Calvin derived the *triplex munus Christi* from Martin Bucer, but see my "Erasmianism," *loc. cit.*, esp. pp. 31-37.

37. Sipayłło, *Akta*, I, pp. 46-52.

38. *Ibid.*, p. 40.

39. *Ibid.*, p. 47.

40. *Ibid.*, p. 48.

41. *Ibid.*, pp. 53-78.

42. Théodore de Bèze, *Correspondence*, 7 vols. ed. by H. Aubert, *et al.* (Geneva, 1960-73), II, pp. 213-19.

43. *OC*, XVI, no. 2445.

44. *OC*, XVI, no. 2446.
wechsel, no. 73.
45. Bèze, *Correspondence*, II, pp. 84f.; Wotschke, *Briefwechsel*, no. 73.

46. *OC*, XV, no. 2373b.

47. The letter of Cruciger *et al.* is in *OC*, XVI, no 2445; that of Lismanino, no. 2431. Later Lismanino would publish some Swiss letters, *Exemplum litterarum* (Pińczów, 1559), but the *memoriale* of Calvin is not among them. Cf. Sipayłło, *Akta*, I, p. 1, no. 2, p. 63; II, p. 39, n. 2.

48. *OC*, XVI, no. 2470.

49. Boner to Calvin, May 1556; *OC*, XVI, no. 2458, Tarnowski to Calvin, June 1556; *OC*, XVI, no. 2489; Zborowski to Calvin, July, 1556; *OC*, XVI, no. 2504.

50. Preserved by Lubieniecki, *Historia*, pp. 65f.

51. *OC*, XVI, no. 2513.

52. *OC*, XVI, no. 2514.

53. I have recently dealt with the legatine president eventuel of the III Period of the Council of Trent, "Cardinal Hosius," *Shapers of Tradition in Germany, Switzerland, and Poland* (New Haven: Yale University Press, 1981), ch. 5.

54. Sipayłło, *Akta*, I, pp. 172-74.

55. *OC*, XVI, no. 2599.

56. *OC*, XVI, no. 2602.

57. Giorgio Biandrata, once a member of the Italian congregation in Geneva (1556-58), well known to Calvin, to whom he presented his theological views in the form of queries and from whom he received a thoughtful response, was court physician for both Sigismund August and his sister Isabelle, Queen and then regent for her son, eventually Unitarian King of Transylvania. Joseph Tylenda, "The Warning that Went Unheeded: John Calvin on Giorgio Biandrata," *Calvin Theological Journal*, XII (1977), pp. 24-52, translates in two appendices the Queries and the *Responsio*, having placed the exchange in context.

58. *Libri sententiarum*, III, dist. xvii, 7; *Patrologia Latina*, CXCII, cols. 797f.

59. This phrase should be credited to Professor Georges Florovsky.

60. Sipayłło, *Akta*, I, pp. 179-207. After Iwanowice, where Łaski first appeared in synod, there were synods in Krzcięcice, 9 March 1557, and in Pełsznica, 13 May, from which Łaski was absent, the first welcoming Lismanino as a major participant in future, the second with the Confession of the Czech Brethren. *Ibid.*, pp. 175-78.

61. *Ibid.*, pp. 208f. On the competition between *Catechismus* and *Confessio*, i.e., a pure *Reformed* Church and a pan-*Protestant* Church, see *ibid*, pp. 136, 208.

62. *Ibid.*, pp. 216-22.

63. *Ibid.*, pp. 223f.

64. The letter of Cruciger is lost. That of Calvin is in *OC.*, XVI, no. 2745.

65. Sipayłło, *Akta*, pp. 240-50.

66. *OC.*, XVI, no. 2744.

67. Sipayłło, *Akta*, I, pp. 225-37; letters were sent by the Czechs remonstrating; the other meetings *ibid.*, pp. 249f.; 256.

68. *Ibid.*, pp. 335-37.

69. *OC*, XVII, no. 2876.

70. *OC*, XVII, no. 2924. For the synod of Książ, presided over by Cruciger as superintendent, see Sipayłło, *Akta*, I, pp. 263f.

71. *OC*, XVII, no. 2931.

72. For the synod, see Sipayłło, *Akta*, I, pp. 265-82.

73. *OC*, XVII, nos. 2959, 2969.

74. Teodor Wierzbowski, *Uchansciana*, 5 vols. (Warsaw, 1884-95), I, p. 32, Wotschke, *Briefwechsel*, no. 158.

75. *OC*, XVII, to Uchański, no. 2983; to Tarnowski, no. 2984; to Ostoróg, no. 2980.

76. *OC*, no. 2981; the whole postscript about Biandrata is translated by Tylenda, *op. cit.*, pp. 35f.

77. Although he would become *archipresbyterus*, i.e., general Elder of the Reformed Church in Poland, then in Transylvania an adorant Unitarian against non-adorant Bishop Francis Dávid, I do not regard Biandrata as a *politique*. He was in fact, an earnest lay theologian, who had doubtless been influenced by his possession of a copy of the *Restitutio Christianismi* of Servetus. Although in the bitter fight against his former ally and editorial collaborator, Dávid, from his base in the Báthory court of Transylvania (later orator of Báthory at the Diet Election in Wielka Wola, 1575), Biandrata still upheld in 1578-79 in Transylvania what he less openly set forth during Łaski's superintendency: a philosophically undefined Apostles' Creed. *Politiques* did not write seriously on dogma. Cf. my "The Christological Issue between Dávid and Socinus," *Studia Humanitatis*, ed. Tibor Klaniczay, VI (1980).

78. *OC*, XVII, no. 3002.

79. Sipayłło, *Akta*, I, pp. 283-94.

80. *OC*, XVII, no. 3004; partly translated by Tylenda, *op. cit.*, pp. 36f.

81. We know this from a later letter of Statorius to Calvin, *OC*, XVII, no. 3098, col. 600.

82. Sipayłło, *Akta*, I, pp. 295f.

83. Wotschke, *Briefwechsel*, no. 167.

84. Sipayłło, *Akta*, I, pp. 297-300.

85. *Ibid.*, pp. 304-09.

86. Lismanino informs the ministers of Zurich about this, 1 September 1559. Wotschke, *Briefwechsel*, no. 174.

87. Sipayłło, *Akta*, I, pp. 310-14.

88. It is most accessible in Wotschke, *Briefwechsel*, no. 174.

89. Wotschke, *Briefwechsel*, no. 174 ; no. 203.

90. Bullinger to Calvin, 27 May 1560, *OC*, XVIII, no. 3204, col. 94.

91. *OC*, XVII, no. 3098, partly translated by Tylenda, *op. cit.*, p. 37.

92. *OC*, XVII, no. 3100.

93. Sipayłło, *Akta*, I, pp. 313f.

94. *OC*, XVII, no. 3134; translated and discussed by Conradt, *op. cit.*, p. 43; by Tylenda, *op. cit.*, p. 38.

95. Sipayłło, *Akta*, I, pp. 315-18.

96. *Ibid.*, II, pp. 1-6.

97. *Ibid.*, II, pp. 8-12.

98. Wotschke, *Briefwechsel*, no. 179.

158

99.   *OC*, XVIII, no. 3168.

100.   Wotschke, *Briefwechsel*, no. 184.

101.   Rodolphe Peter and Jean Rott, eds., *Les Lettres à Jean Calvin de la collection Sarrau* (Paris, 1972), pp. 59-63. The second quotation from Cruciger is from this letter.

102.   Sipayłło, *Akta*, II, pp. 15-22.

103.   Trecy is a young hopeful of the conservatives. He will be sent to Switzerland for further study.

104.   Andrew Wzgierski, *Libri quattuor Slavoniae Reformatae* (Amsterdam, 2nd ed. 1579; facsimile edition, Warsaw, 1973), p. 126. See further my "The Stancarist Reformed Schism (1561-70), centered in Dubietsko in Ruthenia," *Essays in Honor of Omeljan Pritsak*, ed. by Francis Cleaves, Ihor Ševčenko, *et. al.* (Cambridge: Harvard University Press, 1980).

105.   See further my Introduction to Stanislas Lubieniecki, *The History of the Polish Reformation*, Harvard Theological Studies, (ca. 1981) and *The Polish Brethren, 1601-1685*, Harvard Theological Studies, XXX (Missoula, Montana: Scholars Press, 1978).

106.   Both these references are to be found in Calvin's Letter to Bullinger, 1 February 1561; *OC*, XVIII, no. 3332, col. 349.

107.   Calvin to Sarnicki, *OC*, XIX, no. 3559, "gentem vestram non amarem." Cf. Calvin to Trecy, *OC*, XIX, no. 3889, col. 607.

9

THE FUNCTION OF LAW IN THE POLITICAL THOUGHT
OF PETER MARTYR VERMIGLI*

Robert M. Kingdon

One of the great values of the monumental edition of
Calvin's *Institutes of the Christian Religion* superintended by
John T. McNeill and containing the felicitous translation and
the splendid indexes prepared by Ford Lewis Battles is that it
helps place that theological masterwork within its sixteenth-
century context. Its critical apparatus reminds us of the
significant fact that Calvin's *Institutes*, as important as it
was, was not written or used in isolation. It was accompanied
by the works of many other Reformed theologians which helped
to elaborate, document, and occasionally even to modify
slightly the message of the greatest leader of Reformed Protestantism. Of these other works, I suspect the most important
was the *Loci communes* of Peter Martyr Vermigli. It was not
the work of Vermigli himself but was rather a compilation of
many of the short treatises and pericopes scattered throughout
his Biblical commentaries. It was prepared by Robert Masson,
a French minister in London and was deliberately arranged to
follow the same organizational pattern as the *Institutes*.
Editors and publishers of the two works clearly expected them
to be used together. The first Latin edition of the *Institutes*
to appear in England, the Vautrollier edition of 1576, was
even keyed to the *Loci*, with dozens of marginal cross-references. All of these valuable cross-references are tabulated in
the author and source index to the McNeill-Battles edition of
the *Institutes*. In fact Augustine is the only author allowed
more space than Vermigli in that index.[1]

Vermigli's most important contribution to Reformed theology was probably in the field of eucharistics. He developed a
highly subtle eucharistic theology in the course of debates
with Catholic spokesmen at Oxford and he further refined it in

later publications from Strasbourg and Zurich. Calvin appreciated Vermigli's insights on eucharistics and seems to have used them in his own later writings. The cordial letters which the two exchanged, when they go beyond reports of news, tend to dwell particularly on this branch of theology.[2]

But Vermigli made an additional contribution, whose significance is only now winning attention, to yet another branch of Reformed thought. This is the field of Reformed thought on politics.[3] The space given politics in Vermigli's *Loci communes* reflects an extraordinary expansion of attention to this domain. Some rough comparisons will make this point clear. The classic form for Protestant collections of Common Places was set, of course, by Philip Melanchthon. This collection systematically surveys all theology and concludes with a consideration of the human institutions through which the divine message is mediated, specifically the church and state. In the earliest edition of his *Loci communes*, of 1521, this consideration is limited to a single section, the next to the last, which considers both ecclesiastical and secular magistrates, allowing only a page or so for secular authorities. In the last edition of this work which he prepared, of 1559, this part of the general analysis is substantially expanded. Now there are several chapters on the church and a full chapter, toward the end, containing a considerably developed analysis of secular government alone.[4] This same format was adapted for the Reformed branch of the Protestant movement by Calvin in his *Institutes*. Now an entire book, the last of four, is devoted to the human institutions through which God works His will. But of these institutions, the church clearly interests Calvin more than the state. In the final edition of the *Institutes* which he saw through the press, the French edition of 1560, some nineteen chapters of the fourth book deal with the church while only one, the last, deals with secular government.[5] When one turns to the *Common Places* of Vermigli, however, one finds a quite startling shift in proportions. This collection ends, like the *Institutes*, with a fourth book on human institutions. But now eight (or nine) of the twenty (or twenty-one) chapters are devoted to secular government, often, to be sure, in its relation to the church, rather than the one chapter of Melanchthon and Calvin. The Vermigli collection thus devotes several times as much space to politics as the two earlier collections to which it is most comparable. Not all of Vermigli's *loci* on politics, furthermore, are included in the *Common Places*. There are additional ones in several of his published Biblical commentaries, particularly in his commentary on Judges, which was printed in several independent editions.[6]

To me this constitutes an important justification for a

study of the political thought of Peter Martyr Vermigli. His
political ideas are not strikingly original or unusual. But
they are presented in a much more extended and systematic form
than in most of the comparable reference works of the period.
Clearly the political ideas of Vermigli were among the most
developed of those widely circulated in the Reformed community
of the late sixteenth and early seventeenth centuries.

Another important justification for a study of the political thought of Peter Martyr Vermigli can be found in their
form. All of his *loci* are documented with unusual precision.
We can discover not only the precise sources Vermigli used to
develop his argument, on occasion we can even discover the
relative weight he attached to each.

For purposes of analysis, one can distinguish three main
categories of authority upon which Vermigli built his political arguments: ancient philosophers, particularly Aristotle;
the Bible; law, particularly as codified by the ancient Romans
and by the Roman Catholic Church. The use of Aristotle and
the Bible runs through all of Vermigli's writings and has been
pointed out by every other specialist. But the frequent use
of law in his political *loci* has not been pointed out until
very recently[7] and came as a real surprise to me when I began
work on these writings. This paper is an exploration of that
use.

But first let me describe the general form of Vermigli's
political argument. A typical political *locus* begins with the
definition of a term. Examples include the magistrate, war,
sedition. The term is first examined linguistically, in good
humanist fashion, with explanations of its meaning in Latin,
Greek and Hebrew, ornamented with examples. The term is then
explored logically, often at considerable length. The definition of sedition, for example, runs through seven sections of
a chapter in the *Common Places,* and is finally encapsulated in
a summary definition which even Vermigli himself admits is
"very full" (L. C. IV:20, 2-8). By this point, each term
within the definition has been carefully analyzed and explained, typically using Aristotelian categories and vocabulary. Quite often these definitions use the four Aristotelian
categories of causation for a pattern of analysis. Vermigli's
definition of just war, for example, is summarized in these
words: "hostile dissension whereby through the Prince's edict
mischiefs are repressed by force and arms, to the intent that
men may peaceably and quietly live by justice and godliness."
It is then immediately followed by the observation that the
definition "comprehends" the four kinds of Aristotelian cause:
"The form is hostile dissension; the matter are the mischiefs
which ought to be repressed; the efficient cause is the magis-

trate; the end is that we may live justly and godly" (L. C. IV: 16, 1).

After developing a definition, Vermigli then proceeds to flesh out an argument. The argument is often explicitly anti-Catholic, frequently attacking a position developed in the canon law of the Roman Catholic Church as codified by Gratian. Vermigli clearly knew the *Corpus Iuris Canonici* very well and used it constantly, both as an authoritative source of official statements of the Catholic position and as a useful collection of relevant quotations from the church fathers and other authorities. The substance of his argument to counter the Catholic position is drawn primarily from the three types of authority I have already indicated.

His material from Aristotle is taken largely, as one would expect, from the *Politics*. Probably Vermigli's most striking use of that work is his adoption of Aristotle's analysis of the types of government into six categories, according to the locus of sovereignty in each: three good types--monarchy, aristocracy, and polity--matched by the three bad types into which they tend to degenerate--tyranny, oligarchy, and democracy.[8] This pattern of analysis is applied to both the church and the state. The church, Vermigli argues, conforms closely to the classical ideal of a mixed government, incorporating the best features of the three good types. It is monarchic in that Christ is its King and remains its supreme legislator, even though He is in heaven. It is aristocratic in that it is ruled by "bishops, elders, doctors," and others, chosen by merit rather than by wealth, favor, or birth. It is popular in that some of its most important decisions, for example as to whether to excommunicate a notorious sinner, should be "referred unto the people" (L. C. IV:5, 9). This church, of course, is the one Vermigli believes to be the only true church, the Reformed church. Vermigli does not insist that the secular state, on the other hand, be mixed or conform to any one type. There are three possible models for the state, each equally valuable, and three possible corrupt forms, each equally dangerous. What is important to him is that the state, however it is organized, be good (L.C. IV:13, especially 2).

If material from Aristotle supplies much of the substance of Vermigli's political thought, even more comes from the Christian tradition, primarily as it is expressed in the Bible. All of these *loci*, we must not forget, were first written as glosses on specific verses in the Bible, and even though Vermigli could wander quite far from his text, and would occasionally go on for pages without mentioning it, he seldom forgot it completely and often analyzes it quite closely. Vermigli

furthermore followed common Protestant practice in using
Scripture to interpret Scripture. There are frequent marginal
references to other Biblical verses, in both the old and new
testaments, to support nearly every step of his argument. Discussions of political resistance theory, for example, inevitably carry a cross-reference to the verses of Romans 13, the
locus classicus of all Christian discussion of that subject.
In developing his interpretation of Scripture, furthermore,
Vermigli relies heavily on the Church Fathers, using patristic
writers as authoritative explanations of what specific verses
really mean. The particular passages from the Fathers which
he uses are often very well-known ones, clearly lifted from
the *Corpus Iuris Canonici* or some collection of that sort.
But they are sometimes not as obvious, and suggest some independent reading in the Fathers. Vermigli relies with particular frequency on St. Augustine, quoting him lavishly, usually
with approval, although occasionally in disagreement. This
should come as no surprise in a man trained as an Augustinian
religious, particularly given the fondness for Augustine displayed by most of the early Protestant Reformers. Another
Father Vermigli often quotes is St. John Chrysostom. In his
discussions of resistance theory, for example, he uses, in
company with other sixteenth-century commentators, Chrysostom's
homily number 23 on the first verses of Romans 13.

Material drawn from Aristotle and the Christian tradition
did not exhaust Vermigli's supply of documentation. He also
included material drawn from law. By this he most often meant
the Roman civil law, as codified in the *Corpus Iuris Civilis*,
particularly in the *Codex* and the *Digests*. He frequently
cited passages from these compendia, usually with considerable
precision. One law which he cites with particular frequency
and which he uses in ways I find especially intriguing, is the
Roman law of treason called the *lex Julia maiestatis*. This
law was enacted either by Julius Caesar or Augustus and defined treason as conspiracy against the life of the emperor,
libel or slander of the emperor, or adultery with a member of
the emperor's family. Two chapters containing summary statements of this law can be found in the *Corpus Iuris Civilis*, in
the *Digests*, 48:4, and in the *Codex*, 9:8. In going through
Vermigli's political *loci*, I have found at least five citations
of this law, generally drawing from both chapters. It is used
for an example of executive clemency, when Vermigli points out
that Augustus Caesar relied on its provisions to waive the
normal death penalty for treason (L. C. IV:14, 28). It is
used, along with other allegations, to establish the authority
of a prince to wage war and punish the wicked (L. C. IV:16, 2).
It is used, obviously enough, to define treason, again with
legal allegations and also patristic and classical sources

(L. C. IV:16, 29). It is again combined with other legal, Scriptural, and classical authorities to justify the death penalty for sedition (L. C. IV: 20, 9). And it is alluded to in Vermigli's most important *locus* on the obligation of inferior magistrates to lead resistance to a tyrannical government (L. C. IV:20, 13).

Vermigli also drew material from other bodies of law. He could use allegations from the canon law of the Roman Catholic Church in constructive ways, as well as to build straw men for demolition. And he refers a few times to contemporary constitutional law, in ways which I find particularly interesting. These references become really crucial, in fact, when he discusses the right of inferior magistrates to lead resistance to tyrannical governments.

This leads me to consideration of the relative importance of these three sources of documentation to Vermigli's political argument. How did he measure the relative value of appeals to classical philosophers, pre-eminently Aristotle, to the Holy Scriptures as interpreted by the Church Fathers, and to secular law, primarily as codified by the Romans? It is tempting to guess that he always preferred a proof drawn from Scripture. This is very likely what he himself would have said, in common with almost all Protestant theologians of the sixteenth century. The principle of *sola scriptura*, after all, was one of the most fundamental of the Reformation and was held to apply in practically every branch of thought, including politics. A close look at Vermigli's political *loci*, however, reveals that this obvious conclusion does not always hold. It is particularly instructive to look at passages in which he actually balances different types of authority against each other, not always reaching the predictable conclusion. This is especially striking in his discussion of the resistance problem. I would like to supply several examples. In the first Vermigli is discussing tyrannicide as the obvious solution to the problem of tyranny. He concedes that in ancient times pagan leaders "appointed rewards for such as killed tyrants." But he cannot accept this argument based on classical authority, pointing out that "godliness and the Holy Scriptures allow not the same," citing the usual verses from the New Testament requiring obedience even to an evil government (L. C. IV:20, 13). In my second example Vermigli is discussing the legitimacy of resistance to a tyrant if led by duly created inferior magistrates. He concedes at the beginning that this sort of resistance cannot be justified by an appeal to the Bible. But he nevertheless concludes that it can indeed be justified by an appeal to contemporary constitutional arrangements. Let me quote his conclusion: "But thou wilt say: by what law do inferior princes resist either the emperor, or kings, or else public wealths [republics], when as they defend the sincere religion and true faith? I answer by the law of the Emperor, or by the law of the king, or by the law of the public wealth. For they [the inferior princes] are chosen of emperors, kings, and public wealths as helpers to rule, whereby justice may more and more flourish. And therefore were they ordained according to the office committed unto them, rightly, justly, and godly to govern the public wealth. Wherefore they do according to their duty, when in cause of religion they resist the higher power" (*Judges* 1, 36). In my final examples, Vermigli becomes even more precise and practical, naming types of inferior magistrates who may legitimately lead resistance to a tyrannical prince. The type he finds most persuasive is drawn from contemporary German constitutional theory. Specifically he argues that the Electors of the Holy Roman Empire are legally entitled to lead resistance to the Emperor. One finds this argument in two of his political *loci*, on Romans 13 and on Judges 3. The latter form of the argument is more extended, is the one included in the *Loci communes*, and is the one for which Vermigli became best known. Here is the heart of that argument: "There be others in the commonweale, which in place and dignity are inferior unto princes, and yet in very deed do elect the superior power, and by certain laws do govern the commonweale, as at this day we see done by the Electors of the Empire, and perhaps the same is done in other kingdoms. To these undoubtedly if the prince perform not his covenants and promises, it is lawful to constrain and bring him into order, and by force to compel him to perform the conditions and covenants which he had promised, and that by war when it cannot otherwise be done." Here we see not only a striking statement of a theory justifying resistance by inferior magistrates, resting on an analysis of the German constitution; we also see a contract theory of resistance, reminiscent of those developed later and at more length by theorists in France and England. In the *locus* Judges 3, incidentally, Vermigli goes on to line up additional precedents for legitimate resistance, drawn from classical Roman practice, recent Danish practice, and medieval English practice as reported by Polydore Vergil. None of these additional precedents, however, is analyzed as fully, as confidently, and as rigorously as the argument from the German constitution (L. C. IV:20, 13).

These examples should make it clear, I hope, that for Vermigli legal arguments on political questions could be decisive, superseding arguments based on appeals to Scripture. There remains the problem of explaining how Vermigli came by his knowledge of law and his respect for its authority. It is becoming increasingly obvious to American specialists that the law and its study were of pervasive importance during the

Reformation. William Bouwsma has demonstrated the importance
of lawyers in European society throughout the early modern
period.[9] Donald Kelley has demonstrated the importance of
legal thought in the rise of modern historiography during the
sixteenth century.[10] Ralph Giesey and his students have demonstrated the importance of legal principles in political thought
of the period, particularly thought on the problem of resistance.[11] The importance of legal training in forming several
of the most prominent intellectual leaders of the Protestant
movement has been known for some time. Martin Luther was beginning a course of study in law when he decided to transfer
to theology and become a monk. John Calvin finished a course
of study in law and later used his legal talents to draft
ordinances for the city of Geneva. Theodore Beza, Calvin's
chief assistant and successor, was also trained as a lawyer.
None of these theologians trained as lawyers, however, retained great respect for the authority of the law. Luther and
Calvin both tended to insist that the law must conform to
Scripture and that only holy writ could have ultimate authority in human argumentation. Vermigli agreed. But how did he
occasionally come to a different conclusion?

Vermigli's position is a particular surprise in view of
the fact that he, unlike Luther, Calvin, and Beza, had not received formal training in the law. In fact it remains something of a mystery to me where Vermigli did acquire both his
considerable knowledge of law, particularly as it is revealed
in his precise citations of the Roman civil law, and his considerable respect for the authority of the law. From the
posthumous biography drafted by his friend Simler, in consultation with Vermigli's personal secretary, we know something
of his early studies in Italy.[12] At Padua he studied both
philosophy, of the Aristotelian type then favored there, and
theology, primarily as systematized by Thomas Aquinas and
Gregory of Rimini.[13] Although the biography does not mention
this, I think it likely that he learned the canon law as a
part of his course of study in theology. The biography also
reveals that he made informal arrangements outside the curricu-
lum to learn ancient languages, Greek in Padua, Hebrew in
Bologna. It says nothing, however, about any study of civil
law. Bologna, to be sure, was an important center for the
study of both laws. Conceivably Vermigli first began reading
law there.

My own theory, however, is that Vermigli taught himself
law in Strasbourg, during his second stay there, from 1553 to
1556. I can find no decisive evidence for this theory, but
a number of facts point me in this direction. The most extended and the most sophisticated of the political *loci* of Vermigli come from his commentary on the book of Judges. That in-

cludes both the most important of those included in the *Common Places* and a number that were left out. This commentary on Judges was based on lectures delivered in Strasbourg between 1553 and 1556, prepared for publication by Vermigli himself in 1561, after he moved to Zurich.[14] His choice of Judges as a subject for commentary marked a departure from his practice at Oxford which had been to focus on the books of the New Testament which were general favorites of the Protestant Reformers, particularly on Pauline epistles such as the ones to Romans and Corinthians. This choice was dictated in part by the curricular needs of the Strasbourg Gymnasium in which Vermigli was teaching. It needed a professor of Old Testament and had asked him to lecture on its books during his earlier stay in the city. The Gymnasium now wanted him to return to this subject matter. This does not explain, however, why Vermigli chose Judges from among the books of the Old Testament for his commentary in 1553. I suspect that this choice may have been suggested in part by the political situation in which Vermigli found himself teaching. The book of Judges lends itself much more than most parts of the Bible to reflection on political problems, since so much of it recounts the history of the tribes in Israel during a period of political turmoil when there was considerable debate about the appropriate form of government for the community. And there were many within Strasbourg, among Vermigli's students and colleagues, who were unusually concerned about political matters in 1553. Local citizens were concerned about the politics of the Holy Roman Empire, of which the city was a member, as a free imperial city. Strasbourg was then still recovering from the attempts of the imperial government to force upon all of Germany the compromise settlement knows as the Interim. The city was soon to benefit from the efforts of resisting princes when a new Emperor granted full toleration of established Lutheran churches in the Religious Peace of Augsburg in 1555. In Strasbourg Vermigli was surrounded, furthermore, by exiles from other countries determined to promote resistance at home. A number of his English students and friends had followed him from Oxford, and were busily conspiring to overthrow the Catholic government of Mary Tudor, justified and rationalized by the tracts of men like John Ponet. A number of French scholars, increasingly upset with the French crown's repression of Protestantism, also joined Vermigli's circle in Strasbourg. The best known of them is François Hotman, who was later to develop in his *Franco-Gallia* one of the sixteenth-century's most influential appeals for political resistance to a tyrannical government.[15]

At about the time Vermigli began lecturing in Strasbourg on Judges, we know that he obtained a number of law books.

After he died, his entire library was offered to Geneva, to establish the initial core of the library of its new Academy. Most of Vermigli's books which were sent to Geneva are still there, in the rare book collections of the *Bibliothèque publique et universitaire,* and have been examined recently by several scholars. Among these books are a copy of the Justinian *Codex* published in Paris in 1550 and a copy of the *Digests* also published in Paris, 1548-1550, both containing marginal annotations in Vermigli's own hand.[16] The dates and place of publication of these books suggest that he obtained them on his return to Strasbourg in 1553. It seems to me quite probable that he obtained them for use in his lectures on Judges.

We also know that Vermigli was associated with a number of prominent legal scholars in Strasbourg during these years. Among his colleagues at the Gymnasium were the irenic French Protestant François Baudouin and the militant French Calvinist François Hotman, who were named successively to the chair of law there in 1555 and 1556. More important for the shaping of Vermigli's thought, I suspect, was yet another colleague, the historian Johann Sleidan. Sleidan was also trained as a lawyer, in Orleans, in the same faculty where Calvin and Beza studied. He then became a diplomat, accepting a number of assignments in both France and Germany, following closely the development of religious policy in the period of tension between the Schmalkaldic League and the imperial government. He spent the last years of his life in Strasbourg, on diplomatic assignments for the city government and writing an extended history of Germany under Charles V. These years coincided closely with Vermigli's second stay in the city. Vermigli's biography reports briefly that Sleidan was one of the friends who welcomed him back to Strasbourg in 1553.[17] Sleidan's *History* includes towards its end a sympathetic account of Vermigli's departure from Strasbourg, under pressure from militant Lutherans.[18] Those same militants apparently also provoked Sleidan to leave the city, only a few months before the publication of his masterwork and his death.

Finally, although Sleidan's *History* is never cited in Vermigli's political *loci,* on at least one crucial question I see the strong possibility of its direct influence on his thought. Sleidan was fascinated by the development of Lutheran resistance to the imperial government. He describes it in considerable detail in his *History*, inserting the texts of relevant documents in support of his account. He follows the development within the Saxon chancery of the argument that the Electors, of course including the Elector of Saxony, choose the emperor and choose him conditionally, stipulating that he must abide by certain rules and maintain certain rights. This argument was then used to support the claim that Charles V had violated the conditions of his election by seeking to force Saxony to return to Roman Catholicism, and that this violation made it possible for the Elector to lead armed resistance to the imperial government. Sleidan even describes the dramatic meeting at Torgau in 1530, when Luther himself had been persuaded to accept this argument. Until this time, Luther had always insisted that the Bible, in particular Romans 13, made any resistance to legitimate government impossible. He specifically included within this prohibition resistance by inferior magistrates. The Christian oppressed by a tyrant, according to Luther, can only pray for divine deliverance, accepting martyrdom if that be necessary. Armed resistance is never justified. At Torgau Luther listened to the arguments of lawyers who held that the German constitution permitted resistance in certain circumstances, if led by an Elector. He finally agreed to sign a memorandum conceding that in these circumstances the rules drawn from the Bible did not apply and that statesmen would have to decide on legal grounds whether or not resistance was justified.[19]

In his *loci* on resistance, Vermigli in effect adopts the position of the Saxon lawyers, illustrating the point with the example of the Electors of the Holy Roman Empire. He concedes, like Luther, that the New Testament does not allow any sort of armed resistance to a legitimate government. But he argues that this prohibition does not apply in states whose laws, like those of the Holy Roman Empire, permit resistance if led by duly constituted inferior magistrates. This position was first stated by Vermigli in a rather rough and tentative way in his commentary on Romans, based on lectures he delivered at Oxford shortly before returning to Strasbourg, but published in a version he prepared himself after he settled in Zurich.[20] It was elaborated, refined, and stated several times in his commentary on Judges, delivered in Strasbourg while he was in touch with Sleidan, although again published only after he settled in Zurich.[21] It is my contention that the influence of Sleidan is quite probable on the argument as developed in the Judges commentary, and even possible on the argument as developed in the Romans commentary.

My main conclusion, then, is that human law, as codified by the Romans and as further described by contemporary custom lawyers, fills a function of critical importance in the political thought of Peter Martyr Vermigli. It is my further conclusion that Vermigli probably learned to appreciate and use arguments drawn from law in Strasbourg, between 1553 and 1556, perhaps from Johann Sleidan.

NOTES

* This is a revised version of a paper first read at the spring meeting of the American Society for Reformation Research, held as a part of the Fourteenth International Congress on Medieval Studies at Western Michigan University, Kalamazoo, May 6, 1978. It is a sequel to a paper, "The Political Thought of Peter Martyr Vermigli," hereafter cited as Kingdon, "Political Thought," prepared for a conference on Vermigli and the cultural impact of Italian Reformers organized at McGill University by Joseph C. McLelland, September 27-30, 1977, and scheduled for publication in a symposium volume of papers read at that conference.

1. John T. McNeill, ed., *Calvin: Institutes of the Christian Religion,* vols. 20 and 21 in *The Library of Christian Classics* (Philadelphia, Westminster, 1960), I, xlviii; II, 1526, 1628-1632. See also the publisher's letter to the reader in S. T. C. 4414, the 1576 Vautrollier edition of Calvin's *Institutio.*

2. Joseph C. McLelland, *The Visible Words of God: An Exposition of the Sacramental Theology of Peter Martyr Vermigli, A.D. 1500-1562* (Grand Rapids, Michigan: Eerdmans, 1957), pp. 278-281.

3. Marvin W. Anderson, "Royal Idolatry: Peter Martyr and the Reformed Tradition," *Archive for Reformation History,* 69(1978), 157-201, hereafter cited as Anderson, "Royal Idolatry," provides an admirably detailed introduction to Vermigli's writings on politics, based on his exceptionally complete knowledge of the entire corpus of Vermigli's work. I am indebted to Professor Anderson for providing me with an advance copy of this article. My own conclusions are based on an independent reading of Vermigli's political writings.

4. In Robert Stupperich, ed., *Melanchthons Werke in Auswahl,* see vol. 2/1-2 (Gütersloh: Bertelsmann, 1952-1953), Hans Engelland, ed., *Loci communes von 1521,* pp. 158-161, "De magistratibus," and *Loci praecipui theologici von 1559,* pp. 689-732, "De Magistratibus civilibus et dignitate rerum politicarum."

5. See the fine critical edition of Jean-Daniel Benoît, *Jean Calvin: Institution de la Religion Chrestienne* (Paris: Vrin, 1957-1963), 5 vols., especially vol. IV.

6. In preparing this paper, I used microfilm copies of the *Loci communes* in Latin of 1583 (S. T. C. 24668), hereafter cited as L. C.; the *Common Places* in English of 1583 (S. T. C. 24669); the *Romans* commentary in English of 1568 (S. T. C. 24672); the *Judges* commentary in English of 1564 (S. T. C. 24670)—all published in London. I have also used a copy of the *Judges* commentary in Latin of 1571, published in Zurich. References to L. C. are to chapter and section numbers in the Latin text, Part IV. Occasionally I have added variant numberings from the English text in parenthesis. References to the commentaries are to the Bible verses glossed. My quotations are from the sixteenth-century English translations, with spelling and punctuation modernized. I have prepared a critical edition with commentary of many of these texts: Robert M. Kingdon, *The Political Thought of Peter Martyr Vermigli* (Geneva: Droz, 1980).

7. By Anderson, "Royal Idolatry," *passim,* e.g. pp. 190-191, and by Kingdon, "Political Thought."

8. Aristotle, *Politics,* III, v.i-iv.

9. William J. Bouwsma, "Lawyers and Early Modern Culture," *The American Historical Review,* 78 (1973), 303-327.

10. Donald R. Kelley, *Foundations of Modern Historical Scholarship: Language, Law, and History in the French Renaissance* (New York and London: Columbia, 1970).

11. See, *inter alia,* Ralph E. Giesey, "The Monarchomach Triumvirs: Hotman, Beza, and Mornay," *Bibliotheque d'Humanisme et Renaissance,* 32 (1970), 41-56. See also the dissertations and articles of Richard R. Benert, Lawrence M. Bryant, William F. Freegard, Richard A. Jackson, and Sarah H. Madden.

12. *Oratio de vita et obitu. . .Vermilii. . .Iosia Simlero,* in unpaginated forematter to L. C. and in unpaginated appendixes to the English translation, hereafter cited as Simler, *Oratio.*

13. See the extended commentary on his studies at Padua in Philip McNair, *Peter Vermigli in Italy: An Anatomy of Apostasy* (Oxford: Clarendon, 1967), chapter IV, pp. 86-115.

14. Simler, *Oratio.*

15. On Vermigli's second stay in Strasbourg, see Marvin Walter Anderson, *Peter Martyr, a Reformer in Exile (1542-1562)* (Nieuwkoop: de Graaf, 1975), chapter IV, pp. 161-209, hereafter cited as Anderson, *Martyr*.

16. Alexandre Ganoczy, *La Bibliothèque de l'Académie de Calvin* (Geneva: Droz, 1969), items 341 and 342. See also John Patrick Donnelly, *Calvinism and Scholasticism in Vermigli's Doctrine of Man and Grace* (Leiden: Brill, 1976), pp. 208-217, an appendix which reconstitutes Vermigli's library from Ganoczy and other sources, especially p. 217 for Vermigli's law books.

17. Simler, *Oratio*. On Sleidan's career, see the biographical article in the Herzog-Plitt-Hauck *Real-Encyklopädie für protestantische Theologie und Kirche*.

18. Quoted in Anderson, *Martyr*, p. 379.

19. Johann Sleidan, *De statu religionis et reipublicae Carolo V. caesare, commentarii* (Geneva: Badius, 1559), and other editions in several languages. On the Torgau episode, see lib. 8, fol. 119v. For the text of the Torgau memorandum and some commentary, see the Weimar edition of Luther's *Werke* (1883--), *Briefwechsel*, V, 661-664. For a useful survey of the copious literature on Luther's ideas on resistance, see W. D. J. Cargill Thompson, "Luther and the Right of Resistance to the Emperor," in Derek Baker, ed., *Church, Society and Politics*, vol. 12 in *Studies in Church History* (Oxford: Blackwell, 1975), pp. 159-202.

20. Vermigli's commentary on *Romans* 13:3, "For rulers are not a terror to good works, but to the evil."

21. Vermigli's last *locus* on *Judges* 3:29-30, included in L. C. IV:20, 12-13.

10

THE STATE OF THE FREE
Romans 13:1-7 in the Context of Paul's Theology

Markus Barth

"The world needs brave people, and it would be sad if it were just the Christians who did not wish to be such people."

"Free remains only he who makes use of freedom. . .The state promotes the participation of the citizens in political decisions."

"The criterion of the nation's power is the welfare of the weak. . .The state endeavors to establish an order in which the rights and claims of the social groups, the use of property, and the interests of producers and consumers are balanced."

"The state acknowledges the limits of political power, and the duty to cooperate in favor of world-wide peace. . .and a just international order."

These sentences are beautiful and brave. The first stems from Karl Barth's Gifford Lectures (*Knowledge and Service of God,* 1938, p. 232); the others are found in the 1977 draft of a new Swiss Constitution, which--like the present Constitution-- begins with the formula: "In the name of God Almighty." In the times of the English, American, French, and other revolutions, die-hard supporters of unlimited state authority, of national chauvinism, and of the privileges of property-holders, have had misgivings and have protested against such statements. But a freedom loving citizen will cherish them.

All the more may we be inclined to criticize and reject what the apostle Paul wrote to the Christians in Rome during the early years of Emperor Nero's rule:

> "Let every person be subject to the governing
> authorities. For there is no authority except
> from God. . . Therefore he who resists the
> authorities resists what God has appointed,
> and those who resist will incur judgment. . .
> He who is in authority. . .does not bear the
> sword in vain. . . Therefore one must be sub-
> ject. . ."
>
> (Rom. 13:1-5, RSV)

Such words look ill-suited to the needs of the present time, a
comfort only for reactionary characters. The apostle seems to
adorn an outmoded *status quo* with a religious halo and to call
for nothing better than a servile spirit and blank submissive-
ness--even for an attitude which flatly contradicts the self-
consciousness and social concern of all those who would be
real men and worthy women. He appears to have not even one
word to say in favor of freedom and political responsibility,
not to speak of social progress and reform.

No wonder that "Romans 13" has been used by church leaders
and learned laymen alike for justifying and supporting not
only reasonable and beneficial but also barbarous and tyrannical governments. How often have harsh and scandalous political
rulers been left untouched--at least as long as they left to
the churches and their members, on the basis of throne-and-
altar agreements and concordats, a minimum of space to develop
in a protected corner "a quiet and peaceful life." But was
this life also "godly and respectable in every way" as 1 Tim.
2:2 suggests? Only by the building of schools, poorhouses,
and hospitals did Christians show concern for the good of the
total population. On the other hand, governments were encouraged to suppress religious liberty, and outrageous acts
against non-Christians were instigated or condoned. The
Crusades of the Middle Ages, Luther's support of the Princes'
way to handle the Peasant Revolt, the German and Swiss Reformers, use of state power to persecute and execute Anabaptists
and other heretics have still analogies in the present time.

The words quoted from Romans 13 seem to condemn not only
open rebels such as John Knox, Oliver Cromwell and Dietrich
Bonhoeffer, but also citizen's initiatives such as those taken
by peaceful demonstrators against racial discrimination, the
Vietnam War, or atomic power plants. They also appear to declare illicit the conscientious objectors' dearly paid decision
against military service.

For the reasons given, it is unquestionable that Romans
13 can irritate, exasperate or even disgust Christians and

other readers of the Bible. However, it is not sure whether
in the tradition of the church and after the first impression
on a modern reader the apostle has been rightly understood. A
new look at Paul's political ethics may reveal how ill advised
are our complaints against the apostle. This man, a Jew and a
Roman citizen, an eyewitness of Jesus Christ and a martyr for
his faith, may still have things to say which contradict and
refute our traditional understanding of his message and make
us realize that we have cared too little, not too much, about
the substance and intention of his words. Five points call
for consideration.

I

Paul wrote to the Romans in A.D. 55 or 56, a time when
the political situation in Rome was totally unlike the conditions described in Revelation 13 and 16-18. The Emperor to
whose court Paul appealed in Acts 25:11 was not the animal
from the Abyss, nor could the city be depicted as a prostitute
guzzling the blood of the saints. Though for certain periods
Nero's predecessor Claudius had expelled Jews and Jewish
Christians from the city of Rome, there were still good reasons to consider the Roman Empire a state bound internally by
the wisdom of Roman Law, and externally by the endeavor to
establish and uphold the *Pax Romana*. Even pious and devoted
Jews such as the Pharisees and Rabbis acknowledged the beneficial role of the Roman Empire.

However, not all Christians shared this attitude. From
Paul's words to the Romans, "One must be subject. . .Pay all
of them their dues, taxes to whom taxes are due. . .respect to
whom respect is due," it must be deduced that some Christians
in Rome were about to ponder or start a toll-and tax-payers'
strike, combined with a public disdain for the state officials
and their work. Had they not heard the message of the liberation from Satanic rule and sin through Jesus Christ? The consequence of God's grace, which Paul had formulated in his
letter to the Galatians, "In Christ. . .there is neither Jew
nor Greek, neither slave nor free, neither male nor female"
(Gal. 3:28), appeared to call for enthusiastic social emanci-
pation--not only in Rome. The slave Onesimus ran away from
his master in the Asia Minor city of Colossae, as the letter
to Philemon shows. The strictures imposed upon the conduct
of men and women in the Corinthian epistles reveal that male
members took sexual liberties, while women demonstrated their
emancipation in their dress and in loud behavior during the
meetings for worship.

In the letters to Philemon and to the Corinthians, Paul discusses early forms of slaves', men's, and women's "lib" movements, and in Romans a corresponding political freedom adventure. All the main topics of Romans, such as justification by faith, the relation between Israel and the church—and between the strong and the weak—are provoked by very specific occasions and conditions in the Roman congregation. Although Romans has sometimes been considered a testament of Paul, and Romans 13 has been converted into an abstract, timeless Pauline "philosophy of the state," an increasing number of scholars maintain that this letter—as much as the other Pauline epistles—is a pastoral letter with a very particular *Sitz im Leben*. Another situation would have compelled the apostle to use other words and say other things.

Does Paul, then, falsify in Romans 13 the conviction of those Christians who are convinced that there is a connection between faith in Christ and life in freedom? In that case Paul would contradict his own message as conveyed to the Galatians and other congregations, "For freedom Christ has set us free. . .you were called for freedom" (Gal. 5:1, 13; cf. 1:4; 2:4; 4:7, 21-31; Rom. 6:18, 22; 8:2, 21; 2 Cor. 3:17; cf. John 8:32, 36; James 1:25; 2:12)? It is much more likely that he resists and refutes only *excesses* in the enjoyment of freedom, by showing that not every demonstration of liberty is an expression of the freedom granted by God. In his pronouncements about the State, Paul by no means revokes the glorious affirmation made in Rom. 6:15, "You are not under the law but under grace." On the contrary, the words "by the mercies of God" (Rom. 12:1), found in the headline above all counsels and commands assembled in Rom. 12-15, are an explicit reminder of God's work of salvation and liberation as it was described in Rom. 1-8. The political passage, Rom. 13:1-7, is immediately preceded by the appeal to overcome evil and enemies by doing good, and is followed by the excursus on love for the neighbor (12:14-21; 13:8-10). The "eschatological" verses 13:11-14 remind the Christians that they live in a special time: the last hours before Christ's parousia. To stand its stress, the Christians are equipped with a wonderful weaponry, "the armor of light." Thus indeed the "mercies of God" form the basis and fill the time of the Christian's life, and love of the enemy and of the neighbor is the ground-swell of that life, even in regard to its political dimensions. Misuse of the best gifts is the worst squander. To transform grace and love into libertinism, egalitarianism or rejection of any social responsibility—this was the temptation faced in Rome. Paul did not deny but affirmed the gospel of freedom when he called for a responsible political attitude. Freedom shall not be misused as "an opportunity for the flesh" or "a pretext for evil" (Gal. 5:13; 1 Pet. 2:16).

II

A brief study of the term "authority" and its use in the
Pauline epistles is necessary before the proper use of freedom
in the political realm can be unfolded. The Greek term
(*exousia*), translated in Romans 13 by "authority," has more
than one meaning. When used in the singular, it signifies
freedom to act, right to dispose, ability or power—such as exerted by a ruler or an expert. Closely related to it is the
term *archē* (beginning, dominion, or principle). When Paul
uses plural forms of these or similar terms, they denote angelic or demonic forces, even the so called "principalities
and powers." In Rom. 13:1-3 both the plural and the singular
are used; once (in vs. 3) the "powers" are identified as "the
rulers" (*archontes*), that is, by a term which certainly signifies earthly rulers, but which in 1 Cor 2:8 as well as in
gnostic writings also denotes "cosmic powers." These poten-
tates are invisible; they are localized "in heavenly places"
above the earth (Col. 1:16, 20; Eph. 1:10; 6:12, etc.); and
yet they make themselves felt palpably in the daily experience
of mankind. Far from belonging to an obscure and outmoded
world of fairies, ghosts or spooks, they appear to correspond
to entities that are carefully studied in 20th century social
science and psychology. In Rom. 8:38-39 Paul identifies some
of them as "death" and "life," highflying dreams or elated
happenings, depressive fears or crushing defeats, powers of
the past, obsessions in the present, fantasies anticipating
the future. In other passages the law and human traditions,
the slave system and male superiority complexes are found in
their company. Therefore the Pauline references to authorities, principalities, and powers point to the influence over
body and soul, over individuals and society that is attributed
by modern psychologists to the conscious and the unconscious,
the libido and the archetypes, to traumata and utopias—and also
to the role which according to sociologists is played by the
"institutions and structures" of societal life. Modern examples of the latter would include State and Church, Law and
Order, Reaction and Revolution, but also Oil, the Dollar, and
Swiss Banks. By capitalizing such terms we indicate that behind the people seen and met on the street or in an office,
there is a power greater than meets the eye—a power incorporated in, but not exhausted by its earthly representatives.

Among the many utterances of Paul about these powers,
three affirmations are pertinent to the interpretations of
Romans 13. (1) They are creatures of God and are related to

Christ from the beginning because through and for him they
were created (Col. 1:15-17); therefore they are not absolute,
free or uncontrolled beings. (2) They have been idolized by
humankind so much so that many among them became subject to
vanity and wield a power destructive of humanity; yet they are
not bad in themselves but moan and groan in their longing for
liberation from their subjection to vanity (Rom. 8:19-22).
(3) They cannot resist the superior power of God, and they
are incapable of keeping human beings separated from God's
love or to prevent reconciliation among human enemies (Rom.
8:38-39; Eph. 2:14-18).

When and how was their rebellion overcome? Paul mentions
the coming, the death, the resurrection, the ascension and/or
the parousia of the Messiah promised to Israel as the date and
instrument of their subjugation (Col. 1:18-20; 2:14-15; Eph.
1:10, 19-22; 2:15-17; 4:8-10; Phil. 2:9-11; 1 Cor. 15:24-28;
cf. Heb. 1:5-13; 2:6-9). The good news which the apostle
preaches is not exhausted by the pronouncement of the love,
justification, forgiveness, reconciliation, sanctification,
and redemption brought to Jews and Gentiles by Jesus Christ.
For God does more than only care for human souls and inter-
human relations. His love and grace also affect all those
forces that influence and determine the physical and spiritual,
cultural and social life of men, women and children. Even
the powers of disease and death, of law and custom, of prejudices and lusts are in his hands. The gospel does not only
say what good God does to humankind, but also proclaims his
power over nature, ideologies, and institutions.

If already human love is strong as death (Song of Songs
8:6), it is the privilege of God and his love to prove even
mightier--that is, to overcome all enemies, including the
strongest and last enemy: death (1 Cor. 15:26). In Rom.
8:31-39 and Eph. 1:19-23; 2:4-7 Paul mentions love and power(s)
in the same context. Love without power might be sheer
sentimentality, and power without love tends to be brutal. The
omnipotence of God's love, even God's dominion over "all
things," powers and people is an essential element of the gospel (Rom. 11:32, 36; 1 Cor. 8:4-6; 10:18-19; Eph. 4:8-10, etc.).
Humankind cannot overcome the powers mentioned. But just as
the Old Testament promised that God through the Davidic King
would free Israel by overcoming the hostile and idolized
powers (Ps. 2; 8; 68; 82; 94; etc.), so Paul proclaims the
victory won by God through the Messiah Jesus for the benefit
of the people. The words translated in the RSV "(authorities)
instituted by God. . .appointed" refer to God's victory over
both, the invisible political principalities and powers *and*
their human incorporations. They are placed under Christ's
feet and are no longer free to pretend to be gods or to resist

the power of God's love for those by whom they have been idolized and whom, in turn, they have oppressed.

Psalms and Prophets agree in stating: it is the special duty of Israel's king to let justice rule by the protection of orphans and widows, of the poor and the needy; the care for those weak is in the Old Testament called "righteousness" (Ps. 45:7-8; 72:1-4, 7, 12-13; 85:10-12; Is. 9:7; 11:5; 32:1, 16-18; Jer. 22:3, 13-15; 23:5-6 Ez. 34; Deut. 17:18-20; Prov. 31:4-5). The administration of justice is also expected from pagan rulers and judges, as Ps. 82:2-4 shows:

> "Give justice to the weak and fatherless;
> maintain the right of the afflicted and destitute.
> Rescue the weak and the needy,
> deliver them from the hand of the wicked."

Through the Persian king Cyrus, such righteousness (or its equivalent: salvation) shall rain from the skies and sprout from the earth (Is. 45:1-8). Even under the rule and the grip of the King of Babylon, the Israelites are encouraged to "seek the welfare of the city where I have sent you into exile, and pray to the Lord on its behalf, for in its welfare you will find your welfare" (Jer. 29:7).

The apostle Paul's statements about the institution and purpose of the state are equivalent to the quoted Old Testament injunctions on the kings of Israel and other nations. Just as Nebuchadnezzar was called a "servant" of God (Jer. 27: 6), Paul calls the persons representing the state (e.g., the Emperor, the legislators, judges, revenue officers) "servants" and "ministers of God," and regards them as placed into their positions and functions by God himself (Rom. 13:1b, 2a, 4a, 6b). According to the Fourth Gospel, Jesus has informed Pontius Pilate of the same fact: "You would have no power over me unless it had been given to you from above" (John 19: 11). When Jesus declared the "sin" committed by Jude the traitor "greater" than that of Pilate who handed him over for crucifixion, he still did speak of the official's sin. In Romans 13, however, Paul does not even take into consideration a possible failure of the State in protecting the innocent and persecuting only the guilty. He calls for subordination to a State that actually does punish wrong-doers and rewards those doing what is good (Rom. 13:3-4).

How great is Paul's confidence in God's universal reign over all powers: there are no authorities untouched by the coming of the promised Messiah; none of them are free to form a divisive wall between human groups; they cannot separate the

faithful from the love of God (Eph. 1:19-21; 2:14-16; Rom. 8:
37-39)! This conviction is the basis of Paul's political
ethics. The Eastern Churches' ikons depicting Christ the Pan-
tocrator, the Christus-Victor theology of G. Aulen, also the
Christ-King festival instituted by Pope Pius XI might have reminded the Christians in the whole world of this substance of
the gospel. It is impossible to accept, to cherish, and to
praise Paul's doctrine of the justification of the sinner,
and, at the same time, to reject the apostle's proclamations
of the cosmic victory of Christ and of the ensuing political
implications and applications for the life of the redeemed.
For "justification" signifies that on the cross and in the
resurrection of Jesus Christ, God alone is judge, above all
other judges, and that his love is stronger than any other
power. Justification is in itself an act of creative power:
God liberates his children--to a freedom which presupposes
the victory over the powers of sin and death. The subordination of these "authorities" to God's gracious will has been
revealed by the fact that even the Jewish and pagan officials'
decision to kill Jesus had to contribute to the redemption of
God's people.

Admittedly, the subjugation of *all* powers is "not yet
seen" (Heb. 2:9); it is not yet completed and waits for the
day of the parousia (1 Cor. 15:25). But the same is true of
justification, sanctification, and the new creation: "We walk
in faith, not by sight" (2 Cor. 5:7). Paul's political ethics
are a call to walking in faith. To use a German formulation,
Handeln aus Glauben is the basis of *all* parts of Pauline exhortation.

The interpretation of Romans 13 here proposed is at vari-
ance with other expositions. Mostly it is assumed that the
political institutions and the submission of which this chapter speaks have nothing to do with the new order established
by Jesus Christ's victory. Indeed, reference is made to an
order of creation, to a law contradicting the gospel or to a
government by God's left arm that is allegedly opposed to the
gracious rule of his right hand, or, to a sphere of reason
which is wider than the sway of the gospel. A revelation of
God in nature and history is presupposed which can be perceived by the eye of reason; and a law identical with, or
approximate to, God's will is stipulated that is innate even
in Gentiles. Pauline passages such as Rom. 1:19-20; 2:14-15
(also Acts 17:22-28) are used to undergird a "Natural Theology," a "Natural Revelation," and a "Natural Law." Without
hesitancy these doctrines then are juxtaposed to the apostle's
Christ-centered proclamation and ethics. Thus, a bifurcation,
even a fundamental internal contradiction, is construed and

attributed to Paul's thought, whereupon the interpreters of
Paul are urged either to imitate his supposedly doublesided
limp, or, to engage in "substance criticsm"--be it of (the
fiction of) his ethically useless justification doctrine or of
his anti-democratic political stance. Here is not the place
to display arguments (1) why each one of the selected proof-
texts is misused when pressed into the service of Natural
Theology and Law, (2) why the concatenation of these passages
is arbitrary, and (3) why a fundamental contradiction in Paul
is most unlikely. By the assumption that Paul was an exponent
of a double allegiance, more problems are created than solved.

     Less complicated is another interpretation. Because Paul
speaks of a "necessity" (RSV Rom. 13:5 translates the term by
"one must") to be subject, it was held that the apostle--
impressed by useless rebellions such as Spartacus' (in 73 B.C.)
--argued on the basis of fatalism. Or, it is assumed that he
was determined so much by the expectation of the near end of
the present world (to which indeed he refers in Rom. 13:12)
that he did not really care for social change and progress in
the time left. In both cases the vss. Rom. 13:1-7 are understood as the voice of a desperate person who scarcely succeeds
in hiding his laziness and cowardice behind a veil of pious
phrases and who is satisfied if only the Christians can secure
for themselves a minimum of peace or respectability, even at
the expense of what is good for all humankind. Actually, the
same man who warned of "righteousness by works" was not only
an activist who "had worked harder than any" to proclaim the
gospel and to establish confessing churches (1 Cor. 15:10),
but also insisted that all Christians "work out their salvation" by pondering and doing "whatever is just, pure, lovely,
gracious, excellent, worthy of praise" (Phil. 2:12; 4-8).
While, indeed, his ethics is an Interim-Ethics, designed for
the time between Easter and the parousia, it urges the Christians to assume responsibility for all people, not to shun it.

     Only if there were no way at all to interpret Romans 13
in agreement with Paul's central message and total attitude,
could the escape-hatch chosen by a last group of expositors be
recommended: they declare the vss. Rom. 13:1-7 a forgery, in-
serted by a (Jewish influenced?) scribe after the apostle had
finished the genuine parts of the epistle. In the absence of
overwhelming reasons to follow this suggestion, the interpretation of the text itself can now be continued.

III

The RSV translation of Rom. 13:1 and 5 contains the words, "be subject. . .one must be subject" (cf. Eph. 5:21-22, 24). When elsewhere (in 1 Pet. 2:18; 3:1; Tit. 2:5; 3:1) slaves, wives or all Christians are addressed in view of their relation to masters, husbands or rulers, the RSV uses the term, "be submissive." While "subjection" sounds bad enough for the readers of the Bible engaged in the struggle for equality and dignity in human relations, "submissiveness" has an even worse ring; it reminds them of the attitude of a beaten dog.

Fortunately, it was something else that Paul intended to say at a time when Christian citizens, wives, and slaves had to decide how to behave toward non-Christian government agents, husbands, and slave-owners. For he uses the same Greek verb *hypotasso*, which indeed means (e.g., as a military term) "to subordinate," in two different ways.

When the apostle speaks of God's or Christ's action taken against rebellious principalities and powers, the verb (*hypotassomai*) means to subjugate, to subdue, to defeat or to reduce to the state of a servant. Since the institutions and structures as such are beings to whom the gospel cannot be preached and who cannot respond to it by faith, hope, and charity, God talks to them and acts on them in the only way they understand: by (brute) power. Of course, a student critical of Machiavelli or Nietzsche might be inclined to subscribe to the thesis of Jakob Burckhardt, saying that "all power is evil." The apostle Paul, on the contrary, even adopts hymnic terminology when he speaks of the beneficial force by which God has subjugated all those powers (e.g., of evil and death, of the State and other forms of dominion) to which humankind appears to be extradited. In Eph. 1:19-21 he writes (in the version of the Anchor Bible), ". . .how exceedingly great is God's power over us believers. For that mighty strength is at work which God has exerted in the Messiah when

> He has raised him from the dead.
> He has enthroned him at his right hand in the heavens
> above every government and authority,
> power and dominion, and any title bestowed,
> not only in this age but also in the age to come.
> He put everything under his feet."

According to this text and to similar passages in Colossians

and Philippians, God alone possesses the capability to subjugate everything, the resurrection and enthronement of Christ
are the means of his victory, and the principalities and
powers are the victims of his action: they meet their master
and are put in their place. They *suffer* subordination. But
the same is not said about God's relationship to humanity.

Another use of the same verb "subordinate" occurs in con-
texts where Christians are told to "subordinate themselves."
Now *they* are the agents, not God; and they subordinate *themselves*, not the powers. The mutual subordination of Christians, and the subordination of women to that which is decent
and orderly during divine worship, of wives to their husbands,
of all church members to those bearing a specific responsibility among the saints, of Israel to the righteousness of God, of
the church to Christ, and of Christ to God--these are examples
(Rom. 10:3; 1 Cor. 14:34, 40; 15:28; 16:16; Eph. 5:21-24).
In each case, and therefore also when Paul asks for political
subordination, a voluntary action is meant. Presupposed are
the faith and the love of those subordinating themselves--faith
in the power and victory of God over divisive and destructive
institutions; and love of God and of those redeemed by him.
God has created a realm and a climate in which self-assertion,
private revolutions and wars have become pointless. The bene-
ficiaries of the mighty acts of God, who by their faith and
love participate in God's victory over the powers, Paul calls
"more than conquerors" (Rom. 8:37). A spirit is at work in
them that makes them free and humble at the same time--to subordinate themselves voluntarily not only to God but also to
fellow Christians and exponents of the defeated powers.

Paul's call for the Christians' subordination has parallels in the passages (e.g. in Eph. 4:2) where the apostle
speaks of lowliness and meekness, patience and forbearing. In
his exhortation to slaves he speaks of a service rendered "with
fear and trembling, in singleness of heart. . .from the heart
. . .with a good will" (Eph. 6:5-7). He could hardly have
found stronger or clearer words to express the voluntary character of self-subordination.

What is it, then, that makes the difference between Paul
and any upholder of law and order, who sees in the *status quo*
the best of all possible social orders because everybody, both
the high and the low, remains in his place? The apostle of
Jesus Christ starts out from the presupposition that all Christians have a specifically high calling: all are freed by
Christ, all are children of God himself, all are citizens of
the kingdom that is not of this world (Eph. 4:1; 1 Cor. 7:22;
Rom. 8:14-17; Phil. 3:20). The same people whom he has called

184

to humility and mutual subordination in Eph. 4:2 and 5:21, he
describes in Eph. 6:10-20 as people equipped with a rich
officer's weaponry, not as military subordinates. Just because of their freedom and dignity, not despite their high
standing in God's eyes, he expects them to be humble.

In order to explain what at first sight looks paradoxical,
a reference to United States congressional custom might be in
place. A Senator may gallantly "yield" his right of speech to
a fellow Senator without in any way losing face. Equally, a
wise educator of princes will tell his majestic nobility not
to show off, but to be polite from the heart. The apostle,
however, uses a stronger argument in Phil. 2:3-13: Jesus
Christ himself is the solid ground and binding example of the
inseparable connection between divine freedom and voluntary
self-subordination. Why will Christians abstain from "selfish-
ness and deceit" in favor of "humility"? Why will the "interests of others" be for them at least as important as their own
good? Because their attitude and actions shall be determined
by the spirit of the one who was and is equal to God in rank
and who even as the bearer of this dignity took the form of a
servant! If it is good enough for Jesus Christ to prove his
majesty in humility, then humility is good enough for the
Christians. But it is not only "good enough." For even this
is their salvation, and there is no other way to live according to ("to work out") their salvation.

No one would say that God's Son was "submissive" to human
nature, the human predicament, the worst human death, when he
obeyed the Father, became man, and died on the cross. Rather,
the way he chose was to place himself at the service and disposition of others, to reveal his love and might in caring for
the weak, in short: to become poor in order to make others
rich, and to show the perfection of his power in weakness (2
Cor. 8:9; 12:9). When Paul tells the Christians in Rome to
"subordinate themselves" to the political authorities, he
means a voluntary condescendence, the assumption of responsibility for others, even when it means to bear a burden. The
words "subordinate yourselves" in Rom. 13:1 may, therefore, be
paraphrased "place yourselves at the disposition, at the service, of," or, even more pointedly, "cooperate voluntarily."

Does this interpretation adumbrate, if not neglect, the
military origin and *Sitz im Leben* of the term "subordinate"?
In the Greek text of Rom. 13:1-2, 5, derivates from the stem
"order" (*tassō, taxis*) are used with a frequency that is not
transparent in the RSV rendering "be subject," "instituted,"
"resist," "appointed." Indeed, a ring of force and unilateral
command is notorious in the Greek terms. But precisely this
connotation confirms rather than confounds the exposition here

proposed. For the forceful reduction of deified invisible
"powers" to useful "servants" and "ministers" of God can be
called a military victory of God which replaces chaos by
order. Also the appeal to voluntary, responsible cooperation
fits the military imagery--as soon as it is realized that
"self-subordination" is not an attitude of puppets, automatons
or the lowest military rank. Rather, it is expected of high-
ranking officers who under a supreme command contribute by
their own wisdom and courage to the success of the day. It
was already said that the militant Christians described in
Eph. 6:10-20 (cf. Rom. 13:12; 1 Thess. 5:8) bear the weapons
of officers. Their service of God corresponds to the service
of God rendered by state officials--even when the latter are
not conscious of whom they serve, or when they do their work
unvoluntarily. The Christians make their contribution to the
State as colleagues of the professional political officials,
not as underlings.

The two (military!) meanings of the term "subordinate"
converge, according to Paul, in as far as they have the same
purpose: the service of God to the benefit of all. Christians have the privilege to do voluntarily what state officials do under constraint. The subordination to which the
children of God are invited excels by its humane character.

However, neither Paul nor his fellow believers have a
monopoly on humanizing social relations. Long before the
time of Jesus Christ, Aristotle, and among Paul's contemporaries, several Stoic moralists had written and worked in
favor of a reasonable and equitous relation between rulers and
their subjects, masters and their slaves, husbands and their
wives. Moving testimonies exist that resemble the ethics of
Paul; in their own way, just as much as Paul, they aim at full
partnership. Yet there is one decisive distinction: the
moral philosophers addressed their enlightened wisdom only to
the so-called stronger parties, even to rulers, slave owners
and husbands. They still did not honor and trust the allegedly "weaker sex," the slaves or the commoners enough to expect
of them the same amount and quality of responsibility as of
those holding the reins in their hands. It is a unique feature
of the Pauline proclamation that in the discussions of the
relation between the stronger and the weaker (especially in
the *Haustafeln:* Col. 3:17-4:1; Eph. 5:21-6:9) more energy and
space is given to addressing the weak than the strong. By
accepting and treating those in inferior positions as fully
enlightened and spiritually endowed persons, who are capable
of doing their own thinking and making their own decisions,
the apostle contributed vitally to their elevation from the
state of passive underlings to the dignity of co-responsible
activists, even of social partners in the realm of politics,

economics, and family life. Thus he sowed the seed of equality and democracy. What had looked like the private domain of
the rulers, was converted to a *res publica*.

This apostle shows that when the gospel is preached, social change in the direction of liberation and of shared
rights and duties cannot be prevented. Wherever the message
of Christ was or is taken seriously, such changes have occurred
and more changes will occur. For voluntary self-subordination
under the rule of God's gracious power means co-responsibility;
and shared responsibility issues in equal rights and duties--
to an extent which probably, even in bourgeois or Marxist
democracies, is not yet reached.

From the study of specific concepts we now turn to the
observation of some structural elements of Romans 13.

IV

The structure of Rom. 13:1-7 follows the pattern of an
inclusio that is, the first thought is after a lengthy excursus resumed at the end. The passage begins with the clear
command, "Every one shall place himself [and herself] at the
service of the governing authorities" (vs. la). Then follows
the extensive main body in which a series of reasons are given
for the initial request (vss. lb-6). The conclusion resumes
and unfolds the imperative found at the opening, "pay them
their dues, taxes to whom taxes are due," etc. (vs. 7).

Among the reasons compiled in the center part, only the
first has been paid serious attention in traditional interpretation: the statement about the institution of all existing authorities by God, and the consequence drawn by Paul,
saying that political resistance is rebellion against God.
Arbitrarily, these grave announcements were separated from the
Old Testament promise and the Pauline teaching concerning the
subjugation of all gods, angels, demons, kings, and created
things to the elect Messiah's feet (see part II, above).
Therefore, they lost their evangelical character and ring.
Just as in Rom 12:1-2 four chapters filled with imperatives
and exhortations are subsumed under the headline, "By the
mercies of God," so the first argument for subordination reminds the readers of one decisive part of those "mercies":
the superiority and dominion of God's power over all enemies
of God and mankind. Since the revolution of the false gods or
deified powers is quenched by God, it is not up to the Christians to take the place of rebellious powers and play god on
their part.

The second argument shows to what purpose the powers were
subdued: to encourage and reward what good is done, and to
punish the evil that is committed (vss. 3-4). What Paul has
in mind is best described by the German term *Rechtsstaat,* i.e.
a form of government that is bound by constitution and law to
administer public affairs with equity: *suum cuique.* We observe the absence of even the slightest indication that a
state, in order to correspond to God's will, ought to be constituted or dominated by only one ethnic group. The notion of
a *völkischer Staat,* founded to secure only one "nation" (in
the sense of anti-Napoleonic or other romantic "nationalists"),
is neither inspired nor supported by the apostle. Rather, the
vocabulary employed by Paul at this place resembles the best
of legal and political philosophy of his time. Therefore the
assumption can be made that he was acquainted with it and took
it up consciously. However, Paul felt free at given occasions
to use another language and to indicate another attitude: in
1 Thess. 2:14-15, he fiercely denounces Jewish authorities,
and according to Acts 16:36-39 he did not condone (or call for
the Christian's support of) an obvious lesion of a citizen's
rights. But in Rom. 13, without using the term "(government
by God's) grace" or employing the word "gratitude," he urged
the Christians to recognize God's grace in good government and
to show their gratitutde for a government observing reasonable
laws. In 1 Tim. 2:1-2, explicit mention is made of "intercession" and "thanksgiving" for a State that contributes to a
quiet and peaceable life.

The third argument of the apostle is hidden in the same
two verses that contain the second. It describes an experience which Christian as well as all other people may have,
and a decision which all of them have to follow. It can be
learned by experience that under good government, crime does
not pay, but virtuous conduct will find recognition. The decision concerns the doing of "what is good" (vss. 3 and 4).
Paul falls into the style of Jewish wisdom teachers when, without explicit reference to the mighty deeds of God, he expresses
his trust in God's people: they will learn from experience to
make the right decisions. "Would you have no fear. . .Then do
what is good" (vs. 3)! "Find out by experience"--so Rom. 12:2
may be translated--"what is the will of God, what is good and
acceptable and perfect." This appeal to follow common sense
and to behave as free and mature persons contradicts any attempt to transform evangelical ethics into casuistry.

Still, Paul's appeals to "place oneself at the service"
(vss. 1 and 5) and to "do what is good" look so vague and general that the question must be asked: does he dodge committing
himself by giving specific, practical advice? The answer is
found in vs. 7. The political passage ends with particular

commands which at first sight look pedestrian, trite and repe-
titious. "Pay all of them their dues, taxes to whom taxes are
due, revenue to whom revenue is due, respect to whom respect
is due, honor to whom honor is due." How does this "catalogue
of duties" qualify the crisp initial command and the subsequent
reasoning?

First, the apostle spoke of awe-inspiring political "authorities" and their immediate relationship to God. Then he
gave each person "in authority" a title fit for angels and
prophets, for pious Jews and Christians, even for Jesus Christ;
he called the office-holder a "servant of God" and elaborated
on his specific functions in favor of the (public) good--so
much that the political figure became a colleague of the
Christians. And at the conclusion (vs. 7), Paul refers only to
the personal relation between the Christians and those whom
we would call revenue and custom officers, mayors and senators,
policement and firemen, not to forget garbage collectors and
street cleaners. Thus the apostle progresses from abstract
terminology to functional description and ends with personal
relationships. This change might be compared with the emotional shift in a prisoner or another oppressed person who at
first would only speak of "them" (as if they were demons),
then begins to distinguish between a policeman, a judge, a
warden, a money lender, and finally is able to realize that he
has to do with fellow men and women. Paul awakens the awareness that the teller at the counter is much more than only an
exponent of "the bank," the mailman is not just "the mail,"
the revenue officer is to be distinguished from the burden of
the tax-system or the pang of a tax-payer's bad conscience.
Rather is each one of the named officials and of the higher or
lower public servants a very specific and unique fellow human
being, a neighbor, a brother or sister in the one family whose
father is God. This transformation corresponds to the interpretation which in scholarly circles is called "de-mythologiz-
ing"; it may be better, however, to speak of a "humanization."
Paul knows well enough and does not dispute that the existing
social structure, the institutions of society, and the wield-
ing of power have intangible, be it demonic or angelic, dimensions. But he does not want the Christians to be fixed upon a
ghostly, if not ghastly, notion of the State. Neither does he
suggest that "the system" deserves nothing better than to be
cheated and beaten. His message is evangelical, liberating,
edifying, because it affirms that ultimately the relation
between Christians and the State boils down to the inter*human*
relationships.

According to Ps. 82:6-7 and Ez. 28:2, 9, God says to the
rulers and judges:

> "You are gods,
> sons of the Most High, all of you;
> nevertheless, you shall die like men. . ."

> "You are but a man, and no god,
> though you consider yourself as wise as a god. . .
> Will you still say, 'I am a god. . .'
> though you are but a man, and no god. . .
> You shall die. . ."

Instead of showing malicious joy in the proud ruler's human nature and its proof: mortality, the prophet Ezekiel continues the quoted chapter with a lamentation, i.e., with the expression of God's and his own compassion with the humiliated person who believed himself to be god-like. The intercession for the state officials, prescribed to Israel and to the church in Jer. 29:4-7 and 1 Tim. 2:1-4, is the test of whether or not God's people care for the humanizing of politics. For their prayer is the backbone of their behavior and action.

Still, it is not only the often demonic realm of public affairs, institutions, and traditions that needs humanization, but also the Christian himself.

V

One of Paul's arguments has, as yet, not been mentioned explicitly. In vs. 5 he writes (in literal translation): "it is necessary to place oneself at the service (of the political officers who are God's servants) not only to avoid wrath, but also because of the conscience." Instead of wrath, the apostle speaks in vs. 2 of judgment. By wrath and judgment, he does not mean arbitrary political oppression or illegal retaliation; rather does he think of God's own response to evil-doers such as can be recognized in equitable verdicts and punishments. In Paul's words, the political and juridical "servant of God. . .does not bear the sword in vain" but in order "to execute God's wrath on the wrongdoer" (vs. 4). The question is now whether the "terror" or "fear" (vs. 3) instilled by the punitive function of the State is the exclusive motivator of a Christian's stance? If so, then the apostle is indeed that authoritative and reactionary man as he is sometimes depicted by those fighting for the liberation of the oppressed--be they ethnic groups, nations, women, children, or other exploited people. In this case, the man who wrote, "for freedom Christ has set us free" (Gal. 5:1), would contradict himself, elevate fear to the rank of a prime mover, and block social progress.

However, the real Paul has other intentions. In Rom.
13:5 he explicitly prohibits the Christians to be dominated
and motivated *only* by the fear of divine and human wrath. Instead, he appeals to the voice and dictates of the "conscience."
What does he mean by conscience? (See the following: Rom. 2:
15; 9:1; 14:5, 14; 1 Cor. 4:4; 8:7, 10, 12; 10:25-29; 2 Cor.
1:12; 4:2; 5:11; also 1 Pet. 2:19; 3:16, 21; 1 Tim. 1:5, 19;
3:9; 4:2; Tit. 1:15; cf. Heb. 9:9, 14; 10:2, 22; 13:18.)

It is unlikely that in Paul's diction this term signifies
a moral sense or criterion innate in every human being. The
one and only passage mentioning the conscience of Gentiles
(Rom. 2:14-15) speaks in actuality of "the law written upon
the hearts" of God's eschatological people as it is described
in Jer. 31:31-34. According to Paul, Gentiles who have heard
and believed the good news of Jesus Christ's death and resurrection have been incorporated into that very people. Already Jesus had called contemporary Jews to repentance by putting before their eyes the example of the pagan Ninevites who
had repented. Paul destroys in Rom. 2:1-29 a false conceit
found among Jews by pointing to some very specific Gentiles,
that is, to Gentile-Christians, who are driven by the Spirit
to do God's will. Whenever in other New Testament passages
Paul or another author speaks of the conscience--be it the
author's own or some other person's, be it good or bad, strong
or weak, clean or unclean--this word signifies a gift of God
found only in elect people. It is that "consciousness (or
awareness) of God" (1 Pet. 2:18) to which appeal can be made
after the message of Jesus Christ has been preached and believed. To a person who is a member of Christ's body ("in
Christ") it "bears testimony in the Holy Spirit" (Rom. 9:1).
It is tied to faith and open towards God. When hearing is
transformed into obeying, when information received becomes
will and decision--then and there the conscience is born.

Jews may speak of the good and the evil "impulse" found
in every human creature, and Gentiles may experience emotional
trouble or pain before or after doing wrong. In fact, Paul
makes use of a Greek concept which has no equivalent in the
Hebrew Old Testament but which is found in the works of Eu-
ripides, Democritus, Xenophon, Menander, and Philo, as well as
in the popular Greco-Roman philosophy of his environment. However, whereas there the term conscience denotes a monitor,
accuser, censor, judge, and revenger concerned with evil deeds
only, Paul fills it with a new meaning. The conscience of
which he speaks has not only a warning or punitive, but also
an edifying function; it is a guide for the future; it cares
for the community, not merely for the peace of the individual
soul. Its life and energy stem from the concurrence of two
seemingly opposite movements: the gospel is taken to heart

and thereby internalized, and the faith thus engendered compels the believer to externalize his or her conviction, i.e., to take a stance and go into action. The claim of the conscience and its right to be heeded are far from being absolute: God's own judgment stands high above it (1 Cor. 4:4), and on the horizontal level, it is limited by love and respect for the fellow Christians, that is, by the concern for the upbuilding and unity of the community (1 Cor. 8:10; Rom. 14:1, 13, 20). Applied to the service of God in the realm of politics, this means:

1. The conscience rejoices in knowing what God has in mind regarding *all* human beings: all of them are to be saved, they are all brothers and sisters "for whom Christ has died" (1 Tim. 2:4; Tit. 2:11; 1 Cor. 8:11; 2 Cor. 5:14; Col. 1:28). From the depth of his heart a Christian will therefore be grateful for the service rendered by the State when it gives temporal protection against crime in any form not just to the church but also to all people, especially to those exposed to exploitation and oppression. The gratitude will increase when the State also sees the "travail" and hears the "groaning" of all other creatures and proceeds to do something for the protection, e.g., of animals and natural resources.

2. The conscience is aware of a brute worse than tigers and skunks: the rapacious and deceitful beast in every human person. It knows that self-discipline is necessary and that the weak flesh is resisted by a strong spirit, but it also acknowledges the need of restraint imposed by others--in some cases by the application of force. Unless the protection of internal and international order entrusted to policemen and soldiers, judges and government agents are misused in favor of personal gain or national grandeur, the conscience considers and treats the public ministers as brothers and colleagues. A soldier dying in defending his country against the onslaught of a tyrant may in his own way resemble the martyrs of the church. Before the invention of the indiscriminate mass-destruction weapons, also before the organization of world-wide agencies for the protection of peace, the majority of Christians had no qualms in following John the Baptist's advice and doing military service (Luke 3:14)--as long as it did not mean participation in wanton violence and idolatry.

3. The conscience is bound by the commandment of love--that love which overcomes with good deeds the evil done or suffered by an enemy, and which is mutual between brothers and sisters (Rom. 12:14-21; 13:8-10). Love does not stop short at the gates of parliaments, city halls, palaces of justice or prisons. For justice is the public form of love, and love is the heart of justice. Unless trust in the power of forgiveness

and hope for a new life within the community is the ultimate
motivator of the judicial system, the law-and-order agencies
are nothing better than primitive instruments of the ruling
society's revenge and self-protection. Certainly, in speaking
of the state's "sword" (Rom. 3:4), Paul presupposes capital
punishment and war. But one of the consequences of his appeal
to conscience is inescapable: in our time Christians cannot
stand up for the execution of criminals nor for a general
theory of "just wars."

4. The conscience as an integrator, motivator, and judge
is irreconcilable with a double or split allegiance which, for
instance, serves God invisibly in the soul while the body is
placed at the state's disposition. Indeed, Paul's reference
to the conscience has a parallel in the Jesus logion, "render
to Caesar the things that are Caesar's, and to God the things
that are God's" (Matt. 22:21). The superiority of God's
claim and right upon man, and the consequence that God must
be obeyed more than man (Acts 5:29) is expressed by that statement. Jesus Christ acknowledged that the power wielded by
Pontius Pilate "had been given from above" (John 19:11). This
utterance is made in fulfillment of Christ's mission "to bear
witness to the truth" (John 18:37), but it does not exhaust
the witness which he gives to Rome's representative. In 1
Tim. 6:13-14, the "good confession" made by Christ before the
administrator is called to mind as the presupposition and example to "keep God's commandment unstained and free of re-
proach." In short, what Caesar needs and what Christians owe
him is the full testimony to the whole truth, and nothing but
the truth. In reminding the State of its subordination to God,
in pointing out where the State's power ends, and in its intercession, the church renders an essential service to the State.
Conscientious Christians cannot avoid clear testimony in public
matters--or else they, rather than the State, are guilty of
the perversion and disintegration of social and political life.
To prevent the pain of a bad conscience, they will therefore
abstain from distinguishing between things that are good in
God's eyes and other matters that are allegedly good in the
State's interests. They cannot give their support and blessings to both.

5. By their conscience Zwingli and Calvin, John Knox and
Oliver Cromwell, Dietrich Bonhoeffer and others were driven to
envisage or enact resistance and rebellion against tyrannic
governments. None of them intended to declare Romans 13 in-
valid. Rather, they were confronted with the possible case or
the actual fact that the head of a State, with or without an
underlying ideology or the consent of the nation, raised the
claim upon religious reverence. There are rulers who wish to

be worshipped as saviors; there are states that usurp the role
of the church; there are worldviews or programs formed with
the intention to make use of the gospel for purposes contradicting peace, love and justice, or to restrict, if not replace, the gospel by another doctrine of salvation and another
chosen people. In all such cases a situation is given that
flatly contradicts the description of the State's nature and
functions in Rom. 13:3-4. The "authorities" have then re-
lapsed into uproar against God, and the criteria of rewarding
good and punishing evil are no longer determined by a constitution and law serving the welfare of all people. The State's
"sword" is then wielded for indiscriminate bloodshed against
people in and outside its frontiers. Then all those hoping,
praying, and working for "a quiet and peaceable life" are confronted with a revolution from above, which they even may be
tempted to admire as long as it promises a better life. Only
a minority of Christians, perhaps only some individuals among
them, and frequently people who are not Christians, may have
their eyes opened to perceive the causes, signs, and effects
of that revolution. A majority may decide to wait, endure,
and suffer until the tide changes. Indeed, there are times
and circumstances when no other way is open. The author of
Revelation 13 called only for "endurance and faith" of the
small Christian congregations. But under the conditions presupposed in his letter to the Romans, Paul suggested a political activity that is entirely different--though not from the
readiness to suffer injustice, yet from a timid and lazy
fatalism or naked fear. The faith of which both Revelation
and Paul speak has nothing to do with irresponsibility and
cowardice. On the contrary, faith drives the Christians to
make brave decisions, stand upright, resist, and if need be,
suffer just as the witness to truth requires under given circumstances. For this reason, time and again Christians have
stood up and followed the dictates of their conscience rather
than of fear. When they encouraged the use of force against
tyrants, they fought *for* the State instituted by God, not
against it. They gave the State that witness to truth which
is among "the things" the church owes to Caesar. And their
testimony was trustworthy because they were willing to give
their lives for truth.

In summary, Paul had to fight a wanton libertinism
which repudiated the political responsibility of the Christians. He called the chosen people into service for the good
of all. The basis of his counsel is evangelical, for it is

an essential element of the good news he preaches: he proclaims the supremacy of God and the victory of Christ the King
over all powers, be they impalpable or tangible. He avers the
dignity of voluntary service, rendered after the example of
Jesus Christ's subordination to the Father. By throwing the
warm light of love and righteousness, peace and respect into
the cold and obscure realm of politics, he offers an alternative to the demonization of the state. Finally, he reminds
his readers to follow their consciences and thus to prove
themselves responsible and free members of the civic community.

Some elements of Romans 13 have been obfuscated in the
course of church history--to the detriment not only of Christians but also of Jews and non-Christians. But as they need
no longer remain hidden or denied, the apostle Paul should no
longer be denounced by those yearning for freedom in responsibility and for the responsibility of the free. Indeed, Paul
spoke as a man of his time to people and conditions of his
time in a language of his time. However, since his message of
Jesus Christ has proved valid over many centuries, his political ethics also cannot be ignored. It may well be that he is
intimating things that are far ahead of present-day democratic
ideals and achievements. He knew that not all people are
Christians. But while he did not yet foresee the Constantin-
ian and later eras in which the church decisively influenced
if not majoritized a State, yet he affirmed that all Christians are citizens of the body politic. He is calling for a
conscience-bound stance of free people--certainly not for
saturated *bourgeois*, but all the more for courageous *citoyens*.

BIBLIOGRAPHY OF THE PUBLISHED WRITINGS

OF FORD LEWIS BATTLES

Peter De Klerk

1949

"Hugo of Saint-Victor as a moral allegorist" *Church History* 18 (1949) 220-240.

1950

A translation and critical study of the first book of the homilies of Gregory the Great: on the prophet Ezekiel. Ph. D. dissertation. Hartford, Conn.: The Hartford Seminary Foundation, 1950. c, 427 leaves.

Review of *Ignace Goldziher memorial volume.* Part 1. Ed. by David Sámuel Löwinger and József Somogyi. Budapest, 1948. *The Muslim World* 40 (1950) 65-68.

1952

"A hymn for seminaries" *The Hartford Seminary Foundation Bulletin* No. 13 (June 1952) 2.

"A hymn of praise" *The Hartford Seminary Foundation Bulletin* No. 14 (December 1952) 2.

1953

Tr. & ed. "On the pastoral office," by John Wyclif, in *Advocates of reform.* From Wyclif to Erasmus. Ed. by Matthew Spinka. The Library of Christian Classics, 14. Philadelphia: The Westminster Press, 1953. Pp. 32-60. British ed., London: S.C.M. Press, 1953. Pp. 32-60.

Tr. & ed. "On the eucharist," by John Wyclif, in *Advocates of reform*. *From Wyclif to Erasmus*. Ed. by Matthew Spinka. The Library of Christian Classics, 14. Philadelphia: The Westminster Press, 1953. Pp. 61-88. British ed., London: S.C.M. Press, 1953. Pp. 61-88.

Tr. & ed. "The enchiridion," by Desiderius Erasmus, in *Advocates of reform*. *From Wyclif to Erasmus*. Ed. by Matthew Spinka. The Library of Christian Classics, 14. Philadelphia: The Westminster Press, 1953. Pp. 295-379. British ed., London: S.C.M. Press, 1953. Pp. 295-379.

Hartford harmony. A selection of American hymns from the 18th and early 19th centuries. Selected and arranged by Irving Lowens. Text prepared and published by Raymond W. Lindstrom and Ford Lewis Battles. Hartford, Conn.: The Hartford Seminary Foundation Bookstore, 1953. Reprinted in 1955.

Review of *A history of the crusades*. Vol. 2, *The kingdom of Jerusalem and the Frankish East 1100-1187*. By Steven Runciman. Cambridge: Cambridge University Press, 1952. *The Muslim World* 43 (1953) 209-210.

1955

Magna charta latina. The privilege of singing, articulating and reading a language and of keeping it alive. By Eugen Rosenstock-Huessy with Ford Lewis Battles. Pittsburgh: Pittsburgh Theological Seminary, 1955. Revised edition dated 1973. Reprinted in Pittsburgh Reprint Series, 1. Pittsburgh: The Pickwick Press, 1975.

"Stanzas for communion" (Poem) *The Hartford Seminary Foundation Bulletin* No. 21 (Winter 1955/56) 0.

1959

Locutionum cotidianarum glossarium. A guide to Latin conversation. By Goodwin Batterson Beach and Ford Lewis Battles. Hartford, Conn.: Hartford Seminary Press, 1959. Second revised edition dated 1961. Third revised edition dated 1967.

"Some axioms of church history" *The Bulletin of the Hartford Seminary Foundation* No. 26 (February 1959) 49-66.

1960

Tr. *Institutes of the Christian religion*. 2 vols. By
John Calvin. Ed. by John Thomas McNeill, tr. by Ford
Lewis Battles. The Library of Christian Classics, 20-
21. Philadelphia: The Westminster Press, 1960. British ed., London: S.C.M. Press, 1960. U.S.A. edition
in its twelfth printing.

1961

Review of *Calvin's doctrine of the knowledge of God*. By
Thomas Henry Louis Parker. Grand Rapids: Wm. B. Eerdmans Publishing Co., 1959. *Interpretation* 15 (1961)
102-104.

"Two dried sausages" (Fragment of a drama in five acts)
Toledoth 1 (May 1961) 5-22. Also in *The Hartford
Quarterly* 2 (Summer 1962) 7-19.

"A litany of the beatitudes" *Toledoth* 3 (December 1961)
7-12.

1962

*The sources of Calvin's commentary on Seneca's De Clemen-
tia*. A provisional index. Hartford, Conn.: The Hartford Seminary Foundation, 1962.

"Is Christ divided?" (Thoughts upon I Corinthians 11, 17-
22) *Toledoth* 4 (May 1962) 4-7. Also in *The Muslim
World* 52 (1962) 259-261.

Review of *Lectures on Romans*. By Martin Luther. Tr. and
ed. by Wilhelm Pauck. The Library of Christian Classics,
15. Philadelphia: The Westminster Press, 1961. *Interpretation* 16 (1962) 321-324.

1963

"Englishing the Institutes of John Calvin" *Babel* 9
(1963) 94-98.

1964

Review of *Studies on the reformation*. Collected papers
in church history. Series two. By Roland Herbert
Bainton. Boston: Beacon Press, 1963. *The Westminster
Bookman* 23 (March 1964) 25-26.

"Some thoughts on church history," by Ford Lewis Battles
and John Jermain Bodine, *The Hartford Quarterly* 4
(Spring 1964) 31-41.

Review of *Reformation studies*. Essays in honor of Roland
Herbert Bainton. Ed. by Franklin Hamlin Littell.
Richmond, Va.: John Knox Press, 1962. *The Hartford
Quarterly* 4 (Spring 1964) 85-88.

"Art and worship: friends or foes?" *The Reformed Journal* 14 (May-June 1964) 7-10.

Review of *Documents of the Christian church*. Ed. by
Henry Scowcroft Bettenson. Second edition. New York:
Oxford University Press, 1963. *The Hartford Quarterly*
4 (Summer 1964) 80-82.

Review of *Medieval political philosophy*. A sourcebook.
Ed. by Ralph Lerner and Muhsin Mahdi. New York: The
Free Press of Glencoe, 1963. *The Muslim World* 54
(1964) 204-205.

"An ancient church historian looks at the Second Vatican
Council" *The Hartford Quarterly* 5 (Fall 1964) 15-28.

1965

Temple or tomb? Reflections on papal history, sketched
in dramatic form. Hartford, Conn.: The Hartford
Seminary Foundation, 1965.

"Against luxury and license in Geneva: a forgotten
fragment of Calvin" *Interpretation* 19 (1965) 182-202.

"Hildebrandine histrionics" *Toledoth* 6 (May 1965) 2-3.

Tr. "Expostulation of Jesus with a man perishing through
his very own fault," by Desiderius Erasmus, *The Hartford Quarterly* 5 (Summer 1965) 64-67.

Tr. "Enthusiasm for Erasmus," by Huldreich Zwingli, *The
Hartford Quarterly* 5 (Summer 1965) 67-68.

Tr. "Academic discourse," by John Calvin. Tr. and annotated by Dale Jay Cooper and Ford Lewis Battles.
The Hartford Quarterly 6 (Fall 1965) 76-85. Revised
version in *Institution of the Christian religion*. Embracing almost the whole sum of piety, & whatever is
necessary to know the doctrine of salvation: a work
most worthy to be read by all persons zealous for piety,

and recently published. Preface to the most Christian
King of France, whereas [i.e. wherein] this book is of-
fered to him as a Confession of Faith. At Basel, 1536
Tr. and annotated by Ford Lewis Battles. Atlanta:
John Knox Press, 1975. Pp. 462-471.

Review of *The four major cults*. Christian Science, Je-
hovah's Witnesses, Mormonism, Seventh-Day Adventism.
By Anthony Andrew Hoekema. Grand Rapids: Wm. B. Eerdmans Publishing Co., 1963. *The Hartford Quarterly 6*
(Fall 1965) 99-100.

1966

*An analysis of the Institutes of the Christian Religion
of John Calvin*. Hartford, Conn.: The Hartford Semi-
nary Press, 1966. Revised edition with same title by
Ford Lewis Battles assisted by John Robert Walchenbach.
Pittsburgh: Pittsburgh Theological Seminary 1970.
Second revised edition dated 1972. Third revised edi-
tion dated 1976. Reprinted, Grand Rapids: Baker Book
House, 1980.

New light on Calvin's Institutes. A supplement to the
McNeill-Battles translation. Hartford, Conn.:
Hartford Seminary Press, 1966.

Stanzas on the trinity. By Ford Lewis Battles & Edward
J. Furcha, Hartford, Conn.: The Hartford Seminary
Foundation, 1966. Reprinted, Pittsburgh: The Pitts-
burgh Theological Seminary, 1968.

"The sources of Calvin's Seneca commentary" in *John Cal-
vin*. A collection of essays. Ed. by Gervase E. Dur-
field. Courtenay Studies in Reformation Theology, 1.
Grand Rapids: Wm. B. Eerdmans Publishing Co., 1966.
British ed., Appleford: Sutton Courtenay Press, 1966.
Pp. 38-66.

"On the poetry of history" *Toledoth* 7 (May 1966) 4-7.

"Milan. A.D. 390" *Toledoth* 7 (May 1966) 14.

"The passion and death of the prophet Mani" *Toledoth* 7
(May 1966) 15-17.

Review of *Misunderstandings between East and West*. By
George Every. Ecumenical Studies in History 4. Richmond, VA.: John Knox Press, 1966. *The Hartford Quarterly* 7 (Fall 1966) 68.

Review of *Preparatory reports*. Second Vatican Council.
Tr. by Aram J. Berard. Philadelphia: The Westminster
Press, 1965. *The Hartford Quarterly* 7 (Fall 1966) 68.

1967

A first course in church history and history of doctrine.
The patristic era [and] the Middle Ages. Pittsburgh:
Pittsburgh Theological Seminary, 1967/68. Revised
editions dated 1968/69, 1969/70, 1971/72, 1972/73 and
1975/76. Seventh revised edition entitled *Itinerarium
fidei*. Outline for a first course in church history to
A.D. 1500. Pittsburgh: Pittsburgh Theological Seminary; Grand Rapids: Calvin Theological Seminary, 1977/
78. 2 vols.

Seventy decisive years in American hymnody (1799-1868).
Hartford, Conn.: The Hartford Seminary Foundation,
1967.

Review of *John Hus' concept of the church*. By Matthew
Spinka. Princeton, N.J.: Princeton University Press,
1966. *The Hartford Quarterly* 7 (Winter 1967) 76-77.

Ed. "Bellamy papers" *The Hartford Quarterly* 7 (Spring
1967) 64-91.

1968

Abelard & Peter Lombard. Study Outline, 11. Pittsburgh:
Pittsburgh Theological Seminary, 1968.

Tr. *Arius: Thalia*. (A hypothetical reconstruction of
the text) Reconstructed Documents, 2. Pittsburgh:
Pittsburgh Theological Semianry, 1968.

Augustine: city of God. Study Outline, 9. Pittsburgh:
Pittsburgh Theological Seminary, 1968. Reprinted in
1973.

Augustine: confessions and other treatises. Study Outline. 7a. Pittsburgh: Pittsburgh Theological Seminary,
1968.

Boethius: theological treatises. Study Outline, 8 (10).
Pittsburgh: Pittsburgh Theological Seminary, 1968.
Reprinted in 1972.

Church and state in the early centuries. Pittsburgh:
Pittsburgh Theological Seminary, 1968.

From the Apostles to the schoolmen. Foundations of church history. Pittsburgh: Pittsburgh Theological Seminary, 1968.

Ed. *Henry and Hildebrand*. Reflections on papal power, with a concluding glimpse at the Avignonese papacy. By A. Burfiend, P. Kamuyu and F. Dole, ed. by Ford Lewis Battles. Pittsburgh: Pittsburgh Theological Seminary, 1968.

Heresy in the early church. Pittsburgh: Pittsburgh Theological Seminary, 1968. Reprinted in 1972.

Tr. *Hilarius: Filius Dei vivi verbum*. Stanzas drawn from Book II on the Trinity. Reconstructed Documents, 3. Pittsburgh: Pittsburgh Theological Seminary, 1968. Reprinted in 1972.

Ed. & tr. *Monasticism and monastic life;* with a translation of *The imitation of Christ*. Book I. Pittsburgh: Pittsburgh Theological Seminary, 1968.

Review of *Memory and Hope*. An inquiry concerning the presence of Christ. By Dietrich Ritschl. New York: The Macmillan Co., 1967. *Perspective* 9 (1968) 80-82.

1969

The apologists. Study Outline, 1. Pittsburgh: Pittsburgh Theological Seminary, 1969. Reprinted in 1972.

Ed. *Athanasius*. By Paul Kokenda. Ed. by Ford Lewis Battles. Study Outline, 6. Pittsburgh: Pittsburgh Theological Seminary, 1969. Reprinted in 1971 and 1972.

Tr. & ed. *Bonaventura to Luther*. Late medieval and reformation piety and dissent. A miscellany. Selected, ed. & tr. by Ford Lewis Battles. Spirituality of the Reformers, 1. Pittsburgh: Pittsburgh Theological Seminary, 1969.

Tr. *Calvin's commentary on Seneca's De Clementia*. By John Calvin. With introduction, tr., and notes by Ford Lewis Battles and André Malan Hugo. Renaissance Text Series, 3. Published for the Renaissance Society of America, Leiden: E. J. Brill, 1969.

Tr. *Institution of the Christian religion*. Embracing almost the whole sum of piety, & whatever is necessary to know the doctrine of salvation: a work most worthy

to be read by all persons zealous for piety, and re-
cently published. Preface to the most Christian King
of France, wherein this book is offered to him as a
Confession of Faith. By John Calvin. New Englished
completely for the first time by Ford Lewis Battles.
Pittsburgh: Pittsburgh Theological Seminary, 1969.
Revised edition dated 1972. Newly revised edition,
Atlanta: John Knox Press, 1975.

Irenaeus. Study Outline, 2. Pittsburgh: Pittsburgh
Theological Seminary, 1969. Reprinted in 1971 and
1972.

John Chrysostom: on the priesthood. Study Outline, 6B
(7). Pittsburgh: Pittsburgh Theological Seminary,
1969. Reprinted in 1972.

Ed. *John of Damascus: the fount of knowledge.* By Daniel
Sahas, with the editorial assistance of Ford Lewis
Battles. Study Outline, 11. Pittsburgh: Pittsburgh
Theological Seminary, 1969. Reprinted in 1973.

Hugo of Saint Victor. Study Outline, 14. Pittsburgh:
Pittsburgh Theological Seminary, 1969. Reprinted in
1973.

Origen: on first principles. Study Outline, 4. Pittsburgh: Pittsburgh Theological Seminary, 1969. Reprinted in 1972.

Peter Lombard. Study Outline, 15. Pittsburgh: Pittsburgh Theological Seminary, 1969. Reprinted in 1971
and 1973.

Ed. *The piety of Caspar Schwenckfeld.* Tr. & comp. by
Edward J. Furcha with the collaboration of Ford Lewis
Battles. Spirituality of the Reformers, 2. Pittsburgh: Pittsburgh Theological Seminary, 1969. Reprinted in 1971.

Tr. & ed. *The piety of John Calvin.* An anthology illustrative of the spirituality of the reformer of Geneva.
By John Calvin. Selected, tr., and ed. by Ford Lewis
Battles. Pittsburgh: Pittsburgh Theological Seminary,
1969. Reprinted with corrections in 1970. Revised
edition dated 1973. Newly revised edition entitled
The piety of John Calvin. An anthology illustrative of
the spirituality of the reformer. By John Calvin. Tr.
and ed. by Ford Lewis Battles. Music ed. by Stanley
Tagg. Grand Rapids: Baker Book House, 1978.

Tertullian & Cyprian. Study Outline, 5. Pittsburgh: Pittsburgh Theological Seminary. 1969. Reprinted in 1971 and 1972.

"Calvin and the computer" in *Summary of proceedings.* Twenty-third annual conference, American Theological Library Association, Pittsburgh Theological Seminary, Pittsburgh, Pennsylvania, June 16-19, 1969. Wilmore, Ky.: Asbury Theological Seminary, 1969. Pp. 87-112.

Review of *Reformers in profile.* Ed. by Brian Albert Gerrish. Philadelphia: Fortress Press, 1967. *Journal of Ecumenical Studies* 6 (1969) 103-106.

Review of *The style of John Calvin in his French polemical treatises.* By Francis M. Higman. Oxford modern Languages and Literature Monographs. New York: Oxford University Press, 1967. *Church History* 38 (1969) 534.

1970

The documents of Vatican II in historical perspective. The background, drafting and implication for the future of the church. Pittsburgh: Pittsburgh Theological Seminary, 1970.

Ed. *Epiphanius panarion.* By Daniel Sahas, with editorial assistance of Ford Lewis Battles. Study Outline, 17. Pittsburgh: Pittsburgh Theological Seminary, 1970. Reprinted in 1972.

Ed. *The formation of the United Church of Christ* (U.S.A). A bibliography by Hanns Peter Keiling with the editorial assistance of Ford Lewis Battles. Bibliographia Tripotamopolitana, 2. Pittsburgh: Clifford E. Barbour Library, Pittsburgh Theological Seminary, 1970.

Tr. *Hymn texts drawn from the Old and New Testaments.* Tr. by Donald E. Gowan and Ford Lewis Battles. Pittsburgh: Pittsburgh Theological Seminary, 1970.

Review of *Geneva and the consolidation of the French protestant movement, 1564-1572.* A contribution to the history of congregationalism, presbyterianism, and calvinist resistance theory. By Robert McCune Kingdon. Madison: University of Wisconsin Press, 1967. *Perspective* 11 (1970) 344-346.

Review of *Calvin et Vatican II.* L'église servante. Par Alexandre Ganoczy. Paris: Les Éditions du Cerf, 1968. *Journal of Ecumenical Studies* 7 (1970) 807-809.

Review of *Melanchthon and Bucer*. By Philip Melanchthon
and Martin Butzer. Ed. by Wilhelm Pauck. The Library
of Christian Classics, 19. Philadelphia: The Westminster Press, 1969. *Interpretation* 24 (1970) 527.

Ed. *New hymns for a new day?* An anthology of new hymnody
to illustrate the search for new hymns. Pittsburgh:
Pittsburgh Theological Seminary, 1971.

Peter Abelard. Study Outline, 13. Pittsburgh: Pittsburgh Theological Seminary, 1971. Reprinted in 1973.

Representative Christian thinkers. From Ignatius of An-
tioch to the end of the Middle Ages. Pittsburgh:
Pittsburgh Theological Seminary, 1971.

Tr. *The sermons of Nestorius*. Tr. into English from the
texts of F. Loofs and F. Nau, by Ford Lewis Battles
with the assistance of Daniel Sahas. Pittsburgh:
Pittsburgh Theological Seminary, 1971. Reprinted in
1971. Third printing with corrections in 1973.

"Anointed of God" No. 10 in *A new song 3*. St. Louis,
Mo.: Published by the Division of Publication, United
Church Board for Homeland Ministries, for the Executive
Council and the Commission on Worship, United Church of
Christ, 1971. Also as No. 120 in *The hymnal of the
United Church of Christ*. Philadelphia: United Church
Press, 1974.

"Bernard of Clairvaux and the moral allegorical tradition"
in *Innovation in medieval literature*. Essays to the
memory of Alan Markman. Ed. by Douglas Radcliff-
Umstead. Pittsburgh: Medieval Studies Committee,
University of Pittsburgh, 1971. Pp. 1-19.

"Christ, our peace indeed" No. 4, "God so rich in mercy"
No. 5, "Creator spirit, come to us" No. 6*, "The carol
of the two Adams" No. 8 and 9**, "Who prays, but hears
prayer?" No. 10***, "A Christian must by faith be
filled" No. 11****, "All speech far transcending" No.
16, "How long, Lord?" No. 17*****, "In boundless mercy"
No. 19****** in *New hymns for a new day?* An anthology
of new hymnody to illustrate the search for new hymns.
Pittsburgh: Pittsburgh Theological Seminary 1971.
Also *as No. 15, and 16, **as No. 6, ***as No. 11, and
****as No. 8 in *A new song 3*. St. Louis, Mo.: Pub-
lished by the Division of Publication, United Church
Board for Homeland Ministries, for the Executive Council

and the Commission on Worship, United Church of Christ, 1971, and as No. 148, **as No. 71 entitled "Two Adams walked upon the earth," ****as No. 168, and ******as No. 251 in *The hymnal of the United Church of Christ*. Philadelphia: United Church Press, 1974.

"Frederick Neumann and his work" in *God's fifth columnist & other writings*. With introductory essays by Peter L. Berger & Ford Lewis Battles. Appleford: Marcham Manor Press, 1971. Pp. 5-10.

Review of *The early Christians after the death of the Apostles*. Selected and ed. from all the sources of the first centuries. By Eberhard Arnold. Rifton, N.Y.: Plough Publishing House, 1970. *Encounter* 32 (1971) 170-171.

Review of *Speech and reality*. By Eugen Rosenstock-Huessy. Argo Books, 112. Norwich, Vt.: Argo Books, 1970. *Perspective* 12 (1971) 279-280.

1972

A *computerized concordance to Institutio Christianae religionis 1559 of Joannes Calvinus*. Based on the critical text of Petrus Barth & Guilelmus Niesel (Books 1-2: 1967 [i.e. 1957]; Book 3: 1959; Book 4: 1962) corrected from the original text of 1559. By Ford Lewis Battles, with the assistance of Charles Miller. Pittsburgh: Clifford E. Barbour Library, Pittsburgh Theological Seminary, 1972. Seven microfilm reels. Printed introduction, lemmatic index & other aids. Bibliographia Tripotamopolitana, 8. Pittsburgh: Clifford E. Barbour Library, Pittsburgh Theological Seminary, 1972.

Tr. & ed. *John Calvin: catechism 1538*. By John Calvin. Tr. & annotated by Ford Lewis Battles. Pittsburgh: Pittsburgh Theological Seminary, 1972. Revised edition dated 1974. Reprinted with corrections in 1975 and 1976.

Tr. *Pelagius: the Christian life and other essays*. Reconstructed Documents, 7. Pittsburgh: Pittsburgh Theological Seminary, 1972. Reprinted in 1973 and 1977.

Review of *The constructive revolutionary*. John Calvin & his socio-economic impact. By William Fred Graham. Richmond, Va.: John Knox Press, 1971. *Interpretation* 26 (1972) 351-353.

Review of *John Bunyan*. By Richard Lee Greaves. Courtenay Studies in Reformation Theology, 2. Grand Rapids: Wm. B. Eerdmans Publishing Co., 1969. *Perspective* 13 (1972) 247-248.

Review of *Early Christians speak*. By Everett Ferguson. Austin, Tex.: Sweet Publishing Co., 1971. *Church History* 41 (1972) 401.

1973

Indices to the four books of Sentences of Peter Lombard. Comp. by Ford Lewis Battles. Pittsburgh: Pittsburgh Theological Seminary, 1973.

Three rivers of the spirit hymnal. By John W. Neely, Jr., and Ford Lewis Battles. Pittsburgh: Pittsburgh Theological Seminary, 1973.

Review of *The life and legal writings of Hugo Grotius*. By Edward Dumbauld. Norman: University of Oklahoma Press, 1969. *Perspective* 14 (1973) 59.

1974

"The church of Christ is one" No. 153, "Glory to the Father" No. 316 and 324, "Praise the Father [giving life]" No. 317 and 359, "As you have promised, Lord" No. 321 and 328, and "Glory be to our God in heaven" No. 323 in *The hymnal of the United Church of Christ*. Philadelphia: United Church Press, 1974.

Review of *Arminius*. A study in the Dutch reformation. By Carl Oliver Bangs. Nashville: Abingdon Press, 1971. *Journal of Presbyterian History* 52 (1974) 83-84.

1975

Tr. & ed. *Selected writings of Hans Denck*. By Hans Denck. Ed. and tr. from the text as established by Walter Fellmann, by Edward J. Furcha with Ford Lewis Battles. Pittsburgh original Texts and Translation Series, 1. Pittsburgh: The Pickwick Press, 1975.

Tr. "The placards of 1534" in *Institution of the Christian religion*. Embracing almost the whole sum of piety, and whatever is necessary to know the doctrine of salvation: a work most worthy to be read by all persons zealous for piety, and recently published: preface to the most Christian King of France, whereas [i.e. wherein] this book is offered to him as a Confession of Faith. By John Calvin. Tr. and annotated by Ford Lewis Battles. Atlanta: John Knox Press, 1975. Pp. 437-440.

Tr. "Martin Bucer on the Lord's Prayer" in *Institution of the Christian religion*. Embracing almost the whole sum of piety & whatever is necessary to know the doctrine of salvation: a work most worthy to be read by all persons zealous for piety, and recently published: preface to the most Christian King of France, whereas [i.e. wherein] this book is offered to him as a Confession of Faith. By John Calvin. Tr. and annotated by Ford Lewis Battles. Atlanta: John Knox Press, 1975. Pp. 441-461.

Review of *Erasmus and the seamless coat of Jesus*. De sarcienda ecclesiae concordia (On restoring the unity of the church). With selections from the letters and ecclesiastes. By Desiderius Erasmus. Ed. by Raymond Himelick. Lafayette, Ind.: Purdue University Studies, 1971. Reviewed by Donald Morrison Conroy and Ford Lewis Battles. *Journal of Ecumenical Studies* 12 (1975) 272-273.

1976

Tr. *Enchiridion*. Of commonplaces of John Eck against Martin Luther and his followers. By John Eck. Now Englished for the first time by Ford Lewis Battles. Pittsburgh: Duquesne University, 1976. Revised edition published, Grand Rapids: Calvin Theological Seminary, 1978.

"The future of calviniana" in *Renaissance, reformation, resurgence*. Papers and responses presented at the Colloquium on Calvin & Calvin Studies held at Calvin Theological Seminary on April 22 and 23, 1976. Ed. by Peter De Klerk. Grand Rapids: Calvin Theological Seminary, 1976. Pp. 133-173.

Review of *The Christian tradition*. A history of the development of doctrine. Volume 2, *The spirit of eastern christendom (600-1700)*. By Jaroslav Pelikan. Chicago: The University of Chicago Press, 1974. *Christian Scholar's Review* 5 (1975/76) 408-409.

Review of *The spirituality of John Calvin*. By Lucien Joseph Richard. Atlanta: John Knox Press, 1974. *Journal of Presbyterian History* 54 (1976) 281-282.

1977

Adjutorium ad cultum divinum. A supplement to the *wor-
shipbook* of the United Presbyterian Church in the
United States of America for use in the chapel of the
Pittsburgh Theological Seminary. Comp. under the direction of the Committee on Worship by Ford Lewis Battles, N. Mikita and M. Ioset. Pittsburgh: Pittsburgh
Theological Seminary, 1977.

Semita ad perspicendam mentem sancti Augustini. A student's guide to the formative controversies in the life
& thought of Aurelius Augustinus, bishop of Hippo Re-
gius. Comp. by Ford Lewis Battles with the assistance
of Robert Benedetto. Pittsburgh: Pittsburgh Theological Seminary, 1977. 4 parts.

"God was accommodating himself to human capacity" *Interpretation* 31 (1977) 19-38.

"The consultation on ecumenical hymnody," by Ford Lewis
Battles and Morgan Simmons. *The Hymn* 28 (1977) 67-68,
87.

Review of *The Patristic roots of reformed worship.* By
Hughes Oliphant Old. Zürcher Beiträge zur Reformations-
geschichte, 5. Zürich: Theologischer Verlag, 1975.
Church History 46 (1977) 398-399.

1978

Calculus fidei. Some ruminations on the structure of the
theology of John Calvin. Grand Rapids: Calvin Theological Seminary, 1978.

Tr. *Six Psalms of John Calvin.* Psalms 25, 36, 46, 91,
113 and 138. Words by John Calvin. Tr. by Ford Lewis
Battles. Harmonizations by Stanley Tagg. Grand Rapids:
Baker Book House, 1978.

The theologian as poet. Some remarks about the 'found'
poetry of John Calvin. Grand Rapids: Calvin Theological Seminary, 1978. Also in *From Faith to Faith*, essays
in honor of Donald G. Miller on his seventieth birthday.
Ed. by Dikran Y. Hadidian. Pittsburgh Theological
Monograph Series, 31, Pittsburgh: The Pickwick Press,
1979. Pp. 299-337.

"Introduction: Frederick Neumann (1899-1967)" in *Where
do we stand?* A selective homiletical commentary on the

Old Testament. Vol. 1, *Law and revelation*. The Torah. By Frederick Neumann. Brooklyn, N.Y.: Theo. Gaus, 1978. Pp. ix-xi.

"Introduction" in *Where do we stand?* A selective homiletical commentary on the Old Testament. Vol. 2 *Faith and reality in history*. The historical books and the prophets. By Frederick Neumann. Brooklyn, N.Y.: Theo. Gaus, 1978. Pp. 1-2.

Review of *An introduction to the reformed tradition*. A way of being the Christian community. By John Haddon Leith. Atlanta: John Knox Press, 1977. *Interpretation* 32 (1978) 218, 220.

Review of *The reformation*. A narrative history related by contemporary observers and participants. Ed. by Hans Joachim Hillerbrand. Grand Rapids: Baker Book House, 1978. *Calvin Theological Journal* 13 (1978) 257-258.

1979

"An exchange" in *Bibliography Paul Leser*. On the occasion of his 80th birthday on February 23, 1979. Ed. by Absalom Vilakazi. West Hartford, Conn.: The University of Hartford, 1979. [Pp. 44-49].

Review of *John Calvin*. A biography. By Thomas Henry Parker. Philadelphia: The Westminster Press, 1975. *The Journal of Religion* 59 (1979) 254-255.

198

"Notes on John Calvin, Justitia and the Old Testament Law" in *Intergerini Parietis Septum* (Eph. 2:14); essays presented to Markus Barth on his 65th birthday. Ed. by Dikran Y. Hadidian. Pittsburgh Theological Monograph Series, 33, Pittsburgh: The Pickwick Press, 198 .

LIST OF CONTRIBUTORS

Markus Barth, Professor of New Testament at the University
of Basel, is the author of *Die Taufe--ein Sakrament?*
(Zurich, 1951) and the Anchor Bible Commentary to
Ephesians (2 vols., Garden City, N.Y., 1974). In
addition to his New Testament scholarship, he has a
major concern for Jewish-Christian relationships.

James K. Cameron, Professor of Ecclesiastical History at St.
Mary's College, University of St. Andrews, has a special
interest in relations between Scotland and Continental
Europe in the Reformation period. He has edited *Letters
of John Johnston and Robert Howie* (Edinburgh, 1963) and
The First Book of Discipline (Edinburgh, 1972).

Peter De Klerk, Theological Librarian at Calvin Theological
Seminary, Grand Rapids, is well known to Calvin scholars
for his editing of the annual Calvin Bibliography in the
Calvin Theological Journal. He is also currently engaged
in bibliographical work on the Book of Revelation.

B. A. Gerrish is Professor of Historical Theology at the
University of Chicago and Co-editor of the *Journal of
Religion.* He has written *Grace and Reason: A Study in
the Theology of Luther* (Oxford, 1962; reprint ed.,
Chicago, 1979) and *Tradition and the Modern World:
Reformed Theology in the Nineteenth Century* (Chicago,
1978).

I. John Hesselink is President and Professor of Theology at
Western Theological Seminary, Holland, Michigan. He is
a Calvin specialist and has worked extensively on Calvin's
understanding of law and the two testaments. Among his
previous studies on these themes are: "The Law of God,"
Guilt, Grace, and Gratitude, ed. Donald J. Bruggink (New
York, 1963), pp. 169-208; "Calvin and *Heilsgeschichte,*"
Oikonomia: Heilsgeschichte als Thema der Theologie, ed.
Felix Christ (Hamburg, 1967), pp. 163-170.

Robert M. Kingdon is Professor of History and Director of
the Institute for Research in the Humanities at the
University of Wisconsin, Madison. He is the author of
*Geneva and the Coming of the Wars of Religion in France,
1555-1563* (Geneva, 1956) and *Geneva and the Consolidation
of the French Protestant Movement, 1564-1572* (Geneva and
Madison, 1967). His essay in the present volume comes
out of his current interest in Peter Martyr Vermigli.

John H. Leith, Pemberton Professor of Theology at Union
Theological Seminary in Richmond, Virginia, is the
author of *Assembly at Westminster: Reformed Theology
in the Making* (Richmond, 1973) and *Introduction to the
Reformed Tradition* (Richmond, 1977). He has also edited
a widely-used source book, *Creeds of the Churches:
A Reader in Christian Doctrine From the Bible to the
Present* (Garden City, N.Y., 1963; rev. ed., Richmond,
1973).

Donald G. Miller, formerly President of Pittsburgh Theological
Seminary, has his principal area of current interest in
New Testament studies. Besides the Layman's Bible Com-
mentary on Luke (Richmond, 1959), he has published *The
Way to Biblical Preaching* (Nashville, 1974).

Robert S. Paul, Professor of Ecclesiastical History and
Christian Thought, Austin Presbyterian Theological
Seminary, is a specialist in the politics and religion
of seventeenth-century England. Among his publications
are *The Lord Protector: Religion and Politics in the
Life of Oliver Cromwell* (London, 1955), *The Atonement
and the Sacraments* (Nashville, 1960), and *The Church
in Search of Its Self* (Grand Rapids, 1972).

Joseph N. Tylenda is Assistant Editor of *Theological Studies,*
Georgetown University. A Calvin specialist, he has
published two earlier articles on the Calvinistic doctrine of the Lord's Supper: "Calvin and Christ's
Presence in the Supper--True or Real?" *Scottish Journal
of Theology* 27 (1974): 65-75, and "A Eucharistic Sacrifice in Calvin's Theology?" *Theological Studies* 37
(1976): 456-466.

George Huntston Williams, Hollis Professor of Divinity,
Harvard University, has written extensively on the
Radical Reformation and has made a special study of the
church in sixteenth-century Poland. Best known for *The
Radical Reformation* (Philadelphia, 1962), and his most

recent book, *The Mind of John Paul II: Origins of His Thought and Action* (New York, 1980).